Borderline Personality Disorder

FOR

DUMMIES®

by Charles H. Elliott, PhD
Laura L. Smith, PhD

WILEY

Wiley Publishing, Inc.

Borderline Personality Disorder For Dummies®

Published by
Wiley Publishing, Inc.
111 River St.
Hoboken, NJ 07030-5774
www.wiley.com

WILEY

About the Authors

Charles H. Elliott, PhD, is a clinical psychologist and a Founding Fellow in the Academy of Cognitive Therapy. He is also a member of the faculty at Fielding Graduate University. He specializes in the treatment of adolescents and adults with obsessive-compulsive disorder, anxiety, anger, depression, and personality disorders. Dr. Elliott has authored many professional articles and book chapters in the area of cognitive behavior therapies. He presents nationally and internationally on new developments in the assessment and therapy of emotional disorders. Dr. Elliott is coauthor with Dr. Laura Smith of the following books: *Obsessive-Compulsive Disorder For Dummies, Seasonal Affective Disorder For Dummies, Anxiety & Depression Workbook For Dummies, Depression For Dummies,* and *Overcoming Anxiety For Dummies* (Wiley), *Hollow Kids: Recapturing the Soul of a Generation Lost to the Self-Esteem Myth* (Prima Publishing), and *Why Can't I Be the Parent I Want to Be?* (New Harbinger). He also is a coauthor of the Behavioral Science Book Club selection *Why Can't I Get What I Want? How to Stop Making the Same Old Mistakes and Start Living a Life You Can Love* (Davies-Black).

Laura L. Smith, PhD, is a clinical psychologist who specializes in the assessment and treatment of adults and children with obsessive-compulsive disorder, as well as personality disorders, depression, anxiety, AD/HD, and learning disorders. She is often asked to provide consultations to attorneys, school districts, and governmental agencies. She presents workshops on cognitive therapy and mental health issues to national and international audiences. Dr. Smith is a widely published author of articles and books to the profession and the public, including those coauthored with Dr. Elliott.

Drs. Elliott and Smith are members of the New Mexico Psychological Association Board of Directors and affiliated training faculty at the Cognitive Behavioral Institute of Albuquerque. Their work has been featured in various periodicals, including *Family Circle, Parents, Child,* and *Better Homes and Gardens,* as well as popular publications like *New York Post, Washington Times, Daily Telegraph* (London), and *Christian Science Monitor.* They have been invited speakers at numerous conferences, including the National Alliance for the Mentally Ill (NAMI), the Association for Behavioral and Cognitive Therapies, the International Association for Cognitive Psychotherapy, and the National Association of School Psychologists. They have appeared on television networks, such as CNN and Canada AM. In radio, they are often featured as experts on various NPR programs, as well as *You, the Owner's Manual Radio Show, Doctor Radio* on Sirius Satellite Radio, the *Franker Boyer Radio Show,* and *The Four Seasons Radio Show.* They have committed their professional lives to making the science of psychology relevant and accessible to the public.

Drs. Smith and Elliott are available for speaking engagements, expert interviews, and workshops. You can visit their Web site at www.PsychAuthors.com or their blog ("Anxiety & OCD Exposed") at blogs.psychcentral.com/anxiety.

Dedication

We dedicate this book to our children and their spouses: Alli, Brian, Grant, Nathan, Sara, and Trevor. And, of course, to our grandchildren: Alaina, Cade, Carter, and Lauren. Thanks for the excitement.

Authors' Acknowledgments

We'd like to thank our excellent editors at Wiley — our project editor, Tim Gallan, our acquisitions editor, Lindsay Lefevere, and our copy editor, Amanda Gillum — as well as our agents, Elizabeth and Ed Knappman.

We also wish to thank our publicity and marketing team at Wiley, which included David Hobson and Adrienne Fountain.

We appreciate the hard work and dedication of Erika Hanson in keeping track of our literature base. Thanks to Scott Love of Softek, LLC for his unwavering computer and Web site support. Thanks to Trevor Wolfe for keeping us up on pop culture, social media, blogging, and tweeting on Twitter.

We want to thank Deborah Wearn and Pamela Hargrove for finally figuring out how old Judy is (private, inside joke). Thanks to Sadie and Murphy for taking us on much-needed walks.

To Drs. Brad Richards and Jeanne Czajka from the Cognitive Behavioral Institute of Albuquerque, thanks for including us on your affiliated training faculty. To Dr. Brenda Wolfe, thanks for your enthusiastic support. We're anxious to see your next book.

Finally, we are especially grateful to our many clients, both those with BPD and those without. They helped us understand personality issues in general, as well as BPD. They also taught us about courage and persistence.

Publisher's Acknowledgments

We're proud of this book; please send us your comments through our Dummies online registration form located at http://dummies.custhelp.com. For other comments, please contact our Customer Care Department within the U.S. at 877-762-2974, outside the U.S. at 317-572-3993, or fax 317-572-4002.

Some of the people who helped bring this book to market include the following:

Acquisitions, Editorial, and Media Development

Senior Project Editor: Tim Gallan

Acquisitions Editor: Lindsay Lefevere

Copy Editor: Amanda M. Gillum

Technical Reviewer: Lin Ames

Editorial Program Coordinator: Joe Niesen

Editorial Manager: Michelle Hacker

Editorial Assistants: Jennette ElNaggar, David Lutton

Cover Photos: Diamond Sky Images

Cartoons: Rich Tennant (www.the5thwave.com)

Composition Services

Project Coordinator: Kristie Rees

Layout and Graphics: Christine Williams

Proofreaders: Amanda Graham, Jessica Kramer, Nancy L. Reinhardt

Indexer: Palmer Publishing Services

Publishing and Editorial for Consumer Dummies

Diane Graves Steele, Vice President and Publisher, Consumer Dummies

Kristin Ferguson-Wagstaffe, Product Development Director, Consumer Dummies

Ensley Eikenburg, Associate Publisher, Travel

Kelly Regan, Editorial Director, Travel

Publishing for Technology Dummies

Andy Cummings, Vice President and Publisher, Dummies Technology/General User

Composition Services

Debbie Stailey, Director of Composition Service

Contents at a Glance

Table of Contents

Introduction

Sometimes we watch a news show that features a daily commentary called "Worst Person in the World." During this segment, the reporter chooses a few people who've said or done something that he thinks deserves his haughty contempt. Not so long ago, many mental health professionals may have labeled people with borderline personality disorder (BPD) as "Worst Patients in the World."

Until recently, no one knew which treatments really help people with BPD. Furthermore, people with BPD are incredibly scary to treat because they tend to have a lot of rage directed at themselves, the people they care about, the world, and even their doctors and therapists. Borderline rage can occur anywhere and anytime. Mental health professionals want to protect and help their clients, but people with BPD are hard to keep safe and frequently block therapists' best efforts. In fact, about 75 percent of people who have BPD hurt themselves in some way, and one out of ten succeeds in suicide.

On the other hand, if you're lucky enough to treat, know, or care about someone with BPD, you may want to consider that person one of the "Best People in the World." People with BPD can be highly intelligent, enthusiastic, and kind. Some therapists find that persistent effort over time results in a surprisingly gratifying metamorphosis in their patients with BPD.

The contrast between the good and bad in a person with BPD is like the contrast between black and white. Or, as Henry Wadsworth Longfellow said about the girl with the curl in the middle of her forehead:

> *When she was good,*
> *She was very good indeed,*
> *But when she was bad she was horrid.*

About This Book

If you or someone you care about suffers from BPD, we appreciate the challenges and painful obstacles you face. The purpose of this book is to provide a comprehensive look at the symptoms, causes, and treatment of BPD. We strive to help people who have BPD and the people who care about them gain understanding about this complicated mental illness. Because treating

BPD requires professional intervention, this book isn't designed as a stand-alone self-help program. However, you can certainly use it as an adjunct to psychotherapy. We share the belief with other professionals that clients benefit from being informed about their disorders, the suspected causes, and the treatments that work.

An Important Message to Our Readers

People with BPD often have greatly heightened sensitivity to criticism and disapproval. Thus, we're aware that a few of you are likely to take offense to the *For Dummies* part of this book's title. From time to time, people approach us and express concern about the meaning of *For Dummies*. We understand the concern. *Borderline Personality Disorder For Dummies* is our sixth psychology book in the *For Dummies* series. Our intent is to produce books that cover topics that an intelligent audience wants to know about without all the jargon and the technicalities.

Thus, we humbly offer you a clear, comprehensive overview of BPD. We vow to make this coverage serious and in-depth.

Conventions Used in This Book

We believe that stories and examples provide the best way to convey many ideas. Therefore, we use a lot of examples to illustrate our points throughout this book. The stories and cases we describe here represent composites of people with BPD whom we've known in our personal lives as well as in our practices. However, none of these stories depicts a true, recognizable portrayal of a specific person. Any resemblance to a specific person, alive or deceased, is completely coincidental. We bold the names of the individuals affected by BPD in each story the first time they appear to highlight that a case example is unfolding.

Borderline personality disorder is a bit of a mouthful, so we shorten the term to BPD throughout this book. In addition, we often use phrases like "most people with BPD" or "people with BPD generally do this or that." We absolutely realize that BPD plays out differently in each person. In some ways, there's no such thing as "typical" or "most" in the BPD world. However, we'd need another thousand pages to thoroughly discuss each variant and permutation involved in BPD. (See Chapter 3 for a discussion of the many symptom constellations of BPD.) So, just to be clear, we don't mean "everyone who has BPD" every time we say "most."

If you're using this book in collaboration with a therapist, we suggest that
you take notes and write out your responses to the exercises we provide —
whether on your computer, Blackberry, or iPhone or in an old-fashioned notebook. You probably also want to password protect or guard your material
because, after all, your notes are for you (and your therapist) and no one else.

What You're Not to Read

We stuff this book with loads of information about BPD, and we lay it out so
you can pick and choose what to read in any order you like. Use the table
of contents and index to jump into whatever you want to know. Or, take the
conventional route of starting with Chapter 1 and reading straight through
from there.

Sidebars contain information about interesting studies or other stuff that we
think is intriguing, but, in truth, not critical for understanding the material in
the rest of the chapter. Sections marked as Technical Stuff are similar to sidebars, but they relate specifically to the discussion in the chapter they appear
in. You can skip those, too, if you want.

Foolish Assumptions

We're going to take a wild guess here and assume that most people who read
this book are interested in BPD. That interest may stem from your own emotional issues, or you may have concerns for someone you care about who has
BPD-like symptoms.

On the other hand, you may be a professional who's looking for some accessible information that you can pass along to your clients. Or, maybe you want
a few hints about dealing with difficult therapeutic issues. You may also be
a student of psychology, counseling, social work, or psychiatry looking for a
clear introduction to this complex problem.

How This Book Is Organized

We divide *Borderline Personality Disorder For Dummies* into seven parts with
28 chapters, plus two appendixes. Here's a brief overview of each part.

Part I: Mapping the Boundaries of Borderline Personality Disorder

Part I introduces you to the notion of personality and its connection to BPD. Chapter 2 takes a close look at the characteristics that make up a healthy versus an unhealthy personality. Chapter 3 provides an overview of the symptoms of BPD compared to the symptoms of other types of personality disorders, such as paranoid, narcissistic, and obsessive-compulsive personality disorders. We also discuss some of the other emotional problems that often accompany BPD. Chapter 4 describes the cultural, biological, and psychological causes of BPD.

Part II: Taking Note of the Major BPD Symptoms

The six chapters in this part explore the major areas of dysfunction associated with BPD: impulsivity, emotional dysregulation, identity problems, relationship conflicts, thinking styles, and difficulties in perception. This material helps you more fully appreciate the magnitude of the issues that people with BPD must deal with in their everyday lives. If you have BPD, this understanding can help you identify the key areas of your life that you may need to work on. If you care about someone who has BPD, this in-depth exploration can clear up the confusion you've probably been experiencing for a long time.

Part III: Making the Choice to Change

Part III prepares you for treating or dealing with BPD. People with BPD and their loved ones need to know what treatments are available and which ones mental health professionals have found to be effective. Chapter 11 reviews the types of BPD treatment and the various mental health professionals available to provide these treatments. Chapter 12 describes the common obstacles that people must overcome before engaging in treatment. Chapter 13 illustrates how to explain BPD to other people and helps you decide just how much you want to reveal to whom. Chapter 14 looks at keeping physically healthy during the treatment process.

Part IV: Treatments for BPD

In this part, we draw from the various treatment strategies that professionals have found to be effective for BPD and apply them to the core areas of dysfunction that people with BPD exhibit. Chapter 15 discusses how to address problems associated with impulsivity, including self-harm and risk taking. Chapter 16 shows various strategies for improving your ability to regulate out-of-control emotions. Chapter 17 reviews ways to develop a clear sense of identity. Chapter 18 takes a look at how people with BPD can improve their abilities to put themselves in other people's shoes. Chapter 19 provides ways to form more adaptive states of mind and new types of thinking. Finally, Chapter 20 discusses some of the medication options associated with treating BPD.

Part V: Advice for People Who Care

This part is for people who encounter others who have BPD. Chapter 21 tells partners how to set limits and relate more effectively to the ones they care about who have BPD. Chapter 22 speaks to people who have friends with BPD. Chapter 23 discusses what parents who may have adolescents with emerging BPD can do and what they need to look for in their kids. Chapter 24 talks to adults who grew up with BPD parents and attempts to show them how to relate and better understand their parents. Finally, Chapter 25 talks to mental health professionals who treat people with BPD.

Part VI: The Part of Tens

This part gives you some quick tips on calming hot emotions. We also tell you ten ways to say you're sorry. Finally, we list ten things *not* to do when you're trying to overcome your BPD.

Part VII: Appendixes

Appendix A offers numerous resources for more information and help. Appendix B provides several blank forms and exercises that we reference in other parts of the book.

Icons Used in This Book

This icon appears to alert you to a specific insight or strategy for dealing with BPD.

This icon warns you about possible pitfalls or dangers that you need to be on the lookout for.

This icon highlights the take-away message. Pay attention to paragraphs marked with this icon.

This icon marks stuff that you don't have to read unless you're interested. We provide a little extra explanation next to this icon for those of you who like to delve into the discussion a little more.

Where to Go from Here

We intend *Borderline Personality Disorder For Dummies* to provide a comprehensive overview of this complex emotional and behavioral problem. Most readers without BPD will find that this information helps them to better understand the problem and to know how to relate to people with BPD better than they did before. People in close relationships with people who have BPD may find that a therapist can provide additional support.

If you have BPD, this book will help you better understand yourself and the people you care about. However, we strongly recommend that you also enlist the help of a mental health professional who is trained in treating BPD. BPD is one problem you don't want to deal with on your own.

If you're a therapist, this book can help you spot people with BPD more quickly and set better boundaries when you're treating them. However, if you're new to the treatment of BPD, you'll definitely want additional training and education about this disorder.

Part I

Mapping the Boundaries of Borderline Personality Disorder

In this part, we provide an overview on the part in...
a personality disorder (BPD). It explains the characteristics
people respond and form how the one what a pattern
pattern person who has a borderline personality disorder...
with others discussed in this part...

The 5th Wave By Rich Tennant

"You're so intolerant and I *can't* *stand* *that!*"

In this part . . .

1 n this part, we provide an overview of what borderline personality disorder (BPD) is and briefly discuss a couple of treatment options. We also discuss what a healthy personality looks like to help you better understand what's missing for people who have BPD. We describe the major symptoms of BPD and cover the major causes of this complicated disorder.

Chapter 1

Exploring Borderline Personality Disorder

....

In This Chapter

▶ Taking a look at the characteristics of BPD

▶ Searching for BPD's causes

▶ Calculating the costs of BPD

▶ Seeking help for BPD through psychotherapy and medication

▶ Knowing how to help someone who has BPD

....

A charming, exciting, intimate, intelligent, fun person suddenly turns mean, sluggish, angry, self-defeating, and dismal — a radical change in an instant for no obvious reason. What causes the unpredictable ups and downs from fear to rage, intimate intensity to distance, and drama to downfall that some people experience on a daily basis? Borderline personality disorder (BPD), the most common and debilitating of all the personality disorders, causes chaos and anguish for both the people who suffer from the disorder and those who care about them.

This book takes you inside the world of BPD and shows you what living with this disorder is really like. Unlike some books and articles about BPD, we strive to maintain a compassionate, kind perspective of those people who are afflicted with BPD. You may be reading this book because you know or suspect you have BPD or some of its major symptoms. If so, expect to find a wealth of information about BPD, its causes, and some effective treatments.

Perhaps you're a reader who cares about or loves someone who has BPD. By reading this book, you can discover why people with BPD do what they do as well as see how you can better relate to them. Finally, even if you're not in a close relationship with someone with BPD, you no doubt have a co-worker, neighbor, supervisor, or acquaintance who suffers from BPD, or at the very least, a few of its prominent symptoms. Even superficial relationships with people who have BPD can pose surprising challenges. This book can help you better understand what's going on and how to deal with the problems BPD creates for you.

If you're a therapist, you can use this book to expand your understanding of BPD. You can see how to deal with difficult therapeutic issues. You can also figure out how to set better boundaries while you simultaneously take care of both yourself and your clients.

In this chapter, we describe the basics of BPD in terms of how the disorder affects both the people who have it and the people who have relationships with them. We present what's known about the causes of BPD. We also tally up the costs of BPD for both the people who have it and the society they live in. Finally, we overview the major treatment options for BPD and show those of you who care about someone with BPD what you can do to help.

Breaking Down Borderline Personality Disorder

Personalities are the relatively consistent ways in which people feel, behave, think, and relate to others. Your personality reflects the ways in which other people generally describe you — such as calm, anxious, easily angered, mellow, thoughtful, impulsive, inquisitive, or standoffish. All people differ from their *usual* personalities from time to time, but, for the most part, personalities remain fairly stable over time (check out Chapter 2 for more on personality).

For example, consider someone who has a generally jolly personality; this person enjoys life and people. However, when this person experiences a tragedy, you expect to see normal grief and sadness in this generally jolly person. On the other hand, someone with a personality disorder, such as BPD, experiences pervasive, ongoing trouble with emotions, behaviors, thoughts, and/ or relationships. The following sections describe the core problems that people with BPD frequently experience.

The American Psychiatric Association has a manual that describes specific symptoms of BPD. The manual groups these symptoms into nine categories. Here, we condense these nine categories into four larger arenas of life functioning that are impacted by the symptoms of BPD in one way or another.

Although BPD has an identifiable set of symptoms, the specific symptoms and the intensity of those symptoms varies greatly from person to person. Chapter 3 reviews each of the nine symptom categories separately and covers how BPD manifests itself in a wide variety of presentations.

Rocky relationships

People with BPD desperately want to have good relationships, but they inadvertently sabotage their efforts to create and maintain positive relationships over and over again. You may be wondering how they continually end up in rocky relationships. Well, the answer lies in the fact that their desire for relationships is fueled by an intense need to fill the bottomless hole that they feel inside themselves. People with BPD ache to fill this hole with a sense of who they are, a higher level of self-esteem, and high amounts of outside nurturance, unconditional love, and adoration. But no one can fill such a huge personal chasm. Partners and friends are defeated the moment they enter the relationship. Their attempts to make their friends who have BPD happy inevitably fail. The people with BPD respond to their friends' efforts with disappointment, derision, or rage.

This intense negative reaction confuses partners of people with BPD because people with BPD typically start out relationships with enthusiasm, warmth, and excitement. New partners may feel entirely enveloped by love and caring at the beginning of their relationships, but, ultimately, things go terribly wrong.

What happens to turn a relationship so full of love and excitement into something full of pain and confusion? Well, many people with BPD fear abandonment above almost anything else. Yet, at the same time, they don't believe they're worthy of getting what they really want. They can hardly imagine that another person truly does love them. So, when their partners inevitably fail to fulfill their every need, they believe the next step is abandonment. This conclusion fuels BPD rage, and, as a result, they push their partners away. Better to push someone away than to be pushed away, right? This series of reactions is extremely self-defeating, but it's born out of fear, not malice. See Chapter 8 for more information about BPD relationships and Chapter 18 for how you can work to improve them.

Reckless responses

Human brains have built-in braking systems, which, in theory, are a lot like the ones that five-ton trucks use to slow down as they roll downhill. These brake systems come in handy when the trucks drive down steep mountains, or, in terms of the human brain, when the intensity of emotions flares up in certain situations. Unfortunately, most people with BPD have brake systems that are adequate for golf carts — not five-ton trucks — which are hardly enough to handle the weighty emotions that often accompany BPD.

Brain brakes, as we like to call them, keep people from acting without first thinking about the consequences of their actions. Like rolling dice in a game of craps, behaving impulsively rarely results in winning in the long run. Common impulsive behaviors in people with BPD include the following:

- Impulsive spending
- Gambling
- Unsafe sex
- Reckless (but not wreckless) driving
- Excessive eating binges
- Alcohol or drug abuse
- Self-mutilation
- Suicidal behavior

See Chapter 5 for a tour of the dangerous, reckless world of people who have BPD and Chapter 15 for how to start inhibiting such impulsivity.

Yo-yo emotions

The emotional shifts of people with BPD can be as unpredictable as earthquakes. They can also be just as shaky and attention grabbing. After people with BPD unleash their emotions, they usually don't have the ability to regain steady ground.

The rapidly shifting emotional ground of people with BPD causes the people around them to walk warily. In the same day, or even the same hour, people with BPD can demonstrate serenity, rage, despair, and euphoria. See Chapter 6 for more information about this emotional drama and Chapter 16 for how to try to control it.

Convoluted thoughts

People with BPD also think differently than most people do. They tend to see situations and people in all-or-nothing, black-and-white terms with few shades of gray. As a result, they consider events to be either wonderful or awful, people in their lives to be either angels or devils, and their life status to be either elevated or hopeless.

Sometimes the thoughts of people with BPD travel even closer to the edge of reality. For instance, they may start thinking that other people are plotting against them. They may also distort reality to such a degree that they may seem briefly incoherent or psychotic. They sometimes feel so out of tune with reality that they perceive their bodies as being separate from themselves. See Chapters 9 and 10 for more information about the thought processes of people who suffer from BPD and Chapter 19 for how to form more adaptive ways of thinking.

Exploring the Origins of BPD

If you trip over a log and break your leg, the cause of your broken leg is pretty obvious. And the pain in your leg will likely get better gradually as long as you take proper care of your leg. Similarly, if you spend the weekend with someone who has the flu and you get sick a couple days later, the culprit is pretty clear. In the case of the flu, you may have an upset stomach, body aches and pains, and a fever. You need to rest and drink fluids, but in a few days or a week, the symptoms will go away.

In contrast, BPD doesn't seem to have a specific cause, a consistent pattern of symptoms, or even a consistently predictable response to treatment. Nevertheless, different factors do seem to combine to increase a person's chances of getting BPD. These risk factors include the following:

✔ **Trauma:** People with BPD often — but *not* always — have histories of abuse, neglect, or loss.

✔ **Genetics:** BPD tends to run in families.

✔ **Parenting:** Some people with BPD report having parents who told them that their feelings weren't important or accurate.

✔ **Culture:** Family instability, a culture that fosters individual needs and desires over those of the community, and even the angst of adolescence may all contribute to the high incidence of BPD in certain populations, at least in the Western world.

✔ **Biology:** People with BPD appear to have differences in the way their brains work and the way the neurons in their brains communicate.

The multiple causes of BPD should increase compassion for the people who suffer from the disorder because these causes prove that people don't go through life asking for BPD. They acquire the disorder for reasons beyond their control. For more information on causes of BPD, refer to Chapter 4.

Counting the Costs of BPD

BPD inflicts an amazing toll on sufferers, families, and society. For a long time, experts assumed that about 2 to 3 percent of the general population had BPD. However, recent findings suggest that this estimate may have greatly underestimated the extent of the problem. An extensive survey that appeared in the *Journal of Clinical Psychiatry* in 2008 concluded that close to 6 percent of the population may warrant receiving this diagnosis at some point in their lives.

The next sections take a look at the personal costs, both physical and financial, of BPD for the people who suffer from BPD and the people who care about them.

In spite of the bleak topics we cover in the following sections, many people with BPD manage to have brilliant careers and live long, fairly successful lives. Furthermore, the passage of time typically results in reduced severity of BPD symptoms, and therapy can accelerate this process. In other words, don't give up, because you have many reasons for hope!

Health costs

Experts consider BPD one of the most severe mental illnesses. About 10 percent of the people with BPD eventually kill themselves, and many more of them seriously injure themselves in suicide attempts. Multiple studies conducted from the 1940s to the present have consistently found that people with severe mental illnesses (such as BPD) die young — shockingly, studies show that people with BPD live lives that are 20 to 25 years shorter than the lives of people without mental illnesses.

Many factors contribute to these premature deaths. First, people with mental disorders, including BPD, often resort to smoking cigarettes — an obvious risk factor — as a desperate coping strategy. Furthermore, people with mental illnesses usually have greater difficulty controlling impulses and, thus, find quitting even more daunting than other people do.

In addition, researchers find higher rates of obesity and diabetes among sufferers of BPD — researchers now consider both of these conditions to be almost as bad as cigarette smoking in terms of the health risks they pose. Additional risks that people with BPD carry with them include heightened probabilities of heart disease and stroke. Unfortunately, some of the medications that mental health professionals use to treat mental illnesses make matters worse by leading to additional weight gain (and its accompanying increased risk for heart disease, stroke, and diabetes; see Chapter 20 for more on medications and BPD treatment). Furthermore, people with chronic mental illnesses usually receive inadequate basic healthcare because they lack financial resources.

Accidental death rates and death from violence are also significantly higher in people with mental illnesses such as BPD. Risky, impulsive behaviors may result in unintentional deaths because of traffic accidents, drug overdoses, or sexually transmitted diseases (see Chapters 8 and 15 for more on impulsivity and BPD). People with mental illnesses are also more likely to be homeless, which in turn creates additional risks due to poor nutrition, lack of health-care, poor living conditions, and victimization.

Financial and career-related costs

BPD can exert a ruinous effect on employment and careers. People with BPD tend to be chronically underemployed — in part, because they may start out idealizing new job possibilities, only to end up disillusioned and disap-pointed when jobs don't live up to their inflated expectations. As we explain in Chapter 7, people with BPD often experience problems with knowing who they are, which often causes them to drift from job to job because they don't know where they want to go in life. Finally, because many people with BPD struggle to get along with other people, they often lose or quit their jobs because of relationship problems in the workplace.

On the other hand, some people with BPD are highly successful in their careers. They may be unusually skillful and gifted. Most of these surprisingly accomplished people still relate to their co-workers in problematic ways. For example, they may misinterpret co-workers' intentions and react to the slightest provocation with oversensitivity and anger. Their successful careers stand in stark contrast to their failed relationships.

The toll on family and friends

Marriage isn't as common among people with BPD as it is among people with-out the disorder. And, when people with BPD do marry, not as many of them choose to have children compared to the general population. Perhaps sur-prisingly, their rate of divorce doesn't appear to be strikingly different from the rate among the rest of the population.

Family members of people with BPD suffer right along with their loved ones. Watching their loved ones cycle through periods of self-harm, suicide attempts, out-of-control emotions, risky behaviors, and substance abuse isn't easy. Partners, parents, and relatives often feel helpless. Friends often go from trying to help to walking away in frustration and anger.

Furthermore, families of people afflicted with BPD must deal with the frustra-tions of scarce treatment programs, discrimination, and stigmatization. Even when families do secure treatment, the treatment process is prolonged and costly. Clearly, BPD casts a wide net of anguish that captures a lot of people in addition to its specific victims.

The effects of BPD on the healthcare system

BPD costs the worldwide healthcare system a lot of money, and, surprisingly, BPD possibly costs more money when it isn't treated than when it is. Some of these costs result from the personal health problems that often accompany BPD (we describe these health issues in the "Health costs" section of this chapter). These health problems cause people with BPD to go to the doctor more often, and because of chronic underemployment, a disproportionate number of people with BPD receive their healthcare at emergency rooms, which is the priciest source of medical care.

BPD is associated with at least 10 percent of all mental health patients. We strongly suspect that this estimate is low because many mental health professionals are reluctant to assign this diagnosis to their patients. This reluctance is a direct reaction to concerns about stigmatizing patients as well as the fact that some insurance companies refuse to pay for services associated with personality disorders.

Furthermore, BPD accounts for 15 to 20 percent of all inpatients in mental health hospitals. Inpatient mental health treatment tends to be extremely expensive, so costs mount quickly. Politicians often view these costs as prohibitive — a view that results in the underfunding of such services. Because publically financed mental health treatment programs are woefully inadequate, some people with BPD end up homeless or in prisons and jails rather than in hospitals or outpatient settings.

Treating BPD

For many decades, most therapists viewed BPD as virtually untreatable. Studies were few and far between, and the ones that researchers did conduct failed to demonstrate reliable, positive outcomes. Fortunately, the past 20 years have produced a small handful of approaches that hold significant promise. Several specific types of psychotherapy appear to be the most effective forms of treatment.

Psychotherapy

Psychotherapy refers to a wide variety of methods used to help people deal with emotional problems as well as difficulties in their lives and relationships. Psychotherapy takes place in the context of a relationship between a client and a therapist. Techniques involve dialogue, suggested behavior changes, provision of insights, communication, and skill building. A wide range of professionals, including social workers, counselors, marriage and family therapists, psychiatrists, psychologists, and psychiatric nurses, provide psychotherapy to some of their patients.

If you have BPD, you don't want to seek just any psychotherapy because many approaches to psychotherapy haven't proved effective for this particular diagnosis. Instead, you want to obtain therapy based on strategies that have generated at least some empirical support for their efficacy in treating BPD.

As of this writing, the psychotherapies with at least preliminary support for their effectiveness in treating BPD include the following (see Chapter 11 for more information about each of these therapies):

- ✔ Dialectical behavior therapy (DBT)
- ✔ Mentalization-based therapy (MBT)
- ✔ Cognitive behavioral therapy (CBT)
- ✔ Transference-focused psychotherapy (TFP)
- ✔ Schema therapy (ST)

Researchers have developed some of these therapies, such as DBT, specifically with BPD in mind. They've also modified some other traditional therapeutic approaches, such as CBT, to enhance their applications to BPD. After reviewing these approaches, we didn't find anything inherently incompatible among them. In fact, we've been struck by how they overlap more than by how they diverge.

Thus, as you can see in Part IV of this book, we take an integrated approach to treating BPD. In other words, we select ideas and strategies from several of the validated treatments and use them to alleviate specific BPD-symptom clusters. However, we don't explain which treatment each technique is based on because doing so would be too confusing. Furthermore, a few of the strategies we use appear in some form in more than one treatment approach.

This book isn't a comprehensive self-help book for BPD. Such a book would likely have double the number of pages. And, more importantly, self-help alone isn't sufficient for treating BPD. However, you're likely to find that Part IV, which describes different treatment approaches, provides a useful supplement to therapy.

Medication

The purpose of psychotropic medications is to lessen or alleviate emotional pain. Prescription drugs can be lifesavers for many people with emotional problems. However, in the case of BPD, medications don't seem to be as helpful as they are for other emotional problems. Even so, most people being treated for BPD take some form of medication. And sometimes they take a surprisingly large number of medications. Mental health professionals often give their patients these medications with the hope that they'll reduce some of their patients' symptoms of BPD. However, to date, research provides only limited support for the usefulness of using psychotropic drugs to treat BPD. For more about medications and BPD, refer to Chapter 20.

Many people with BPD also have other disorders, such as depression or anxiety disorders, that have been successfully treated with medication. Thus, using medications to treat other disorders in people with BPD can be a useful form of treatment.

Helping People Who Have BPD

If you're a concerned friend or family member of someone with BPD, learning about the symptoms, causes, and treatment of BPD can help you better understand the complexity of the disorder. In Chapters 21, 22, 23, and 24, we provide detailed information for partners, parents, friends, and adult children of people with BPD. In the meantime, here are a few tips to keep in mind:

✔ **Step back and try not to take BPD behaviors personally.** Realize that BPD makes controlling emotions a difficult task. However, people with BPD sometimes mistreat the people they love. By telling you not to take things personally, we aren't suggesting that you allow yourself to be abused — either mentally or physically.

✔ **Have a support group or therapist help you maintain your physical and mental health and keep your thinking clear.** People with BPD can make the worlds of the people around them highly confusing and chaotic, so you need to maintain some connection to reality.

✔ **Don't try to be a therapist.** You can't solve the problems that your loved one with BPD is experiencing. In fact, you can make matters worse by trying to do so.

✔ **Understand but don't accept.** You need to fully grasp what's going on and why, but you also have to know your limits — don't let someone with BPD run you over.

If you're a therapist who works with people with BPD, or are hoping to do so at some point in your practice, check out Chapter 25 for more information on how to relate to patients with BPD. And don't go at it alone; seek supervision or consultation — these cases can be challenging and sometimes confusing. Objective input from others can keep you on track.

Chapter 2

Defining Personality to Understand BPD

In This Chapter

▶ Picking apart personality

▶ Figuring out what's healthy and what's not

▶ Uncovering personality problems

Personality — you hear that word a lot. Most people assume they know what it means. For example, for many of us, the following three phrases are easy to understand and succinctly convey considerable information about a person:

✔ **She has a bubbly personality.** This woman probably laughs a lot, loves fun, and enjoys being around people.

✔ **He has no personality at all.** This man likely comes off as flat and boring, and he avoids hanging around other people.

✔ **He has an irritable personality.** This man probably loses patience quickly and puts people off.

However, you can't really capture a person's complete personality in one or two words — or even a whole sentence. In this chapter, we explore the full meaning of personality. We describe which characteristics make up a healthy personality and which ones identify an unhealthy personality.

This chapter lays the groundwork for understanding borderline person- ality disorder (BPD) and all the other personality disorders that we discuss in Chapter 3. After all, all these disorders have one thing in common — personality.

Digging into Personality

Personality consists of broad, fairly enduring patterns of behaving, relating, and expressing emotions to other people. Some of these patterns are quite healthy and adaptive, while others are not.

The term personality comes from the Latin word *persona,* which means *mask.* People use masks not only to project identities they want others to perceive but also to conceal what actually lies beneath the surface. *Personality* represents an attempt to describe the core essence of a person, yet, somewhat like a mask, that description is determined only by what others perceive. For example, a girl whom others describe as "the life of the party" may feel shy and self-conscious inside. Thus, the personality that others perceive of this girl isn't a direct reflection of her own perception. In contrast, some people have personalities that are quite consistent with their inner feelings and emotions. For example, an adolescent boy may perceive himself as the class clown just as his classmates do.

The next section discusses the core dimensions that distinguish a healthy personality from an unhealthy one.

Differentiating Healthy from Unhealthy

People with healthy personalities report considerable satisfaction with their lives. Others see them as well adjusted to life in general. They manage to obtain most of their goals, face challenges with resolve, and bounce back quickly from adversities.

On the other hand, people with unhealthy personalities describe their lives as being unfulfilled and unhappy; they're typically unsatisfied with what life has to offer them. Others usually see people with unhealthy personalities as poorly adjusted. These folks struggle to control their emotions, and they often have difficulty relating effectively to other people. People with any one of the personality disorders we describe in Chapter 3 have at least one of the characteristics of an unhealthy personality and relatively few of the qualities of a healthy personality.

However, the line between healthy and unhealthy isn't as black and white as you may think. Most people, even those with healthy personalities, present a mix of healthy and unhealthy qualities. Almost everyone struggles in some areas of life from time to time. You can visualize healthy and unhealthy personalities as lying along a continuum. The following dimensions of personality play a role in whether a personality is healthy or unhealthy:

- ✔ Flexibility
- ✔ Emotional regulation
- ✔ Ability to delay gratification
- ✔ Dependability
- ✔ Interpersonal effectiveness
- ✔ Emotional resiliency
- ✔ Self-acceptance
- ✔ Accurate perception of reality
- ✔ Moderation

These core dimensions that distinguish healthy from unhealthy personalities interact with one another. Thus, people who are quick to anger (in other words, people who lack the ability to regulate emotions) usually also struggle to keep friends (in other words, they have low interpersonal effectiveness). Consequently, after people acquire one or two unhealthy personality traits, they're quick to develop more unhealthy behaviors. The following sections describe these dimensions in detail.

Flexibility: Rolling with the punches

Habits govern a large part of people's lives. For example, you likely sleep on the same side of the bed every night. Perhaps you have a routine for getting ready for work in the morning. You get up, turn the coffee pot on, take a shower, read the paper, and eat breakfast — every day in the same sequence, on autopilot. Habits are good because they allow you to do things more quickly without having to think every action through.

On the other hand, sometimes circumstances call for flexibility. For example, in most countries, you drive on the right side of the road. But if you drive on the right side of the road in Great Britain, you'll likely end up in a head-on collision. For those of you who've tried driving in a country that uses a different side of the road than your own country, you know how awkward the change feels. You have to maintain vigilance and care so that you don't fall back to your old habits.

However, most people manage to make the adjustment. The ability to adapt to changing conditions is *flexibility*. If you can't make such changes, you're at a disadvantage in life. Flexibility is a key dimension of a healthy personality.

Life frequently demands some degree of flexibility. For example, when we walk along the road in Corrales, New Mexico, we habitually say hi and smile at the people we encounter. The people of Corrales expect this courtesy. In contrast, when we walk the sidewalks in New York City, we pass hundreds of people without offering a greeting or even making eye contact. People in New York expect this action, too. If we rigidly adhere to our New Mexico style in New York, people may view us suspiciously.

The people whose personalities are marked by rigidity and inflexibility struggle to adapt to changing expectations. This inflexibility or inadaptability is one dimension of an unhealthy personality. For example, an inflexible man may adhere to strict time schedules for daily activities, such as getting up and having his meals at the same times every day. These schedules work well for him until he goes on vacation with several friends. He gets angry when his friends want to sleep in a little later than he usually does and have meals at different times each day. His rigid rules and anger annoy his friends.

Emotional regulation: Controlling what you express

People with healthy personalities possess the ability to modulate their emotions, which means they express emotions at appropriate times in appropriate ways — not that they're emotionless. They may cry at a sad movie or laugh out loud at a comedy. They may feel anger, but they express it smartly. For example, they may be angry with a police officer who gives them what they see as an unjust ticket, but they don't punch the officer in the face.

On the other hand, people with unhealthy personalities may lack the ability to control their emotions. Irritation easily morphs into rage. Laughter escalates to hysteria. Anxiety leads to panic. For some people with unhealthy personalities, unbridled emotions rule their lives.

Having the ability to control one's emotions carries significant benefits to one's physical health. People who have the ability to moderate their emotions also tend to have

- ✔ Less physical pain
- ✔ Better cardiovascular health
- ✔ Improved immune system functioning
- ✔ Prolonged life expectancy

Ability to delay gratification: Controlling impulses

People with healthy personalities have the ability to persist at tasks and wait for rewards. They know how to save for a rainy day. They improve the quality of their lives through long-term planning and hard work. They know how to tolerate frustration and even discomfort when they're working toward their greater goals.

A hallmark of an unhealthy personality is the inability to wait for gratification. In fact, much of what people think of as immoral involves a failure to control impulses. Consider six of the seven deadly sins. Gluttony refers to excessive consumption and pleasure. Sloth is laziness and lack of discipline. Lust, greed, and envy all consist of unrestrained desire, which in the absence of self-control, leads to immoral behavior. And anger without self-control results in violence.

Dependability: Doing what you say you'll do

Another characteristic of a healthy personality is *dependability,* or conscientiousness. Dependable people do what they say they'll do. They're reliable, disciplined, and motivated. They approach tasks with zeal, enthusiasm, and thoroughness. As you can imagine, they accomplish more than the people who lack this trait do.

In contrast, people with unhealthy personalities may have little motivation. They frequently have great plans and ambitions, but they often do little to follow through with them. Other people may not be willing to count on them. Their lack of dependability and motivation usually prevents them from achieving significant success.

Interpersonal effectiveness: Having good relationships

People with healthy personalities often enjoy good relationships. Others see them as both agreeable and friendly. People who exhibit interpersonal effectiveness trust others without excessive suspiciousness, but they don't approach relationships with naiveté. They're skilled at accurately perceiving the motivations, feelings, and perspectives of other people. They seek and allow closeness with others while maintaining their own autonomy. They end relationships that become toxic, but they work hard to maintain connections with the people they value.

On the other hand, people with unhealthy personalities often have a hard time maintaining, or even beginning, close relationships. For instance, some people avoid relationships altogether — they usually distrust others and keep them at a distance. Others exhibit the opposite problem from avoidance and become extremely dependent on their close relationships. As a result, they often feel extremely insecure in their relationships and feel anxious, clingy, and jealous. They often lack the ability to understand other people's views.

Psychologists have studied the way infants respond to their primary caregivers. Some infants demonstrate what's known as an *anxious* or *ambivalent* attachment style — responding with sadness when their caregivers depart and ambivalence, anger, and reluctance when their caregivers return. Other infants exhibit an *avoidant* attachment style and show little distress when their caregivers leave; they often appear aloof when their caregivers return. In contrast, infants with a *secure* attachment style show distress and are upset when their caregivers depart, but they're easily consoled when they return. You can see similar attachment styles in people's relationships throughout life, although people may change their attachment styles at different points in their lives. People with healthy personalities often exhibit the secure attachment style, while people with unhealthy personalities often exhibit either the anxious or avoidant attachment styles.

Emotional resiliency: Bouncing back from tough breaks

Setbacks, adversity, and even trauma befall everyone throughout life. People with healthy personalities have *resiliency,* or the ability to bounce back. After they encounter disappointments or tragedies, they're better able to collect their resources and move forward than people without this ability. Emotionally resilient people persist even when recovery takes a long time and requires intense effort.

Of course, some events are so horrific or traumatic that recovery remains out of reach even for those people with extremely healthy personalities. However, people with healthy personalities are more likely than others to accept their fate with courage — they don't go down without a fight.

In contrast, people with unhealthy personalities often recover from adversity slowly — if at all. They tend to focus on the unfairness, injustice, and awfulness of their plights. They have a very limited range of coping abilities. They often see themselves as victims in need of rescue.

Self-acceptance: Seeing yourself as you really are

People with healthy personalities view themselves in a manner similar to the way in which others perceive them. They appreciate their strengths, but they also accept their faults. They neither bask in their own glory nor wallow in self-deprecation.

On the other hand, people with unhealthy personalities often think about themselves in extreme terms. They tend to see themselves as either all good or all bad. For example, a *narcissist* — someone who puts himself on a pedestal in relation to other people — exhibits one of the extreme self-views that an unhealthy personality may have. By contrast, other people have extremely low self-esteem and think of themselves as beneath everyone else, worthy of nothing but loathing and despair. Still others flip between these two extremes. See Chapter 7 for more information on how the issue of instability plays out for people with BPD.

Several decades ago, a number of psychologists promoted the idea that seeing yourself as better than reality was actually a sign of psychological health. They believed that possessing an inflated, overly positive self-esteem helped people achieve more, feel better, and have more friends. However, a variety of studies since then strongly suggests that psychologically healthy folks have a generally positive, *accurate* view of themselves that is neither self-aggrandizing nor self-critical.

Accurate perception of reality: Seeing the world as it is

People with healthy personalities tend to see the world around them accurately. They view people and events as they are. They don't view life's ugliness through rose-colored glasses, and they don't gloss over unpleasantries. They take occurrences at face value and don't read negative meaning into other people's intentions. Thus, they rarely personalize comments unless clearly warranted.

For example, imagine that a friend tells you she can't go with you to a movie. If you have a healthy personality, you're likely to assume your friend has a good reason for not going with you. You wouldn't see your friend's intention as a personal slight. But, if that friend says she'll never go to another movie with you again because she hates you, you likely — and reasonably — feel personally insulted.

As you probably guessed, people with unhealthy personalities often do quite the opposite. They magnify negative events and frequently discount positive happenings. They tend to think in terms of black and white, good or bad, and all or nothing. They have either exquisite sensitivity to criticism or blatant disregard for the feelings and rights of other people.

Moderation: Avoiding extremes

Benjamin Franklin, one of the founding fathers of the United States, extolled the virtue of moderation and counseled people to avoid extremes. Similarly, many psychologists have advocated moderation for a healthy personality. For example, someone with a healthy personality is neither overly introverted nor excessively extroverted.

Paradoxically, achieving moderation is sometimes more difficult than swinging between extremes, especially for people with unhealthy personalities. Thus, for many people, going from starvation diets to binge eating is easier than consuming food moderately. For others, completely abstaining from alcohol is far easier than drinking in moderation. This inability to achieve moderation is another dimension of an unhealthy personality.

Even good qualities become unhealthy when taken to the extreme. Honesty, courage, and generosity all sound like positive attributes. Yet, more isn't always better. Too much courage makes people take unnecessary risks, excessive generosity can easily be taken advantage of, and being overly honest may offend others. People with healthy personalities have many good qualities, but they avoid extremes — often unlike their counterparts.

Chapter 3

Describing BPD

. . . .

In This Chapter

▶ Sorting through the symptoms of BPD

▶ Exploring the evolution of BPD diagnosis

▶ Looking at other personality disorders

▶ Knowing the relationship of BPD to other emotional disorders

. . . .

*B*orderline personality disorder (BPD) provokes anger, angst, and agony in the people it afflicts. Their families and friends suffer, too. BPD manifests as a complex mix of long-standing patterns of thinking, behaving, and feeling that destroy happiness, relationships, and productivity. Furthermore, people with this disorder have trouble controlling impulses, relating to others, handling emotional disturbances, and, at times, perceiving reality.

In this chapter, we describe the signs and symptoms of BPD. We give you examples of how these symptoms torment people who have BPD and those who care about them. We also explore the nature of other personality disorders, including histrionic, narcissistic, schizotypal, and antisocial. You may be surprised to find that people often show signs of more than one personality disorder. Finally, we discuss other types of emotional problems that aren't part of BPD but that sometimes occur in conjunction with BPD.

The Nine Symptoms of BPD

Knowing whether you or someone you know has BPD requires careful scrutiny and input from a trained mental health professional. However, even professionals struggle with making this diagnosis because the symptoms of BPD vary dramatically from person to person. In a way, BPD is similar to the countless breeds of dogs that exist today. For example, cocker spaniels, terriers, Bernese mountain dogs, pit bulls, Russian wolfhounds, golden doodles, mutts, and Chihuahuas differ strikingly from each other, but they're all dogs. Likewise, people with BPD don't share all the same symptoms, but they do all have the same disorder.

People who suffer from BPD experience a range of symptoms, which mental health professionals group into nine major categories. Currently, to be diagnosed with BPD, you must show signs of at least *five* of these nine symptoms.

1. Sensation seeking (impulsivity)

To count as a sign of BPD, this sensation-seeking symptom has to involve a minimum of two types of impulsive, self-destructive behaviors. These impulsive behaviors trigger adrenaline rushes and intense excitement and include the following:

- Sexual acting out
- Substance abuse
- Uncontrolled spending sprees
- Binge eating
- Reckless behavior, including
  - Highly aggressive driving
  - Extreme sports
  - Shoplifting
  - Destruction of property

The impulsive behaviors we're talking about here are both risky and self-damaging. They often endanger the lives and well-beings of the people who exhibit them. For instance, sexual acting out may consist of frequent, casual, unprotected sexual encounters with complete strangers, which can lead to STDs or unwanted pregnancies. Uncontrolled spending sprees can involve numerous, unnecessary purchases that max out credit cards and pile up debt. Shoplifting often involves stealing items strictly for excitement and can lead to jail time.

2. Self-harm

Self-harm is a particularly common and conspicuous symptom in people with BPD. People who exhibit this symptom may threaten or attempt suicide and do so often. Others may deliberately burn themselves with cigarettes, slice their arms with sharp blades, bang their heads, mutilate their skin, or even break bones in their hands or bodies. Although this symptom is separate from sensation seeking, it also involves a certain level of impulsivity. People who exhibit this symptom have to be impulsive enough to try to kill themselves again and again. Chapter 5 describes symptoms 1 and 2 in more detail.

A common misperception is that suicidal threats rarely lead to real suicide attempts. In truth, though, you need to take any threat of suicide by a person (whether he's suffering from BPD or not) seriously and seek professional help immediately.

3. Roller coaster emotions

People with BPD experience extreme emotional swings. They may feel on top of the world one moment and plunge into deep despair the next. These mood swings are intense but usually transient, lasting only a few minutes or hours. The emotional flip-flops often occur in response to seemingly trivial triggers.

For example, a co-worker passes by someone with BPD in the hallway without acknowledging her. This unintentional slight can spark powerful anxiety and distress in the person with BPD. Most people who are in a relationship with someone who has BPD find that these mood swings are quite difficult to understand or accept.

4. Explosiveness

Dramatic bouts of anger and rage frequently plague people with BPD. Again, the events that trigger these rages may seem inconsequential to other people. As you can imagine, these explosions often wreak havoc in relationships and may even result in physical confrontations. People with BPD sometimes end up in legal entanglements because of their outrageous behavior. Road rage is a good example of this symptom of BPD, although not everyone who exhibits road rage has BPD.

5. Worries about abandonment

People who exhibit this symptom obsess over the fear that a loved one will leave them. Their terror over abandonment may cause them to appear clingy, dependent, and outrageously jealous. For example, a husband with BPD may check his wife's cellphone logs, e-mails, and car odometer readings daily, always looking for evidence of infidelity. Paradoxically, the obsession with keeping loved ones close usually drives them away.

6. Unclear and unstable self-concept

This symptom describes a failure to find a stable, clear sense of identity. People who exhibit this symptom may view themselves quite favorably at times, yet, at other times, they exude self-disdain. They often have little idea of what they want in life and lack a clear sense of values or purpose. Frequent changes in jobs, religion, or sexual identity may reflect shifting values and goals. Navigating life without a clear self-concept is like trying to find your way across the ocean with no compass.

7. Emptiness

Many people with BPD report feeling painfully empty inside. They have cravings for something more, but they can't identify what that something more is. They feel bored, lonely, and unfulfilled. They may attempt to fill their needs with superficial sex, drugs, or food, but nothing ever seems truly satisfying — they feel like they're trying to fill a black hole.

8. Up-and-down relationships

Relationships involving people with BPD resemble revolving doors. People with BPD often see other people as either all good or all bad, and these judgments can flip from day to day or even from hour to hour.

People afflicted with BPD often fall in love quickly and intensely. They place new loves on pedestals, but their pedestals collapse when the slightest disappointments (whether real or imagined) inevitably occur. People in relationships with people who have BPD (whether they're lovers, co-workers, or friends) experience emotional whiplash from the frequent changes from idolization to demonization. As a result, many people find difficulty in maintaining meaningful relationships with those who have BPD.

9. Dissociation: Feeling out of touch with reality

Professionals describe dissociation as a sense of *unrealness*. People who feel dissociated or out of touch with reality say they feel like they're looking down at themselves and watching their lives unfold without being a real part of them.

When people with BPD lose touch with reality, they usually don't do so for long periods of time. But sometimes when they lose touch with reality, they hear voices telling them what to do. At other times, they may suffer from intense, unwarranted mistrust of others.

As you can no doubt see, these signs and symptoms overlap and feed on each other. Thus, if someone explodes with little or no provocation, demonstrates unusual moodiness, and clings excessively to his loved ones, you can understand why that person's relationships suffer. And when relationships go poorly, self-concept can plummet.

In the next section, we show you examples of people with BPD who have some prominent BPD symptoms (enough to warrant a diagnosis of BPD), but who show no signs of other key symptoms.

Diagnosing BPD: Like Ordering from a Chinese Menu

Because a diagnosis of BPD requires only five of nine major symptoms, you can come up with dozens of combinations using different sets of five symptoms. For example, one person can have symptoms 1, 2, 3, 4, and 5, while another has symptoms 5, 6, 7, 8, and 9. Even with different symptoms, both people can receive an accurate diagnosis of BPD. To better understand this idea, consider the following three examples of people, all of whom carry the diagnosis of BPD.

Renee, a 42-year-old single parent of an 18-month-old boy, has three older children, whom their grandparents are raising. She feels unable to take care of the older kids. Her four children all have different fathers. Renee has been hospitalized five times for suicide attempts — each attempt coming after a breakup and subsequent alcohol binges. She fears she can't live without a man, yet she has never maintained a relationship for more than a year. She frequents local bars and goes home with strangers at the drop of a hat.

Renee excelled in school. She attended four different colleges but never completed her degree in mass communications. She has jumped from job to job and has no life direction or career path. She doesn't know what she wants out of life. Sometimes she basks in the attention she receives from men, but at other times, she feels worthless because of her inability to parent. Renee does seem fairly stable at times — especially when she's pregnant.

Renee demonstrates the following symptoms of BPD (refer to the complete list of symptoms in the section "The Nine Symptoms of BPD"):

1. **Sensation seeking:** Renee binges on alcohol and engages in unsafe sex.

2. **Self-harm:** Renee has attempted suicide multiple times.

5. **Worries about abandonment:** Renee desperately believes that she needs a man in her life to survive.

6. **Unclear and unstable self-concept:** Renee lacks goals and direction. She alternates between feeling good about her worth as a sexual woman and disdain about her inability to parent.

8. **Up-and-down relationships:** Renee has had many tumultuous relationships, none lasting more than a year.

In spite of her many problems, Renee manages to keep her temper in check. She doesn't feel particularly empty or bored, nor does she experience feelings of being out of touch with reality. Her day-to-day moods remain fairly stable with the sole exception of when she feels abandoned.

Frank's story below illustrates a different set of symptoms, yet he has the same BPD diagnosis as Renee.

Frank, a 34-year-old carpenter, loses his temper with little provocation. Although he's a highly skilled craftsman, he can't hold a consistent job because of his frequent outbursts. He lost his last full-time job after he threw a screwdriver at a co-worker. Now he picks up odd jobs wherever he can. Frank's moods swing from neutral to anxious, to dread, to anger, to dark depression — all in the course of a single afternoon. Frank believes in various conspiracy theories and worries that the government is plotting to control the minds of all its citizens.

At times he seems lost in his own world. Although he feels lonely and empty, he has never dated anyone or shown interest in relationships. When feeling especially down, he cuts himself with a razor blade until he bleeds. He wears long pants and long-sleeved shirts to hide the numerous ugly scars on his arms and legs. He reports that the cutting calms him down.

Frank has the following five symptoms of BPD:

2. **Self-harm:** Frank cuts his arms and legs with a razor blade until he bleeds.

3. **Roller coaster emotions:** Frank rarely feels good emotionally, but his moods run out of control. At times, he dwells on his anxieties; at other times, he feels consumed by deep depression.

4. **Explosiveness:** Frank loses control of his temper.

7. **Emptiness:** Although lonely, Frank neither seeks nor desires the company of others. He feels empty and unfulfilled, but he has little idea of what can improve his situation.

9. **Dissociation (feeling out of touch with reality):** Frank distrusts people and has paranoid beliefs that the government is out to get everyone.

As you can see, Frank presents quite a different picture from Renee. Unlike Renee, he doesn't care about relationships or fear abandonment. He has little concern for his self-worth, and he doesn't seek excitement and sensation through sex, drugs, alcohol, or reckless driving.

Maria, like Frank and Renee, also has a diagnosis of BPD, yet she has her own unique mix of symptoms.

> **Maria**, a 28-year-old insurance saleswoman, wins clients easily with her charm. She talks glibly and develops many superficially close relationships. She turns her clients into instant best friends. She puts these new friends on pedestals but dismisses them as demons when they fail to meet her lofty expectations. When she blows up at her friends, she has no awareness of her viciousness. After her outbursts, she desperately tries to make amends by buying gifts and showering her friends with attention. However, her friends eventually hit the road when Maria continues to lose control.
>
> When she makes a sale, Maria often invites the entire office out for dinner and drinks, blowing her hard-won commission. Although Maria earns a lot of money, she maxes out her credit cards and teeters on the edge of bankruptcy. Maria has a weight problem and binges on ice cream when she feels lonely. She follows her binges with starvation diets, but they don't last long. Her moods go up and down like a yo-yo.

Maria demonstrates the following five symptoms of BPD:

1. **Sensation seeking:** Maria goes on uncontrolled spending sprees and has episodes of binge eating.

3. **Roller coaster emotions:** Maria overreacts to both positive and negative events. Her emotions run out of control.

4. **Explosiveness:** Maria blows up at her co-workers and friends. She doesn't understand the impact she has on others.

5. **Worries about abandonment:** Although she's unaware of how she pushes other people away, Maria desperately tries to get them back when they leave.

8. **Up-and-down relationships:** Maria knows when and how to draw people in — during the early stages of a relationship. But when people disappoint her, she reacts with rage.

On the other hand, Maria doesn't cut herself or threaten suicide. Her self-concept remains reasonably stable from day to day. She doesn't dwell on feelings of emptiness, and she doesn't hear voices or suffer from paranoia.

TECHNICAL STUFF

Evolving approaches to diagnosing BPD

Great controversy surrounds the diagnoses for all personality disorders. In particular, mental health professionals like to argue about the diagnosis of BPD. The fact that different individuals with BPD can present such varying pictures has led many professionals to advocate alternative approaches to the diagnosis. Some professionals believe that part of the diagnostic problem relates to the term *borderline*.

Adolph Stern, an early American psychoanalyst, coined the term *borderline* in 1938 to describe patients who seemed to lie on the border between neurosis and psychosis. *Neurosis,* a concept popularized by Freudian psychology at the turn of the 20th century, describes a variety of emotions, such as anxiety, depression, and distress. These troubling emotions ostensibly stem from unconscious conflict. *Psychosis,* on the other hand, describes a loss of contact with reality, such as hallucinations, delusions, and serious problems with rational thought.

Whether mental health professionals will retain the term *borderline* is unclear at the time of this book's writing because professionals seem to be moving toward a narrower definition of BPD. BPD experts, Dr. John Gunderson and Dr. Mary Zanarini, have developed an interview (called the Diagnostic Interview for Borderline Patients Revised) to use for the diagnosis of BPD. In brief, the Gunderson-Zanarini approach focuses on the following four symptoms:

✔ **Unstable relationships:** The relationships of people with BPD tend to be quite stormy and manipulative; they're often characterized by entitlement, a habit for being demanding, and quick flips from idealization to demonization.

✔ **Mood instability:** The moods of people with BPD show heightened sensitivity to events and often shift from one mood to another because of misperceptions of other people's intentions. A sense of emptiness, anger, anxiety, and rage are common as a result of this issue. People with BPD have great difficulty bringing their emotions back to a normal state after they're out of control.

✔ **Impulsivity:** People with BPD often act without thinking in the form of recklessness, self-mutilation, suicide attempts, and/or sensation seeking.

✔ **Cognitive impairments:** People with BPD often have distortions in perceptions and thoughts. Feelings of intense distrust, hallucinations, and delusions are part of this symptom.

The Gunderson-Zanarini approach essentially collapses the usual nine symptoms of BPD into four major categories. Their approach recommends using the term BPD only for those people who exhibit all these symptom clusters. However, the mental health field hasn't yet reached a consensus for how to diagnose BPD. We, therefore, choose to use the current nine-symptom perspective throughout this book. But we do recognize that a narrower (or completely different) definition will likely emerge in the future. Regardless of the ultimate diagnostic criteria that professionals agree on, treatment strategies are likely to remain consistent with the ones we describe in this book.

Renee, Frank, and Maria all exhibit the minimum of five symptoms of BPD, and, as a result, they all receive the BPD diagnosis. However, most people with BPD have more than five symptoms. Furthermore, the vast majority of people with BPD also have one or more other personality disorders. See the "Other Personality Disorders" and "Emotional Disorders that Accompany BPD" sections of this chapter for an understanding of these other emotional issues.

Other Personality Disorders

People with personality disorders of any type have trouble with day-to-day living. Their emotions are out of sync, and they relate poorly to other people. In general, they don't seem very happy.

Mental health professionals have ten distinct labels for describing the various personality disorders as listed in DSM IV. Each label comes with a specific list of symptoms, but symptoms listed for one personality disorder often overlap with symptoms for another disorder. People with BPD almost always carry one or more additional personality disorder diagnoses. Therefore, someone with BPD may exhibit a dizzying array of symptoms, some of which are part of BPD while others are part of another personality disorder diagnosis.

To help you make sense of this dizzying array of symptoms and disorders, the next section reviews each personality disorder in detail. The personality disorders we discuss in the following sections currently fall into three major groupings:

- ✔ Odd and eccentric
- ✔ Dramatic and erratic
- ✔ Anxious and fearful

The odd and eccentric

No doubt you've met people who have one or more of the personality disorders in the odd and eccentric grouping — paranoid personality disorder, schizotypal personality disorder, or schizoid personality disorder. However, you may not have paid much attention to them because people with this kind of personality disorder don't have much need for other people. In fact, sometimes they aren't interested in people at all. They have a lower need for social contact than most people, and their thoughts are often somewhat distorted in that they perceive events differently than most people do.

The following sections take a look at each disorder individually.

Paranoid personality disorder

Paranoid personality disorder is a surprisingly common disorder, afflicting as much as 4 to 5 percent of the general population. Researchers think that genetics play a significant role in the development of this disorder. People with paranoid personality disorder look at their world with suspicion and mistrust. They typically

- ✓ Feel mistreated by others
- ✓ Hold grudges for a long time
- ✓ Criticize and judge others harshly
- ✓ Assume that most people are out to get them
- ✓ Feel like outcasts
- ✓ Doubt the loyalty of friends, partners, family, and lovers
- ✓ Feel jealous and frantically search for signs of betrayal

People with paranoid personality disorder often interpret neutral events as harmful. Thus, they harbor a great deal of resentment and hostility, and they typically blame others for their problems.

In spite of the seriousness of this disorder, these individuals rarely seek mental health treatment unless they're referred by the courts or their problems cause them considerable distress. For the most part, they don't trust other people — friends, lovers, acquaintances, or therapists — so they don't see a purpose in seeking help from others. They believe that any information they divulge to therapists will be used against them. Furthermore, they're driven to appear strong and autonomous and, thus, see therapy as a sign of weakness.

The ninth criteria for BPD is feeling out of touch with reality, which can include feelings of paranoia. However, feelings of paranoia aren't an especially prominent sign of BPD. You can have diagnoses of both paranoid personality disorder and BPD if your behavior shows strong signs of both disorders.

Schizoid personality disorder

Schizoid personality disorder affects about 1 to 3 percent of the population. Once again, genetics appear to play an important role and account for as much as half the risk for developing this disorder.

People with schizoid personality disorder are quintessential loners. They don't have close friendships, and they don't desire them. Other people consider them to be outcasts, and they rarely connect with their own families. They have poor social skills and don't understand the nuances of social interactions. Their emotions are flat and detached. They don't care about praise or criticism.

Furthermore, people with this diagnosis prefer to do almost everything by themselves. They derive little pleasure from most activities that other people enjoy, especially those that stimulate the senses, such as the following:

- ✔ Watching a sunset
- ✔ Listening to the ocean
- ✔ Hiking in the mountains
- ✔ Receiving or giving a hug
- ✔ Having sex with another person

If people with schizoid personality disorder work, they choose jobs beneath their abilities because they lack motivation. Like those with paranoid personality disorder, people with schizoid personality disorder don't often seek mental health services. They see no reason to seek help because they don't feel particularly dissatisfied with their lives. Left to their own devices, they live relatively quiet, aloof lives.

Autism is a spectrum of diagnoses in children that describes a wide range of difficulties with social interactions and restricted interests. Children with the milder diagnoses in the autism spectrum (specifically Asperger's disorder and pervasive developmental disorder) exhibit several of the same characteristics as people who have schizoid personality disorder as adults. Researchers have yet to study this issue in depth, but many mental health professionals believe that adults with schizoid personality disorder may have had one of the milder forms of autism as children.

Schizotypal personality disorder

People with *schizotypal personality disorder* share a major commonality with those who have schizoid personality disorder — they avoid close relationships and lack social skills. However, people with schizotypal personality disorder tend to have more anxiety in social situations than people with schizoid personality disorder. Furthermore, people with schizotypal personality disorder are far more noticeable to others because they have a variety of very odd or eccentric behaviors and thoughts. Examples of this striking strangeness include

- ✔ Beliefs that events in the world revolve around them — newspaper headlines, television (TV) news, and so on.
- ✔ Magical thinking such as strong superstitious feelings, bizarre fantasies, and belief in telepathy.

    Thoughts or beliefs that are a part of a person's culture don't count as magical thinking.
- ✔ Strange perceptions about their bodies, such as feeling like their hands are controlled by outside forces.

✔ Unusual speech or thoughts that others find hard to follow because of vagueness or overuse of metaphors.

✔ Paranoia (once again, symptoms from various personality disorders have a way of showing up in more than one disorder).

How these symptoms affect the lives of people with this disorder varies greatly from person to person. However, the following story gives you a glimpse of what someone with schizotypal personality disorder may look like.

Charlie, who is 37 years old, is known in his neighborhood as The Cap Man. He lives alone in a rundown mobile home in his uncle's backyard. His nickname refers to the many different baseball caps he wears wherever he goes. He owns hats from each major league baseball team and wears the hats in a particular order that only he understands. Charlie believes that the major league players depend on him for advice and that he must wear certain hats to communicate with them during plays. He has a cable system that allows him to watch all the games, and he spends hours alone watching baseball.

Charlie receives a disability check each month because of his mental illness. He has received multiple diagnoses since he was in school, including mental retardation, schizophrenia, and bipolar disorder. Recently, he was evaluated and diagnosed with schizotypal personality disorder.

Charlie has a case manager who helps him buy groceries and keeps track of his health because, without someone to help him, Charlie spends all his time sorting through his hat collection or watching TV. His case manager has referred Charlie for treatment, but Charlie refuses.

Charlie's case reflects the challenges of diagnosing some mental disorders. Although he fits a diagnosis of schizotypal personality disorder, at times in his life, he seemed even more out of touch with reality and was diagnosed with schizophrenia. *Schizophrenia* is considered a more serious condition that frequently involves delusions, severely disordered thinking, and/or hallucinations. The line between the two disorders can be very fine, even for experienced mental health professionals.

The dramatic and erratic

People with personality disorders in the dramatic and erratic grouping are hard not to notice. This group includes antisocial personality disorder, BPD, histrionic personality disorder, and narcissistic personality disorder. People with these disorders draw attention to themselves either by extreme seductiveness, hostile aggression, excessive emotionality, shocking violation of rules, or self-aggrandizing behavior — all of which they typically exhibit without thinking.

These individuals exhibit striking self-centeredness and have difficulty grasping how other people feel. Although BPD belongs in this grouping of personality disorders, we don't describe it here because we cover it in much greater detail in the section, "The Nine Symptoms of BPD."

Antisocial personality disorder

Antisocial personality disorder afflicts about 2 percent of the general population, with men significantly outnumbering women. However, if you go to a prison, you may find that as many as 50 to 80 percent of the inmates have this disorder. You don't want to run into someone with this disorder in a back alley, but, if you do, run.

People with antisocial personality disorder have little regard for other people, their rights, or their feelings. They blatantly break society's rules and frequently end up in jail. Many of them act with extreme violence with no remorse for their actions or compassion for their victims.

On the other hand, some people with antisocial personality disorder aren't particularly aggressive, but they may derive a sadistic sense of pleasure from conning other people. A small percentage of these people even manage to become CEOs of major corporations — but they do so through exploitation and manipulation. Paradoxically, they often exude charm and charisma. Typical symptoms of antisocial personality disorder include the following characteristics (for more about how this disorder can be confused with BPD, especially in men, see the "Gender in the diagnosis of BPD" section of this chapter):

- ✔ Irresponsible
- ✔ Deceitful
- ✔ Dishonest
- ✔ Impulsive
- ✔ Aggressive
- ✔ Irritable
- ✔ Indifferent
- ✔ Guiltless

People with antisocial personality disorder care more about maintaining their power and image than being in close, long-term relationships. At first, they may shower you with affection, but they leave the relationship the moment they feel bored or when you no longer serve their purpose. The antisocial personality disorder is what has prompted so many people to run background checks after meeting new potential employees, clients, or even dates.

Histrionic personality disorder

Although only about 2 percent of the general population has *histrionic personality disorder,* you may think the percentage should be higher because you rarely forget people with this disorder. They seek attention like rising Hollywood stars.

Some common characteristics of people with histrionic personality disorder include the following:

- Uneasiness when they're not receiving attention
- Excessive emphasis on physical appearance
- Extremely dramatic or provocative dress
- Sexually seductive behavior
- Exaggerated show of emotions
- Speaking style that attempts to impress but lacks substance
- Feelings of neediness, dependency, and helplessness
- Shallow and rapidly changing emotions

People with histrionic personality disorder are experts at flattery and flirtation, so people often find them quite interesting and attractive in the beginning. But over time, their self-centeredness wears thin, and their shallowness reveals itself.

Narcissistic personality disorder

Narcissistic personality disorder afflicts about 1 percent of the general population. People with narcissistic personality disorder, like those with histrionic personality disorder, crave attention. However, people with narcissistic personality disorder feel unusually self-important and entitled to special treatment from everyone else. They come off as arrogant and haughty.

Common characteristics of people with narcissistic personality disorder include:

- Consumed with self-importance
- Absorbed in their specialness
- Without empathy
- Exploitive
- Competitive
- Envious

People with narcissistic personality disorder treat others more like an audience than as real people. They fantasize that they have special talents or will achieve great fame or fortune. We bet you can think of someone you know who has a similar problem.

The anxious and fearful

This group of personality disorders is primarily characterized by anxiety, fear, shyness, withdrawal, and overconcern for the opinions of others. These people avoid harm at all costs and are unusually averse to taking risks. This group includes avoidant personality disorder, dependent personality disorder, and obsessive-compulsive personality disorder.

Avoidant personality disorder

At one time researchers considered *avoidant personality disorder* to be somewhat uncommon, but at the time of this book's writing, studies suggest that as much as 2 to 5 percent of the population may have this disorder. These people feel inadequate, shy, and fearful of negative opinions from others. They withdraw from people, not because they lack interest in relationships (as is the case with schizoid personality disorder, which we discuss in the section "The odd and eccentric"), but because they're afraid of rejection and criticism.

Their fears cause them to appear socially awkward and inhibited. They get involved with someone only when they feel almost certain that this someone will accept them. They're passive and lack the ability to be assertive. People with this disorder usually work in occupations that require little interpersonal skill and, thus, often achieve less than they may have done without the disorder.

Dependent personality disorder

Dependent personality disorder occurs in less than 1 percent of the general population. People with this disorder see themselves as helpless and in need of others' care. They're submissive and clingy, as well as desperate for approval. They have a hard time making decisions and ask for excessive advice from others. They avoid taking on responsibilities and, instead, try to get others to carry their responsibilities for them. They may be vulnerable to exploitation or abuse by others because they're so unassertive and unable to stand up for themselves.

People with dependent personality disorder tend to underachieve, a quality they share with people who have avoidant personality disorder. However, their failure is a result of a lack of initiative and feelings of inadequacy rather than avoidance of interpersonal contact. As you can imagine, the excessive neediness expressed by people with this disorder can wear down their friends and acquaintances.

When someone doesn't fit the categories

Like trying to fit round pegs into square holes, people don't always fit cleanly into one personality disorder or another. Sometimes a person has two symptoms of BPD, two symptoms of narcissistic personality disorder, and one strong symptom of histrionic personality disorder. Such a person doesn't fit neatly into any of these three personality disorders, yet he most likely demonstrates chronic difficulties with the handling of emotions, interpersonal relationships, and/or work. This person may also act without considering consequences. Someone who demonstrates these symptoms certainly shows the general signs of a personality disorder, but he doesn't belong in any specific category.

Mental health professionals have come up with one solution for this dilemma; it's called *personality disorder not otherwise specified* (NOS). Professionals use this diagnosis whenever a person's symptoms are mixed and simply don't meet the criteria for a specific personality disorder, such as BPD, histrionic personality disorder, or antisocial personality disorder. In fact, personality disorder NOS is the most frequently used diagnosis in the personality disorder

category because a very large number of people's issues aren't easily categorized.

This chapter describes all the personality disorder diagnoses that our profession has officially accepted at the time of this writing. However, experts continue to study other personality disorders that may eventually become formally recognized. These diagnoses include the following:

✔ **Depressive personality disorder:** Characterized by a chronic, gloomy, brooding, pessimistic outlook

✔ **Passive-aggressive personality disorder:** Characterized by passive resistance to demands, sullenness, and harsh criticism, especially of authority figures

✔ **Sadistic personality disorder:** Characterized by cruelty to others, intimidation, and amused interest in violence

Don't be surprised when you hear professionals discussing other personality disorder diagnoses. The way that mental health professionals view diagnoses evolves over time.

Obsessive-compulsive personality disorder

Obsessive-compulsive personality disorder (OCPD) afflicts perhaps 2 percent of the general population. People with OCPD are orderly, inflexible, and extremely detail oriented. They usually follow the rules excessively. Most people with OCPD have a high devotion to their work. They also tend to overwork, partly because they think they're the only ones who can do their jobs well enough and partly because of their excessive drive and perfectionism. They dwell on details to an extent that most people simply can't imagine. They organize their work and lives ad nauseam. People with OCPD live frugally to a fault.

Even when people with OCPD take on a hobby or other interest, they sap the fun out of it by scrutinizing and studying all the ins and outs of the activity. For example, an OCPD person may decide to travel to a foreign country for recreation. Instead of relaxing and carrying out normal preparations, however, a person with OCPD may

- ✔ Spend months reading every imaginable travel guide
- ✔ Learn the history and culture of the destination
- ✔ Master the language of the destination
- ✔ Fill the trip with an exhausting schedule of museums and historical landmarks

Of course, some of those activities can enrich an adventure. But someone with OCPD doesn't like to spend much time at the beach reading novels for pleasure or taking midafternoon naps. In other words, goals and useful activities supersede enjoyment and relaxation.

Although they have similar names, *obsessive-compulsive disorder* (OCD) isn't the same thing as OCPD. A particularly striking difference is that most people with OCD feel great distress from the effects of their disorder. People with OCPD, on the other hand, usually believe that the way they live their lives is the right, correct way for them to live, and they don't want to change anything about themselves.

For information about OCD, see the "Anxiety" section later in this chapter.

When you ask people with OCPD whether their lives satisfy them, most of them tell you that they feel content with their lives. The following story about Paul depicts a day in the life of someone with OCPD.

> **Paul** begins each day precisely at 5:15 a.m. His shower routine takes exactly nine minutes. He dresses by 5:45 a.m. on the dot. For breakfast, he always eats oatmeal (for his cholesterol), $1/4$ cup of prunes (for regularity), $1/3$ cup of nonfat milk, and a single cup of black coffee. He reviews his schedule book for the day and heads to his office by 6:15 a.m. He's always the first to arrive at 6:55 a.m. He enjoys the quiet time before the other employees arrive at 8:00 a.m. He reviews his schedule a second time and prioritizes each task that lies ahead.
>
> Paul logs on to his computer and checks his retirement funds at 7:30 a.m. and again in the late afternoon. Each Friday he gives himself a treat by completing an online financial checkup. He's pleased to see that all three online retirement analyzers indicate a 98 percent chance of his being able to live in his current lifestyle until the age of 105 or longer. Paul's secretary arrives at 8:00 a.m. She smiles and greets him. Paul simply nods and, without looking at her, says, "I looked over the letter I asked you to write yesterday and I have 17 changes. I want you to make them and run it by me again."

She rolls her eyes but knows that he won't notice because he rarely looks at her. She's worked for him for twelve years and has almost never seen him smile. As far as she knows, he has no real life, family, or friends outside work.

Although you may view Paul as miserable and miserly, he has no complaints about his life. He has no desire for change and doesn't seem to notice his emotional impoverishment. However, a mental health professional can accurately diagnose Paul with OCPD.

Emotional Disorders That Accompany BPD

You can compare the difference between a personality disorder (BPD, for example) and other types of acute emotional disorders to the difference between climate and weather. *Climate* refers to general patterns of weather that are fairly predictable over long periods of time. *Weather* refers to what is happening at any given moment in terms of temperature, wind, rain, and humidity.

For example, Florida's climate is mild with an enduring pattern of sunshine and warm temperatures. But Florida's weather changes from sunny to occasional thunderstorms and hurricanes. Like climate, personality disorders endure over long periods of time. In contrast, the acute emotional disorders, such as anxiety and depression, are more like weather — thunderstorms and hurricanes — in that they typically manifest in more intense and often shorter bursts than personality disorders.

People with personality disorders exhibit long-standing patterns of behavior that interfere with their lives. However, they also often have emotional disorders that roll in like thunderstorms. The following sections briefly describe the emotional disorders that most often occur with BPD — or that people sometimes mistake for BPD.

You may wonder why we devote so many pages to diagnoses that sometimes accompany or can be confused with BPD. Consider this scenario. If you get malaria, you want your doctor to treat malaria, not the bubonic plague. But if you have the bizarre misfortune of coming down with both of these maladies, you want your doctor to treat both of them.

The difference between acute emotional disorders and personality disorders isn't quite as clear and distinct as the analogy to weather and climate. For instance, some people experience anxiety and depression for many years, if not their entire lives, especially if they never seek treatment. Professionals disagree whether personality disorders and other emotional disorders are actually separate entities.

Anxiety

Almost everyone experiences a little anxiety from time to time. *Anxiety* is a sense of uneasiness, distress, worry, or apprehension. Some people feel anxiety in their bodies (stomach tightness or difficulty catching one's breath, for example). Others wake up in the middle of the night with worries running through their heads; and, still others avoid going places that arouse anxious feelings. Anxiety becomes a disorder only when it significantly interferes with someone's quality of life or health.

If you want more information about common anxiety disorders, we recommend you read our book, *Overcoming Anxiety For Dummies* (Wiley). There you can find details about the diagnoses as well as sound advice on how to treat them. Fortunately, treatment for anxiety disorders is typically quite successful.

The most common types of anxiety disorders are

- ✔ **Generalized anxiety disorder (GAD):** This disorder is characterized by an almost constant state of worry and tension that doesn't go away. The worries are generally excessive and exaggerated.

- ✔ **Social phobia:** This disorder centers on fears of public scrutiny and evaluation by others. People with this disorder avoid socializing, public speaking, attending parties, and answering questions posed by instructors.

- ✔ **Panic disorder:** People with panic disorder have intense episodes of overwhelming fear, usually accompanied by physical symptoms, such as shortness of breath, racing heartbeats, and sweating. Many people report that their panic attacks make them feel like they're about to die — in fact, people sometimes confuse panic attacks with heart attacks.

If you experience a sharp panic attack (especially if it's accompanied by chest pain or shortness of breath), you need to see a physician who can help you determine whether your symptoms are related to panic or another physical problem, such as a heart attack. Call 911 immediately. After being evaluated, you and your doctor can work on how to deal with and evaluate future attacks.

- ✔ **Agoraphobia:** This disorder frequently (but not always) accompanies panic disorders. Agoraphobia involves an irrationally intense fear of being trapped and unable to escape from crowds, theaters, or groups of any kind. People with this disorder often constrict their activities to the point that they become housebound.

- ✔ **Specific phobias:** Phobias involve exaggerated fears of specific objects, situations, or animals. The fear causes people to avoid these dreaded things to such a degree that their lives are restricted, somewhat like those with agoraphobia. Common phobias include an intense fear of heights, snakes, spiders, airplanes, insects, and lightning.

✔ **Post-traumatic stress disorder (PTSD):** PTSD often occurs following a life-threatening or horrifying event. This disorder involves unwanted memories or flashbacks, avoidance of reminders or memories of the event, and the feeling of being stirred up and constantly on guard. Traumatic events that may lead to PTSD include car accidents, war, and violent crimes (whether you're a witness or a victim).

Many people with BPD have histories of trauma, so some professionals propose that BPD is a complex form of PTSD. However, most people who experience trauma don't develop BPD and some people with BPD don't have extensive histories of abuse or trauma. Thus, most professionals believe that abuse and trauma can contribute to the problems associated with BPD but that they aren't direct causes.

If you or someone you care about has symptoms of PTSD, consider seeking professional help. It's a treatable condition, but it may never go away if you don't seek help.

✔ **Obsessive-compulsive disorder (OCD):** This complex disorder involves either obsessions or compulsions — or perhaps both. *Obsessions* are unwanted thoughts, images, or urges that are repetitive and disturbing. An example of an obsession is having intense worries about germs or contamination. *Compulsions,* on the other hand, are actions that you take to reduce the fears associated with obsessions. Thus, people with germ obsessions may wash their hands over and over again (an example of a compulsion) to reduce their worries about germs.

OCD is a fascinating, yet highly disturbing and serious disorder. To learn more, read our book *Obsessive-Compulsive Disorder For Dummies* (Wiley).

Mood disorders

Moods are emotional states that, in general, feel either good or bad. Most people's moods relate to what's currently going on in their lives. So, you're probably in a good mood when you're engaged in pleasant activities, such as sailing or eating ice cream. On the other hand, you may be in a bad mood when you see your life savings go up in smoke because of falling stock prices.

However, moods sometimes take on a life of their own. *Mood disorders* are characterized by emotions that run out of control and dominate a person's life.

You can treat mood disorders using a variety of methods, including specific psychotherapies, medications, lifestyle changes, exercise, and even light therapy in some cases.

Although mood disorders come in a variety of types, the main two types are depression and bipolar disorder, which we cover in the next sections.

Depression

Depression is a disorder that is characterized by low moods, lack of pleasure, loss of interests, appetite changes, sleep disturbances, low self-esteem, poor concentration, and often thoughts of suicide. Depression varies in severity, but it's always serious. *Dysthymia* is a somewhat milder form of depression. Dysthymia also involves low moods, but it doesn't have as many of the symptoms of depression. Dysthymia tends to be more chronic than regular depression.

If you or someone you know has experienced significant symptoms of depression for more than a week or two, consider seeking professional help — especially if the symptoms include thoughts of suicide.

Bipolar disorder

Fluctuating moods characterize *bipolar disorder.* Everyone's moods go up and down sometimes. However, sufferers of bipolar disorder experience mood swings that occasionally rise beyond normal, good moods. These episodes are called either *mania* or *hypomania,* depending on the severity of the episode (mania is considered more severe). During a manic phase, the world of someone with bipolar disorder becomes too good. Manic phases typically involve the following symptoms:

- ✔ Racing thoughts
- ✔ Inflated, grandiose self-esteem
- ✔ Poor judgment
- ✔ Decreased need for sleep
- ✔ Rapid speech
- ✔ Irritability
- ✔ High but unfocused energy
- ✔ Risky, impulsive behaviors
- ✔ High distractibility

Most (but not all) people with bipolar disorder also experience phases of depression that can range from mild to severe. The moods of people with bipolar disorder seem to have lives of their own and go up and down independently of what's going on in the lives of the sufferers. Remember that fluctuating moods is also a symptom of BPD, but the moods of people with BPD are usually triggered by positive or negative events.

Most people who run through the highs and lows of bipolar disorder require some type of medication in addition to psychotherapy to help gain control of their mood swings.

Over the past couple of decades, the diagnosis of bipolar disorder has become more and more common. Interestingly, a number of the symptoms of bipolar disorder significantly overlap with symptoms of BPD. In our practice, we have observed that some people who are diagnosed with bipolar disorder actually seem to fit better with a diagnosis of BPD. However, distinguishing between these two disorders may be less important than focusing on treating a person's specific symptoms.

For a lot more information about mood disorders and their treatment, read our book, *Depression For Dummies* (Wiley), or *Bipolar Disorder For Dummies* by Candida Fink and Joe Kraynak (Wiley).

Other emotional disorders

People with BPD often act impulsively, abuse alcohol or drugs, and occasionally lose touch with reality. The following three disorders share some of these symptoms with BPD, but these disorders are considered separate disorders and require separate and specific treatment:

Attention deficit/hyperactivity disorder

Attention deficit/hyperactivity disorder (AD/HD) begins in childhood and is characterized by the following symptoms:

- ✔ Poor focus
- ✔ Forgetfulness
- ✔ Lack of organization
- ✔ Distractibility
- ✔ Fidgetiness
- ✔ Impulsivity

These symptoms cause problems in school, at work, and in relationships. People with BPD may also have AD/HD, but not necessarily. Even though people with BPD tend to be impulsive, they may not show the other critical signs of AD/HD.

Substance abuse

Substance abuse involves frequent overuse of drugs, alcohol, or prescription medications that results in problems at work, problems with relationships, legal difficulties, or dangerous behaviors. People with BPD frequently have substance abuse problems; however, not everyone with BPD abuses substances. Diagnosing and addressing substance abuse is very important when someone with BPD shows any signs of this problem.

Gender in the diagnosis of BPD

More women than men receive a diagnosis of BPD. Professionals disagree on why this trend exists. One possible reason that more women receive a diagnosis of BPD than men is that women seek help for their problems from mental health providers more readily (and more often) than men do.

Gender differences in BPD diagnosis may also occur because mental health professionals, family members, the legal community, and society at large don't view behaviors in men and women in the same way. For example, people interpret violence and aggression differently when the perpetrator is a man rather than a woman. The following two stories about Randy and Tammy illustrate this issue.

> **Randy** finishes his fifth beer at the Mountain Brewery and demands a final beer with a chaser for the road. The bartender says, "Randy, I think you've had enough. I'm turning off the tap. How about a soda?" Randy throws his car keys across the bar, barely missing another patron. He exclaims, "I'm not driving — give me another round!"
>
> The bartender says, "Let me call you a cab. I can't serve you anymore." Randy starts yelling and pushes the bartender. Several patrons dial 911 immediately; police arrive and arrest Randy.

Randy's behavior lands him in jail. In contrast, Tammy's story below shows you how the same behavior from a woman can evoke a completely different reaction and outcome.

> **Tammy** finishes her fifth beer at the Mountain Brewery and demands a final beer with a chaser for the road. The bartender says, "Tammy, I think you've had enough. I'm turning off the tap. How about a soda?" Tammy throws her car keys across the bar, barely missing another patron. She exclaims, "I'm not driving — give me another round!"
>
> The bartender says, "Let me call you a cab. I can't serve you anymore." Tammy starts yelling and pushes the bartender. Several patrons go up to Tammy, and one man puts his arm around her shoulders. He says, "Tammy, let me take you home. The bartender has to follow the rules or he'll be fired. You can have another beer at home."

Tammy and Randy both had too much to drink. They acted aggressively and over the top. However, people usually find aggressive behavior in men more threatening than in women. Tammy and Randy demonstrate identical symptoms (rage and substance abuse) that frequently occur in people who have BPD. However, when a mental health professional sees both of them, he may diagnose Tammy with BPD while diagnosing Randy with antisocial personality disorder (see the "Other Personality Disorders" section for more on this disorder).

The two diagnoses do have some overlapping symptoms. However, a diagnosis of antisocial personality disorder involves behavior that is more outrageous and out of line with society's norms than a diagnosis of BPD. People typically interpret aggressive behavior on the part of a woman as less serious because it doesn't seem as threatening to others as aggressive behavior from a man.

Psychosis

In this chapter's section, "The Nine Symptoms of BPD," we note that one symptom of BPD is occasional loss of contact with reality. People with BPD sometimes hear voices that aren't really there, experience beliefs that others are out to get them, or have strong feelings of detachment or unrealness. People who are diagnosed with *psychosis* have similar experiences, but their episodes usually last longer and involve a more severe loss of contact with reality.

Loss of touch with reality, including hearing or seeing things that aren't there, inability to speak or think logically, and extreme paranoia, are signs of a serious disorder. These symptoms require prompt medical attention.

Chapter 4

Who Gets BPD and Why?

In This Chapter

▶ Looking at the influence of culture on personality

▶ Exploring the contribution of childhood challenges

▶ Uncovering the biological and genetic factors behind BPD

*N*ot everyone who has a horrible childhood experience ends up with borderline personality disorder (BPD). However, most people with BPD report difficult or traumatic childhoods. Recent studies suggest that combinations of genetic influences accompanied by highly challenging developmental events are usually present in people who develop BPD. In addition, culture and society create conditions that either facilitate or inhibit the development of BPD.

Scientists can't pinpoint a single, clear pathway that leads to the emergence of BPD in a particular person. Consider the flu as a rough analogy. People don't come down with the flu every time they're exposed to the flu virus. Other factors, such as the person's genetic makeup, general health, levels of current stress, and past history (having received a flu shot, for example), make a difference in whether or not a certain person will come down with the flu. Similarly, exposure to one or two risk factors doesn't cause BPD in everyone.

In this chapter, we explore the ins and outs of the major risk factors for BPD. We also try to show you how various combinations of factors may contribute to the emergence of BPD.

Considering Culture

Culture is similar to the concept of personality (for more on personality, head to Chapter 2). Personality attempts to capture the essence of a person; culture attempts to capture the essence of a community. *Culture* represents enduring patterns of behavior, attitudes, beliefs, and ways of expressing emotions that are common to a large community of people. Culture transmits strong expectations about the way individual members of a particular community are supposed to live their lives.

Culture also influences the way people express emotional distress. In most poor countries, for example, intentionally cutting oneself is a rare and confusing event. In wealthier cultures, however, the act of self-mutilation is a relatively common occurrence, especially among troubled adolescents.

Some emotional disorders, such as schizophrenia and obsessive-compulsive disorder, occur at about the same rate and in similar ways across most cultures. See Jerome and Irene Levine's *Schizophrenia For Dummies* (Wiley) and our own *Obsessive-Compulsive Disorder For Dummies* (Wiley) for more information about these two disorders. However, BPD symptoms appear at different rates in different cultures. The varying social norms that exist across cultures may explain this difference in the rate of occurrence, at least in part. The next sections discuss the following five issues that differ across cultures and that may impact how frequently BPD occurs:

- ✔ Individualism
- ✔ Adolescence
- ✔ Entitlement
- ✔ Family instability
- ✔ Technology

Individualism: Emphasizing me versus we

Since before the days of the Declaration of Independence, American culture has strongly encouraged individualism. Today parents, teachers, and other role models encourage young people to strive for achievement on their own — to be all that they can be. Success in the United States is measured by how much more you accomplish or how much better you are at a particular skill than everyone else around you.

People in the United States, and in many other modern societies, are movers. People move away from their families to better their own lives or to experience something new. Many modern industrialized countries share the culture that celebrates the individual.

In contrast, more traditional cultures, such as those in the Far East, encourage community, family, and interdependence. These cultures emphasize bringing honor to the family group. In traditional cultures, people have more structure within their communities. Families — both immediate and extended — provide support for one another. Unlike more modern cultures, being part of a group is more important than being an individual in traditional cultures.

What does the emphasis on the individual versus the group have to do with BPD? Researchers have lamented the astonishing lack of studies on BPD across various cultures. Although symptoms of BPD clearly appear at varying rates across cultures, no one knows the exact frequency of BPD around the world. However, a number of researchers have noted that many of the symptoms of BPD occur more often in cultures that emphasize the needs, values, and priorities of individuals over those of the community at large.

Some scientists believe that a concept known as self-absorption supports this observation. *Self-absorption* refers to a narrowed focus on oneself and a heightened concern for evaluating that self. Social scientists have discovered that an excessive focus on oneself substantially increases the risk for a wide range of physical and emotional problems, including

- ✔ Eating disorders
- ✔ Anger
- ✔ Alcoholism
- ✔ Drug abuse
- ✔ Self-harm
- ✔ Depression
- ✔ Anxiety
- ✔ Sensation seeking

In Chapter 3, you can see that most of these problems are common symptoms of BPD. A number of psychologists have suggested that an excessive emphasis on the self creates stress and pressure that lead to these and other similar symptoms. A community with strong social connections and an effective support system may eliminate much of this pressure.

See the "Sleuthing self-absorption" sidebar for more information about the relationship between emotional problems and an excessive focus on the self.

Please understand that we're not blaming people with BPD for being too self-absorbed. No one wants or asks for BPD, and people don't often seek out self-absorption. In our opinion, modern culture encourages this trait among its people. Furthermore, self-absorption is but one of many contributors to the development of BPD.

Sleuthing self-absorption

Sometimes nature creates unexpected experiments. Susan Nolen-Hoeksema, professor of psychology at Yale University, stumbled upon one such experiment during an organized study of her own. In the late 1980s, Nolen-Hoeksema measured a group of college students for their tendency to ruminate about themselves. *Rumination* involves focusing on oneself and the causes of one's problems rather than on coming up with solutions. Fourteen days after her experiment, the area near the college experienced an earthquake. Ten days later, Nolen-Hoeksema's researchers went back to the students they'd previously assessed and measured their levels of depression and symptoms of stress. The researchers assessed the students' levels of stress and depression again seven weeks after the earthquake. They found that students who were ruminators had developed significantly higher levels of depression right after the earthquake than people who weren't ruminators and

that their stress and depression levels were sustained at the final assessment seven weeks after the earthquake.

Many other studies have shown similar trends. For example, several studies have shown that increasing someone's self-focus causes undesirable spikes in depressive and anxious feelings as well as a reduced ability to solve problems. These experiments studied the effects of rumination by using various techniques to increase self-focus. For example, one such experiment asked subjects to spend eight minutes reflecting on their personal traits and emotional states. Another experiment asked participants to look at themselves in a mirror for a particular period of time, and a third experiment asked subjects to write paragraphs that contained numerous references to themselves. All these strategies for increasing self-focus caused an increase in negative feelings and lowered the ability to solve problems.

Adolescence and BPD

Adolescence is a relatively modern concept that refers to the transition period between childhood and adulthood. Adolescence emerged as a consequence of the Industrial Revolution as a way to keep children in school and out of sweatshops — not such a bad idea. However, as it has evolved, adolescence has become a tumultuous and treacherous time for many teens. Arguably, adolescence brings with it large chunks of free time, which means numerous opportunities for teens to engage in self-destructive behaviors. Pressures mount for teens to have more, be more, and be noticed.

Adolescence is a time when psychological disorders, including signs of personality disorders, such as BPD, emerge. Problems with gangs, violence, drug use, sensation seeking, eating disorders, and risky sexual behavior have burgeoned among adolescents in the past four or five decades.

Of course, we're not saying that adolescence itself causes emotional disorders; after all, many adolescents mature into adulthood with no sign of any emotional disorders. However, from a historical perspective, BPD symptoms and behaviors have only been written about in the past century or so — which coincides with the emergence of adolescence as a feature of modern culture. When kids were busy milking cows and gathering crops, much less adolescent angst existed among teens. Perhaps if we can give teens more important tasks than texting, video gaming, and hanging out at the mall, they won't be as easily seduced by self-destructive behaviors.

Entitlement: Feeling too good

In recent years, the value of suffering — both physical and emotional — has diminished. A few hundred years ago, people admired others for their ability to endure hardship. For example, ancient religious writings are full of messages extolling the virtues of suffering. Many people believed that suffering strengthened character and helped people appreciate the gifts of life.

That message has changed dramatically in modern, industrialized cultures. Today, people look to pills to combat the slightest emotional distress, and advertising pushes people to treat their frowns, wrinkles, and splotches like they do diseases. Even normal grief in response to loss has become an abnormal condition in need of medical treatment.

Unfortunately, an inability to accept any negative feelings typically increases a person's vulnerability to being overwhelmed by emotional distress. People who believe that feeling good all the time is a basic human right end up feeling entitled to having all their needs met. As a result, they become sharply disappointed when the world fails to cater to their every whim.

Don't get us wrong; we like feeling good like most other people. We're definitely not promoting the idea of suffering for suffering's sake. However, as we note in Chapter 2, the abilities to tolerate frustration, delay gratification, and recover from adversity are hallmarks of a healthy personality, and people who lack these abilities often struggle to remain calm and buoyant with every little mishap that comes their way.

Family instability

Today, especially in Western cultures, more children grow up in single-parent families than ever before. Although divorce rates have peaked and then decreased slightly in the past 10 or 20 years, they remain much higher than they were in 1950. Furthermore, fewer people marry today than in the past, and when they do marry, they marry later in life.

In addition, large extended families consisting of multiple generations — cousins, aunts, uncles, and grandparents — aren't as common as they were in the past. Today, immediate families (Mom, Dad, and two kids, for example) spread out across the world. As a result, sources of emotional support are much less reliable and stable than they once were. Again, we don't know to what extent family instability contributes to the development of BPD, but social scientists have long known that social support serves as a strong protective force against declining mental and physical health.

Technology and its isolating effects

Technology in the form of computers, cellphones, and the Internet have increased productivity, access to information, and the ability to communicate. Personally, we love computers — they've enabled us to write more and to research with greater ease than ever. Sometimes we spend days at a time holed up in our offices, banging away on the computer and not speaking to other living beings. Yet, because we don't want to lose real, face-to-face communication, we try to monitor our isolation to make sure we don't go overboard with cyber communication.

Unfortunately, some people find themselves drawn into a digital, virtual world that becomes more exciting than their real lives. They spend day after day socializing on MySpace, Facebook, Twitter, and online gaming sites. They lose contact with the people around them, and they become fully absorbed in their virtual selves. Consider the following ways in which many people choose to relate to others:

✔ Joining a World of Warcraft team rather than the soccer team

✔ Participating in live Webcasts rather than meeting up with friends at a local coffee shop

✔ Posting comments on discussion boards rather than communicating face to face in social settings

✔ Conversing via e-mails and text messages rather than phone conversations

✔ Being a part of anonymous online support groups rather than attending local support group meetings

✔ Cybersnooping friends' profiles rather than getting to know them personally

Of course, some of these ways of "techno-relating" are fun and beneficial. The social components of the Web appeal to many people because they offer easier, safer, and quicker ways to connect to others. No one really knows to what extent isolation from overuse of technological ways of relating to other people contributes to the development of BPD or other emotional problems. However, technology can prevent the in-person contact you need to build relationships and trust. To get better, people with BPD need real relationships, real social support, and real feedback about their behavior.

Childhood Challenges and the Increased Risk of BPD

Mental health professionals widely ascribe to the theory that the events of a person's childhood greatly affect mental health in adolescence and adulthood. Parents and the way they parent greatly influence the mental and emotional states of their children throughout their lives. Other family members, peers, schools, neighborhoods, friends, and even strangers also impact children. In addition, random events, such as hurricanes and house fires, can change young people's lives forever.

As important as the impact of childhood is on people, however, keep in mind that children are quite resilient. Many mental health professionals have allowed their opinions to run ahead of the data in drawing connections between childhood problems and disorders in adulthood. As research has shown, the development of BPD involves much more than just poor parenting or even traumatic events. Many kids experience significant traumas as well as neglectful parents, yet they manage to lead emotionally healthy lives. A biological vulnerability usually plays at least a part in the development of BPD (see the "Bringing biology into the BPD equation" section for more information). Nevertheless, difficult childhoods do raise the risks for developing BPD.

The three major factors that can affect childhood negatively and, as a result, can increase risk for BPD in some cases are

- ✔ Parenting styles
- ✔ Abuse and trauma
- ✔ Early separation and loss

BPD has no single cause. Most of the issues we describe in the following sections must occur in extreme forms and/or for a very prolonged period of time to increase the risk of BPD. Even then, they usually require some interaction with biological and cultural factors for BPD to emerge.

Problematic parenting

Most of what mental health professionals know about the parents of people who develop BPD comes from reports made by the people who suffer from BPD. But when people suffer great distress, they tend to focus on and recall negative events far more than positive ones. When they feel better, their memories of certain events have a somewhat more cheerful tone. As a result, researchers quarrel over how much weight to give studies based on such recollections.

Unfortunately, far fewer studies objectively look at parenting styles at a given point in time and then follow the outcomes in terms of how children function in adulthood. Therefore, current professional perspectives on parenting and its true long-term effects remain somewhat murky. At the same time, mental health professionals have reached a reasonable degree of consensus that certain parenting practices do harm children. The next sections take a look at some problematic parenting styles.

Emotional invalidation

Psychologist Marsha Linehan promotes the idea that emotional invalidation plays a critical role in fostering the development of BPD. *Emotional invalidation* refers to a variety of ways in which parents diminish, demean, discount, and disqualify children's emotional experiences.

Parents who emotionally invalidate their kids deliver a wide variety of messages to their kids that ultimately teach them to distrust or disbelieve their own emotional reactions. In the following list, we explore some of the more common messages parents use to invalidate their children's emotions and describe how these messages affect the children's feelings:

- ✔ **You shouldn't feel that way.** Parents send messages like this one when their kids have been hurt or upset. Parents may feel uncomfortable with their children's distress and, thus, attempt to squelch it by using this message. They may think they're helping their kids calm down, but the net effect of the message is to induce guilt and to invalidate the kids' feelings.

- ✔ **What are you crying about?** Most people don't enjoy listening to other people cry. In fact, some parents have a very low tolerance for dealing with the extremely grating noise that crying and wailing generate. Unfortunately, children can't really respond to this question because they're feeling overwhelmed and often simply don't know the answer. With this message, parents imply that distress and sadness aren't acceptable emotions.

- ✔ **You're exaggerating.** This message essentially tells children that they're fundamentally misinterpreting reality. As a result, the kids learn to distrust their perceptions. This message attempts to suppress emotions rather than teach kids how to regulate them.

✔ **That's just not true!** Sometimes children come to parents with opinions about relationships, school, or even politics. Rather than encourage independent thought, parents lead children to distrust their own viewpoints and, instead, rely on their parents' superior knowledge. This statement is also quite a conversation stopper.

✔ **You're just like your father (brother, uncle, aunt, or whomever).** This message invalidates the very identities of children. Generally, the comparisons to other family members aren't particularly flattering. Using this message inhibits children's growth and their capacity to believe in their own abilities.

✔ **I sure wish you could be more like your sister (cousin, father, aunt, or whomever).** This message tells kids that they aren't good enough and that their parents are disappointed in who they are. Again, this message erodes children's identities.

✔ **Grow up!** By nature, children are sometimes loud, annoying, and, well, just kids. Parents who can't tolerate frustration commonly put their kids down for boisterous childlike behavior. This message not only fails to change kids' behaviors but also makes them feel guilty for acting like kids.

✔ **Tell me something good that's happened.** Some parents say this when their kids report an unhappy or sad event. Instead of validating the sadness, these parents believe that redirecting the child to focus on more pleasant events will help them learn to feel better. Instead, this approach teaches kids to suppress their true emotions.

✔ **You're being selfish.** In truth, most kids are a little selfish. They haven't yet learned to fully appreciate the needs, wants, and perspectives of others or to balance those needs with their own. Unfortunately, though, this message doesn't help them become less selfish. Rather, it invalidates kids for being true to their nature.

✔ **You're way too young to try something like that. You could (get hurt, get in trouble, get lost, or whatever). Always ask me first before you do anything!** Some parents use messages like this one because of their own insecurities and desire to protect their kids. Unfortunately, this approach suppresses kids' curiosity, independence, motivation, confidence, and competence.

Growing up in a family in which emotional invalidation dominates the atmosphere can be very hurtful for kids. They learn either to passively withdraw to avoid these messages or to demonstrate extreme emotions and behaviors to obtain recognition and attention.

Emotional invalidation can also lead to more serious situations. Consider how the emotional invalidation a child receives from her mother can contribute to a sexually abusive situation and further harm the child. The following story about Daniela illustrates this point:

"Mommy, please don't go out again tonight," 8-year-old **Daniela** whines.

"I need my fun time without kids getting in my way. Besides, Uncle Gordon is going to watch you," her mother responds.

"But I hate Uncle Gordon," Daniela declares.

"Don't talk about your uncle that way. He's always been good to you," her mother scolds.

"But he's creepy. I don't like the way he smells, and he gives me yucky wet kisses," Daniela says.

"That's not true. He's a nice man. You need to show him respect," her mother argues.

"He always grabs me and makes me sit on his lap. He bounces me up and down like a baby. I don't like it," Daniela pleads.

"Listen. You need to be nice to your family. Uncle Gordon is a nice man. Stop this complaining; I don't want to hear any more about your uncle," her mother admonishes.

Many kids like Daniela know when something is wrong, but they don't have the words to express their concerns fully and completely. Given her mother's invalidating comments, Daniela is likely to stop complaining even as her uncle's inappropriate touching may slowly escalate into full-blown sexual molestation.

Daniela's story doesn't contain enough information for you to conclude that sexual molestation was actually occurring. However, parents can't decide whether a child's concerns are legitimate when they frequently invalidate their kids' emotions and statements. Furthermore, because molestation often begins at a low level and slowly escalates over time, parents have to make sure their children feel totally safe in sharing their concerns with them.

Dysfunctional and disorganized families

An old cartoon depicts a man alone in a huge conference hall with a banner that reads "Worldwide Meeting of Those with Functional Families" draped across the stage. Although we may have slightly misquoted the cartoon, the point is that most people have at least some degree of dysfunction in their families.

In contrast, dysfunction and disorganization dominate in some families. Dysfunction occurs when parents experience high marital discord and conflict. Parents often overtly express that conflict in the form of frequent loud fighting that fills children with anxiety and even fear that one or both parents may leave them. Other parents express that marital discord behind closed doors. In these cases, the parents may cover up and fail to talk about their disagreements. Although this approach may sound less stressful to children, most professionals believe that sweeping conflicts under the rug only makes them fester. Children pick up on the subtle signs of tension, and when parents don't openly resolve their conflicts with each other, their kids fail to learn the skills needed for resolving their own conflicts.

Dysfunction also arises when parents place confusing roles and expectations on their children. Some parents feel virtually incapable of parenting and place excessive responsibilities on their oldest children — virtually turning them into parents of the younger kids. Other parents take the opposite tack and treat their kids as incompetent — essentially infantilizing them.

Some homes are filled with disorganized chaos, something that children also find difficult to understand and manage. Such chaos comes in a wide range of forms, including the following:

- Financial woes, unpaid bills, and bill collectors
- Frequent job changes
- Constant moves from one neighborhood to another
- Conflicts that cause various household members to move in and out
- Substance abuse
- Incarceration
- Neighborhood crime
- Disability, serious illness, or severe emotional disorders in one or more of the parents

These types of chaotic atmospheres challenge children and make understanding their own and other people's emotions very difficult. Disorganized chaos also interferes with a child's developmentally crucial task of learning how to regulate or control emotions.

Abuse and trauma

Numerous studies have demonstrated that people with BPD have a high rate of abuse — inflicted by either their parents or someone else, namely a relative, a bully, or a stranger — in their childhoods. Because of such data, some professionals suggest that BPD is actually a complicated form of post-traumatic stress disorder (also called PTSD, it's an intense anxiety disorder that frequently occurs some time after a highly traumatic event; see Mark Goulston's *Post-Traumatic Stress Disorder For Dummies* [Wiley] for more about PTSD). However, most researchers now contend that BPD is *not* a form of PTSD, even though trauma certainly raises the risk of developing BPD.

One reason researchers believe BPD is separate from PTSD is that BPD can and does develop in people who don't show clear signs of trauma in their childhoods. Biological vulnerabilities (see the "Bringing biology into the BPD equation" section) combine with other difficulties, such as emotionally invalidating experiences or chaotic childhoods (which we explain in the preceding two sections), and lead to BPD in some people.

On the other hand, some people undergo traumatic events and don't develop BPD or even PTSD. Many of the people who demonstrate such resilience to trauma likely do so as a result of their genetic makeup, which enables them to endure hardships that many others can't. Other factors, such as highly supportive families, the presence of an especially involved caring adult, or psychotherapy, may also serve a protective function for some people who experience traumatic events.

Furthermore, the type of trauma children experience makes a difference in whether they develop BPD or other emotional disorders later in life. Trauma inflicted by a trusted family member appears to have a greater impact than trauma inflicted by a stranger. Sexual molestation that goes on for years typically has a greater impact than a single event of molestation. Incest usually increases the risk of BPD and other emotional disorders more than molestation by a stranger does.

Keep in mind, though, that any event involving abuse or trauma of children causes harm. Yet, in the absence of genetic vulnerability or other risk factors, many children eventually manage to overcome some of the damaging effects.

If you have BPD, you shouldn't assume that you were abused as a child. Unlike claims that people have made to the contrary, most instances of trauma tend to be at least partially recalled over the years. Therapies based on the assumption that everyone with BPD was abused often guide people to construct memories of events that evidence later shows never occurred.

Separation and loss

Unexpected losses and separation from one or more parents for extended periods of time contribute to an increased risk of BPD. Such losses can be quite traumatic because they disrupt the development of normal bonding between children and their parents. Children who lose parents often become more anxious and depressed in part because they worry about who will take care of them.

However, much like the case with trauma and abuse, some children lose a parent and overcome the effects of the loss, for the most part. Such recovery is more likely when these kids have an innate biological resilience and don't have the other risk factors of BPD (see the next section for more about how biology affects BPD).

Genetics and Biology: BPD in the Family Tree

Studies confirm that BPD runs in families. If one member has BPD, the chances of a close relative also having BPD are about ten times greater. But keep in mind that many people in the same family live together or have similar childhoods. So childhood rather than genetics may be responsible for the higher rates of BPD in the same family. At this point, you may be wondering how to figure out what's in the genes and what comes from the environment. The following sections take a closer look at biology and its effects on raising the risks for BPD.

Studying twins to find genetic causes

Twins studies help to untangle the heritability question. Remember that identical twins share the same genetic makeup, but fraternal twins don't. Most twins, regardless of whether they're identical or fraternal, share the same environment as children. You can look at the relationship between genetics and BPD by comparing these two types of twins. Subtract the number of fraternal twins who have BPD from the number of identical twins who have BPD, and you can get a decent estimate of the role genetics have in the development of BPD.

Only a few of these types of studies have been done (they tend to be expensive, and scientists have a hard time finding enough twins who have BPD), but the results suggest that 40 to 60 percent of BPD is predicted by genetic factors.

We're not saying BPD is an inherited trait, like blue or brown eyes. Indeed, BPD is much more complicated than that. What someone with BPD may have inherited are tendencies to

- ✔ Be impulsive

- ✔ Have unstable, highly reactive emotions

See Chapter 3 for more information about both of these contributors and the problem of BPD. If you throw together a couple inherited tendencies to be impulsive and have unstable emotions with other risk factors, such as problematic parenting and cultural influences, you may be on the fast track for developing BPD.

Bringing biology into the BPD equation

Genetics influence BPD because of their impact on the brain, but genes don't directly make someone impulsive or highly emotional. Rather, genes alter the brain in ways that increase the likelihood of impulsiveness and strong emotional responses. Researchers are investigating three specific biological areas for their influences on BPD. These biological areas are

- **Brain chemistry:** Nerve cells in the brain communicate through chemical messengers called *neurotransmitters.* Serotonin, one such neurotransmitter, seems to be particularly influential in BPD. Serotonin is involved in aggression, impulsivity, and mood stability. Studies have found that many people with BPD have disruptions in the way serotonin is used in the brain. However, medications that increase the availability of serotonin in the brain haven't been as helpful in treating BPD as they have been in treating other emotional disorders, such as depression and obsessive-compulsive disorder. Therefore, the exact role of serotonin in BPD remains unclear.

- **Brain structures:** The brain has numerous structures that process information, emotions, memories, and events. Recent studies have linked problems in the emotion-regulating circuits of the brain to BPD. People with BPD appear to have excess gray matter (the working cells of the brain) in the emotional interpretation hub of the brain (known as the *amygdala*). They also have less gray matter in the front portion of the brain that inhibits emotions. No wonder people with BPD often react very emotionally to events that others view as trivial and have trouble calming down after they're upset!

- **Brain functions:** *Brain functioning* refers to the tendency of certain brain areas to activate or inactivate under various conditions. The brains of people with BPD function differently than the brains of people without the disorder. For example, a sophisticated system in the brain senses when to be uncomfortable in social situations. This system corresponds to what people generally call street sense or gut reactions. This complex brain system doesn't work properly in people with BPD; thus, they fail to interpret situations and other people's intentions accurately.

  Another brain system, called the *executive system,* helps people make rational, thoughtful decisions. These decisions take into account both past experiences and current information, and they also consider future implications. People with BPD often have executive systems that don't function properly, which results in impulsive decisions.

So, what came first — the chicken or the egg? Did these deficiencies in brain chemistry, structure, and function come before or after BPD? At the time of this book's writing, even mental health professionals don't know. They need more research before they can make an accurate assessment.

Part II
Taking Note of the Major BPD Symptoms

The 5th Wave   By Rich Tennant

"Let's see if we can identify some of the stress triggers in your life. You mentioned something about a large wolf that periodically shows up and attempts to blow your house down..."

In this part . . .

This part zeros in on the major symptoms of borderline personality disorder (BPD). We illustrate how each of these symptoms impacts the lives of people with BPD and those who interact with them. We also show you how incredibly different from each other two people with BPD can appear to be.

Chapter 5

Sensation Seeking and Self-Harm: The Impulsivity of BPD

In This Chapter

▶ Finding excitement in dangerous places

▶ Understanding self-harm and the reasons behind it

▶ Seeking escape through suicide

*E*xcruciating emotional pain is a frequent companion of people with borderline personality disorder (BPD). Attempts to escape from this pain can take many forms, including abusing substances, cutting oneself, and attempting suicide. Although these escape strategies provide momentary relief, in the long run, they cause increased pain for people with BPD and those who care about them. In Chapter 3, we describe the first two symptoms of BPD — sensation seeking and self-harm — as being impulsive in nature.

In this chapter, we elaborate on these two symptoms and the impulsive actions they involve. Self-harm and sensation seeking can cause emotional damage, physical injury, and sometimes even death. First, we look at some of the impulsive behaviors that people with BPD sometimes exhibit as they try to feed a need for excitement or fill a deep emotional emptiness. After exploring the basics of impulsivity, we move on to self-mutilation, a shocking but common feature of BPD that also involves impulsive behaviors. Finally, we describe the thoughts and feelings that lie behind an extreme form of impulsive behavior — suicide threats and attempts.

Living Dangerously: Impulsive Behavior

Impulsivity involves two critical behavior problems. First, people who act impulsively tend to overlook the future, especially the negative outcomes that are likely to result from their present behaviors. Second, impulsive people don't fully process information before acting. In other words, they don't think before they act.

People with BPD have trouble controlling their *impulses,* or immediate wants and desires. They crave excitement and drama, and they crave it now — hence the term *sensation seekers.* They feel driven to fill the deep well of emptiness they feel inside, but with every impulsive behavior, they only increase their feelings of hollowness. The more they try to satisfy their insatiable cravings, the more their cravings grow. After they engage in an impulsive act, they usually report feeling momentarily better. However, those feelings of satisfaction are quickly replaced by enormous guilt, anxiety, and self-loathing.

People with BPD try to satisfy their sensation-seeking urges in many different ways. Here are some of the more common behaviors people with BPD rely on to satisfy their urges:

- **Spending:** Impulsive spending isn't about walking by a colorful package in the grocery store and buying it on impulse. Most people do buy something on impulse from time to time. In contrast, though, problematic, impulsive spending involves out-of-control buying binges. Some people with BPD try to fill a void by purchasing excessive quantities of totally unnecessary *stuff.* Some impulsive spenders pile up debt like a mountain of trash in a landfill. People who spend impulsively may go on extravagant vacations, spend too much on luxuries, and fill closets with clothes they rarely even wear — all to fill the emptiness within them.

- **Gambling:** Gambling is a rapidly growing problem in most developed countries. People who occasionally go to a casino and spend a predetermined amount of money don't qualify as impulsive gamblers. Most people know that the odds of winning are with the casino, not the gambler. However, some people with BPD ignore these odds and gamble with abandon. Sometimes they take out second mortgages to fuel their habits. They may even resort to forgery, embezzlement, and theft to raise the money they need to continue gambling. In most cases, like with impulsive spending, the motivation is to fill the emptiness they feel inside with a rush of excitement, but it never works — at least not in the long run.

- **Binge eating:** People with BPD sometimes try to regulate their emotions and fill their feelings of emptiness by overeating. They gorge on an entire box of cookies, a carton of ice cream, or a huge bag of potato chips. They eat such large quantities that they often vomit, or at least feel acute discomfort, instead of feeling satisfied.

- **Shoplifting:** Occasionally, you read about a movie star or other famous, wealthy person who gets caught shoplifting. You probably wonder why people with loads of money risk jail time for something they can easily afford to buy. The answer lies in their need for excitement. People with BPD who are impulsive shoplifters fill the emptiness in their lives with the excitement — and maybe even fear — that comes with shoplifting. Sometimes they steal relatively worthless items just to give them away. Keep in mind that impulsive shoplifters aren't people who steal because of dire economic conditions.

- ✔ **Reckless driving:** Reckless drivers ignore all the potential consequences of their behavior. They initiate reckless behavior to add excitement and a sense of danger to their lives. People with BPD who exhibit this risky behavior do amazingly dangerous things on the road — gun through stoplights, change lanes without signaling to other drivers, speed well beyond the limit, and execute hair-raising U-turns illegally. If you're wondering whether impulsive reckless drivers end up in more accidents than other people, studies indicate that the answer is yes.

- ✔ **Reckless sex:** For many people, sex is exciting. People with BPD who exhibit impulsive behaviors often attempt to increase their level of excitement by seeking one new partner after another. Even while fearing abandonment by their current partner, they often have affairs and engage in risky, unprotected sexual activities. They may feel seduced by sadomasochistic sex, group sex, partner swapping, or exhibitionism. To people who follow their sexual impulses, sex with someone new may represent an attempt to obtain the validation they didn't receive as kids. Or, they may use sex to try to fill the emptiness they feel in their lives. Obviously, such impulsive sexual behavior greatly increases risks of sexually transmitted diseases, unwanted pregnancies, and sometimes even violence.

- ✔ **Substance abuse:** Substance abuse is one of the most common forms of impulsivity that people engage in, whether they have BPD or not. Furthermore, the consumption of many substances (such as alcohol, marijuana, cocaine, or ecstasy) causes further loss of inhibition and triggers more impulsive behaviors of other types. Some people with BPD abuse substances to try to regulate their out-of-control emotions. Others do so for the rush or high they crave to fill their endless emptiness. Unfortunately, substance abuse raises the risk of suicide in people with BPD who are already at high risk of self-induced death.

Impulsiveness partially explains why most people with BPD don't live as long as people without the disorder. Whether because of suicide, car accidents, substance abuse, or simply unhealthy lifestyles, BPD all too often cuts life short.

Hurting for Help

Self-harm is a more dramatic impulsive symptom of BPD than the behaviors we describe in the preceding section. Many people assume that acts of self-injury or mutilation are suicide attempts; however, a desire to die isn't usually the motive that drives someone to commit self-harm. Although some people who hurt themselves do eventually commit suicide, many people engage in the dangerous behaviors we describe in the following section for decades without ever attempting suicide.

Types of self-harming acts

People with BPD commit a surprisingly diverse range of acts all meant to inflict pain or harm on themselves, including the following:

- ✔ **Cutting:** People who use this method of self-harm most commonly make cuts on their arms, legs, and abdomens. Some cutters try to hide their injuries, while others seek to display them. They use various tools, such as razor blades, scissors, paper clips, staples, needles, knives, and broken glass. Sometimes people even scratch themselves severely with their own fingernails.

- ✔ **Burning:** People often burn themselves with cigarettes, lighters, and matches. Typically, each burning act involves only a small area of the body; however, numerous scars may spread over time.

- ✔ **Blunt force trauma:** This category of self-harm includes pounding fists against walls, punching oneself, banging one's head into something hard, and using a hammer or other tool to inflict pain to one's own body. Blunt force trauma sometimes results in bruises, scars, wounds, and, in rare cases, broken bones.

- ✔ **Skin picking and hair pulling:** These acts include picking at cuticles and scabs, pulling out hair, and pinching the skin until it bleeds. These symptoms also sometimes accompany various other emotional disorders and may be related to obsessive-compulsive disorder.

- ✔ **Intentional accidents:** Behaviors in this category of self-harm may appear *accidental* at first. However, some people with BPD purposely avoid taking reasonable precautions. They may have accidents at work or home that they could easily avoid by being more careful or by using basic safety equipment or clothing. As a result of not being careful, they may fall off ladders that they set up on unsteady ground or burn themselves while using broken sticks to rearrange logs in a fireplace.

- ✔ **Rare behaviors:** This category of self-harm includes rare but certainly not unheard of actions, including the following:

    - Swallowing sharp objects

    - Friction burning

    - Eyeball pushing

    - Biting one's own body

    - Inserting objects into bodily cavities

    - Ingesting harmful but not fatal chemicals

Serious self-harming behaviors like the ones we list here afflict approximately 2 million people in the United States alone, many of whom have BPD. Some acts of self-harm come to the attention of medical professionals only in emergency rooms.

Why hurt yourself?

You may find yourself struggling to understand the idea that engaging in various acts of self-harm can actually provide relief to someone with BPD. Although you may wonder why some people want to hurt themselves, people with BPD and professionals who treat them have developed plenty of theories about the motivations behind these shocking and extremely painful behaviors. These motivations include the following:

- **To get attention:** Many professionals don't believe that this motivation plays a large role in the reasoning behind most self-harming behaviors because most people who exhibit self-harm try to hide what they've done from others. Sometimes, though, people with BPD lack the skills they need to obtain appropriate nurture and support from others. Instead, they feel driven to hurt themselves as a way to seek help. In the end, these attention-seeking acts may elicit the concern and care that people with BPD need, but they're desperate ways to reach this goal.

- **To distract from emotional pain:** Many experts, including ourselves, believe that people with BPD engage in self-harm as a way to deal with unbearable inner or emotional pain. Physical pain pales in comparison to what they feel internally, but it does pull attention away from their overwhelming emotions — at least temporarily.

- **To feel better:** When you injure your body, your brain releases natural pain killers called *endorphins.* These endorphins may facilitate a return to a less distressing emotional state. Thus, ironically, physical pain may actually help some people regulate their emotions. For a much less extreme example of the positive effects of endorphins, some people find appeal in eating hot chili peppers because eating them causes their bodies to release endorphins. Thus, even people who don't suffer from severe emotional disorders can understand on some level the appeal of obtaining a rush of endorphins.

- **To feel something other than numbness and emptiness:** Some people with BPD report that they feel unreal and out of touch with the world around them (see Chapter 10 for more on this symptom of BPD). These people sometimes inflict pain on themselves to feel something "real."

- **To punish themselves:** Although mental health professionals don't know how often this motivation leads people with BPD to self-harming behaviors, some people do report that they believe they deserve punishment and abuse. In these cases, the self-harm may be a way for people to punish themselves.

✔ **To get back at someone:** Some people with BPD are unable to express anger appropriately and, as a result, hurt themselves to make others feel guilty for something they said or did.

✔ **To reenact their own abuse:** Many people with BPD report that they were abused during childhood (see Chapter 4 for more on the causes of BPD). Children often believe that they deserve the abuse they receive, and thus, as adults they sometimes continue the pattern of abuse on themselves.

These motivations represent interesting hypotheses. However, professionals don't have enough data to determine which motives best account for self-harm in people with BPD. The reasons for each individual most likely vary. Although you may find studying the reasons behind self-harming behaviors fascinating, people with BPD who hurt themselves may not find your insight helpful. In other words, insight into why people hurt themselves isn't always enough to help them stop.

Although no situation of self-harm is really *typical,* the following story about Abigail illustrates how one person with BPD engages in this behavior to cope with her distress.

> **Abigail** throws her cellphone across the room. She hears Ryan, her now ex-boyfriend, yelling on the phone. She picks up the phone and screams that he'll be sorry he cheated on her. He pleads with her to settle down; after all, he only talked to someone else at work. She hangs up the phone. Now her rage changes to anxiety. She feels tense and desperate, and she can't seem to catch her breath. The only escape from her searing pain is blood. She pulls the knife from her dresser drawer. The urge grows. Abigail pulls off her t-shirt. She slowly pushes the blade into the skin on her stomach. She experiences a single moment of delicious pain — then nothing. She watches the blood begin to flow and pulls the knife higher, watching more blood pour out of her stomach. She deliberately slices through a scab from the last time. Somehow the sight of blood calms her down and eases her into a state of peace. She slowly rocks back and forth.

In the preceding story, Abigail feels searing emotional pain and doesn't know how to cope. She turns to cutting as a way of distracting herself from her overwhelming emotions. Chapter 16 offers ways to help people cope with their intense emotions in more effective ways.

Self-harming behaviors are always dangerous, and they typically escalate in severity and require treatment. See Part IV for some ideas about how to reduce self-harm.

Suicide: Seeking the Ultimate Escape

People with BPD are at a disturbingly high risk of eventually committing suicide. This risk terrifies the people who care about them and frightens the mental health providers who treat them. Studies suggest that as many as 10 percent of people with BPD eventually commit suicide — and frequently precede the final act with numerous attempts. These suicidal acts are among the most serious and complex of the impulsive behaviors that sometimes afflict people with BPD.

A cry for help or an attempt at revenge?

People who live through suicide attempts usually report that they felt unbearable emotional pain before the attempt. They felt helpless and hopeless about their options and their lives. They didn't see any potential for a better future, and the thought of oblivion left them no alternate option.

Suicide attempts are sometimes desperate calls for help. Unfortunately, for people who succeed at suicide, help comes too late. For other people, suicide attempts seem to involve a need to get back at people in their lives who have wronged, abandoned, or hurt them. In these cases, people with suicidal urges seem to believe that they'll be able to watch their foes feel guilt and remorse after their death.

Who's at risk?

Mental health professionals want to have the ability to predict who has a particularly high risk of suicide and who has a lower risk, but so many factors play into who is at most risk that professionals can't say exactly who will try suicide and who won't. At the time of this writing, however, professionals do know that the diagnosis of BPD greatly increases the risk of suicide. Risks of suicide also seem to increase if a person has made previous suicidal attempts (or parasuicidal behaviors) or has experienced a suicide in the family. Professionals also know that substance abuse raises the risk of eventual suicide. Studies that look at suicide suggest that people with BPD usually don't commit suicide during adolescence or their 20s — suicide in people with BPD is more common during the third decade of life.

Assessing the risk of a given individual is an extremely difficult task, but psychotherapy for BPD does appear to lower the risk of suicide. In addition, whether treated or not, people with BPD usually experience a reduction of symptoms, including suicidal behaviors, in their 40s and 50s, so time eventually becomes an ally.

Although predicting suicide in someone with BPD is extremely difficult, you should seek professional help if your loved one exhibits the following behaviors:

- Shows a sharp loss of interest in things he or she used to enjoy in life
- Talks about feeling utterly hopeless and helpless
- Expresses the view that the world would be better off without him or her
- Talks about committing suicide
- Calls people to say goodbye
- Puts personal affairs in order
- Exhibits unusual calm for no clear reason after extended sadness
- Starts giving prized possessions away without cause
- Has experienced a serious recent loss

No one can reliably predict or prevent all suicides. If someone you care about commits suicide, it's not your fault. But, if you believe that suicide may be imminent, call the police.

If you're experiencing feelings of helplessness, hopelessness, or the desire to end your life, seek help immediately.

Impulsive behaviors encompass only two of the major symptoms of BPD that we describe in Chapter 3. Not everyone who exhibits impulsivity (specifically sensation seeking, self-harm, or suicide) qualifies for a diagnosis of BPD. Some people who present these behaviors have bipolar disorder and only exhibit them when they're experiencing an episode of mania (see Chapter 3 for more information about mania and bipolar disorder). Others have specific diagnoses like kleptomania (impulsive stealing), pathological gambling, or substance abuse and don't show other signs of BPD. Furthermore, not everyone who has a diagnosis of BPD engages in the impulsive behaviors we describe in this chapter, but many do.

Chapter 6

Explosive Feelings and Moods

In This Chapter

▶ Looking at the reasons behind emotions

▶ Exploring emotional regulation or lack thereof

▶ Understanding borderline rage and its effects

Some people with borderline personality disorder (BPD) get angry with little provocation, feel anxious over trivial matters, and experience despair when good things happen. Their feelings may change quickly, and they often have trouble settling down. Mental health professionals refer to these rapidly changing reactions as *emotional dysregulation*. Emotional dysregulation is a core symptom of BPD and causes much pain and chaos for the people who experience it.

In this chapter, we take a look at basic human emotions. We also explore the concept of emotional dysregulation. We explain how problems with dysregulation cause people with BPD to react with intense fear, anxiety, depression, and anger to events that many people may consider trivial. Finally, we review the difficulty that people with BPD have in trying to identify and label the emotions they experience.

Emotions 101

Emotions are mental and physical responses to life events, which include anything that happens in the world as well as memories, thoughts, or images that pass through the mind. Emotions occur universally among all humans. Psychologists have identified six primary emotions that people all around the world experience. You can reliably identify the following primary emotions on other people's faces:

✔ Happiness

✔ Sadness

✔ Anger

- Fear
- Disgust
- Surprise

Numerous words have evolved to discuss various levels and nuances of these six major emotions. Hence, you can describe happiness as joy, elation, and delight; or, you can say it's the state of being upbeat, exhilarated, satisfied, pleased, blissful, radiant, merry, and so on. Words that describe fear include anxiety, terror, horror, nervousness, trepidation, distrust, worry, and alarm.

Cultures across the world vary enormously in the number of words they have for describing each of these major emotions. For example, the English language has more than 2,000 words to describe emotion, whereas Taiwanese has only about 750. In contrast, the Chewong language (spoken by a small group of people living in Malaysia) has only 7 words that describe emotion.

Furthermore, some cultures have words that describe emotions that aren't captured at all in other cultures. For example, the German language uses the word *Schadenfreude,* which means the unanticipated enjoyment a person feels because of the suffering of someone else. The German language goes further to distinguish between a secret Schadenfreude (withheld from the view of others) versus an open Schadenfreude (openly expressed scorn). We bet you can't think of an equivalent word in English.

Emotions, even hateful ones, aren't inherently right or wrong. What makes them healthy versus destructive is the way you express them.

Both philosophers and scientists actively debate about what emotions are, how to categorize them, and what parts of the body they involve. One group tends to focus on the physical changes within the body that occur in conjunction with emotions, and the other group argues that emotions have more to do with thoughts than the body's physical reactions. Both perspectives have value in terms of the role emotions play in BPD. We describe these two approaches to emotion in the following sections.

Primitive emotions

Some professionals approach emotions by looking at the relationship between the body's physical reactions and emotions. They believe people react instinctively with little or no thought to some events — even when they encounter the event for the first time. For example, fears of falling, loud noises, abandonment, and some predators, such as snakes and spiders, seem to elicit certain genetic-encoded, instinctual responses from a person's body, which, in turn, lead that person to feel certain emotions. In other words, these physical responses are preprogrammed to warn people of possible danger and get them ready to respond. The emotions that these bodily reactions cause are called *primitive emotions*. People with BPD may have supercharged physical responses to fears, which, in turn, lead to overreactive emotions. (See Chapter 3 for more on the symptoms of BPD and Chapter 4 for more on the biological influences on the emergence of BPD.)

Normal responses

Professionals in one camp believe that emotions have more to do with the physical body than thoughts (see the "Thoughtful emotions" section for the other side of this issue). They assert that the responses your body has to certain events actually cause your emotions. In other words, you feel sad because you cry or feel anxious because you tremble. Your body sends signals to your mind, which, in turn, causes you to feel particular emotions. The following list provides several bodily responses. The emotions that follow these bodily reactions can include fear, anger, disgust, happiness, sadness, or surprise.

- ✔ Muscle tension
- ✔ Increased heart rate
- ✔ Increased blood pressure
- ✔ Sweating
- ✔ Smiling
- ✔ Laughing
- ✔ Gagging
- ✔ Jumping
- ✔ Pupils dilating or constricting
- ✔ Salivating
- ✔ Frowning

BPD responses

Some research has indicated that people with BPD have more intense startle responses to events than people who don't have BPD. One study looked at the reactions of people when they were startled with unexpected static noise at the same time that they were shown a random series of words that had either neutral meanings (such as regular or collect) or negative meanings (such as abandon or hate). People with BPD were more reactive to the sounds than the other group, especially when the words they saw had negative meanings. This study, which was reported in the journal *Biological Psychiatry* in 2007, concluded that the unstable emotional responses of people with BPD may be related to an exaggerated startle response.

Paradoxically, other research has failed to demonstrate that people with BPD have stronger bodily responses following the same types of events. For example, in one study, people with and without BPD were shown unpleasant images and had the same physical responses (including startle responses and decreased heart rates). These contradicting findings have puzzled scientists because many mental health professionals believe that people with BPD do indeed react with greater emotional intensity than other people. Possible explanations for this inconsistency include

- ✔ People with BPD sometimes dissociate or mentally remove themselves from stressful events. In turn, this dissociation may mute their physical reactions.

- ✔ Some of the methods that scientists have used in studies to trigger emotion may not be equivalent to natural emotion-evoking events. In other words, people with BPD may indeed respond with more intense bodily reactions to real events, but scientists may simply have failed to capture the essence of such events in their studies.

- ✔ People with BPD may not experience stronger bodily reactions to events; instead, they may simply believe or think that their emotions are stronger than those of other people. As a result, they report stronger emotions during studies.

Still other studies have focused on self-reported emotions rather than bodily responses that people with BPD feel in response to various types of events. These studies suggest that people with BPD report more intense emotions than people without the disorder. For example, one study asked participants with and without BPD to carry around devices like personal digital assistants (PDAs) throughout the day. The device beeped at random times during the day, and the participants recorded their emotional states each time they received a signal. This research consistently demonstrated that people with BPD do *claim* to have more intensely negative reactions to events than people without the disorder. Furthermore, people with BPD reported that their emotions were also more variable and unstable.

Thoughtful emotions

Other professionals connect emotions more to thoughts than to the body's responses. They believe that how people interpret events ultimately causes emotions. For instance, a gun pointed at your head doesn't cause you to tremble and sweat profusely; what does cause you to tremble is the meaning that a gun holds for you — danger or even death. If you'd grown up in some remote village where guns didn't exist, you probably would respond to a gun with mere curiosity, not fear, because your thoughts about a gun don't connect it to fear. So, the meaning that people give to events (or things) directly causes emotions.

Studies have shown that people with BPD have a strong tendency to view events more negatively than other people. (See Chapter 9 for more information about the ways that people with BPD view events in distorted ways.) These distortions in thinking can cause substantial emotional turmoil because thoughts play a large role in emotions.

On the other hand, people who are able to regulate their emotions effectively use logic and reasoning to reinterpret events in a less threatening way, which, in turn, leads them to experience less-extreme emotions. For example, a woman with BPD may interpret her husband's business trip as evidence that he's having an affair and is likely to leave her. In contrast, a woman without BPD may have the same initial thought that her husband may be having an affair, but she can quickly dismiss the thought by reviewing the positive aspects of her marriage.

The ancient Greek philosopher Aristotle argued that reason should triumph over emotions in a balanced life. He warned against the danger of excessive emotions as well as overly restrained emotions. See Part IV for numerous ideas about how to follow Aristotle's sage advice.

Emotions — Borderline Style

Tuning into the emotional life of someone with a healthy personality is like listening to a symphony orchestra (see Chapter 2 for more on healthy personalities). The score has high notes and low notes, periods of soft tones and crashing crescendos. The performance as a whole has an ebb and flow. Similarly, emotions may rise and fall in a person with a healthy personality, but the entire experience has a certain coherence — everything seems to fit together.

On the other hand, turning an ear to the emotional life of a person with BPD is more like listening to an orchestra made up of amateurs who have never practiced or played their assigned instruments. Highs and lows come and go at random, crescendos blast louder and last longer than you expect, and coherence is hard to find in the performance.

Numerous studies have shown that people with BPD experience negative emotions more often than people with healthy personalities do. They have more anxiety, sadness, anger, and jealousy than most people. At the same time, they appear to experience less elation or happiness. Their emotions race from 0 to 60 in mere seconds, and calming their emotions takes longer than you may expect.

Furthermore, the events that trigger the negative emotions of people with BPD don't have to be huge or life altering because people with BPD often see the world through a dark, distrusting, and distorted lens. They tend to think the world revolves around them and, as a result, often personalize happenings — big or small — that have little or nothing to do with them. In addition to these distorted thought processes, people with BPD sometimes overreact because they have a genetic predisposition to do so (see Chapter 4 for more information on the biological factors that affect BPD).

People with BPD often rage at the people who care about them the most. They blame others and refuse to accept responsibility for their out-of-control emotions. In the following story, Isabella (a young woman who has BPD) turns what could've been a happy celebration into a nightmare.

> **Isabella** bounces into the kitchen, happy and excited. "Sam, guess what?" she exclaims holding up a letter, "I've been accepted into grad school!"
>
> "That's great news. Let's go out and celebrate. We may not have much time to go out after you start the program," Sam replies.
>
> Isabella frowns, suddenly angry. "What do you mean we won't have time?"
>
> "What? I'm so proud of you — I was just joking," Sam says cautiously.
>
> "You can't say anything positive about anything, can you? You always ruin my success with your sarcasm," Isabella's voice gets louder. "Forget celebrating. You've just wrecked another evening. I can't believe you're so negative all the time!"
>
> "Isabella, please, don't be angry with me. I'm really glad you were accepted. Can't we start this conversation over?"
>
> Isabella stalks off, refuses to talk, and rips her acceptance letter into shreds. Sam knows that her tantrum can last a minute or several hours. He hears her slamming drawers, throwing things, and sobbing in the bedroom, followed by silence. Afraid that she may be cutting herself again, he goes to her. He finds her sitting on the bedroom floor.
>
> "I feel horrible Sam; I'll never be happy. I should forget about grad school and end everything now!" she screeches.
>
> Sam shouts, "Stop it, Isabella! Stop it right now! You're out of control! Calm down!"
>
> "Don't hit me. Don't hit me. Don't hit me," Isabella pleads and sobs. She runs out of the apartment.
>
> Sam shakes his head in disbelief. He's never threatened to hit her, and the thought has never occurred to him.

Isabella is quick to anger, overinterprets the meaning of Sam's neutral comments, and isn't easily talked down from her rage. She shifts from rage to terror in just seconds. Yet, she needs several hours to calm down from her emotional storm. Because of her intense emotions, Isabella acts very impulsively when she thinks about ending her life and runs screaming out of the apartment (see Chapter 5 for more information about impulsivity and how it plays a part in BPD).

Not only do people with BPD have extremely strong emotions, but they also struggle to realize how these emotions affect their lives. The next section discusses the difficulty they have in recognizing and expressing emotions.

Struggling to recognize and express emotions

Many people with BPD suffer from yet another emotional problem — they seem oblivious to their current emotional states. They don't reflect on their feelings or try to label them; instead, they act out their feelings without even being aware of what emotions they're feeling. They lack the insight they need to understand their emotions, which is almost like not having a vocabulary for describing their emotions.

For example, a man with BPD may shout and talk rapidly while shaking his finger, yet at the same time, deny that he feels angry. Or, a woman with BPD may smile while talking about ending her life. Sometimes people with BPD who can't maintain control of their emotions demonstrate a profound disconnection between how they express emotions and what they say they feel. This struggle to recognize and express emotions confuses family members, friends, and even therapists.

In contrast, studies have shown that some people with BPD are unusually sensitive to the facial expressions of other people. When they see pictures of faces of other people, they actually perceive negative emotions with surprising accuracy. However, they also see more negativity than exists in neutral faces.

Having emotions about emotions

People with BPD who exhibit emotional difficulties tend to have more anxiety, depression, jealousy, and rage than most people do. However, they make themselves even more miserable by feeling bad about feeling bad. They become depressed *because* of their anxiety and anger. They wallow in guilt and despair *because* of their jealousy and rage. They get emotional about being emotional, and they get stuck in a cycle of recurring — and often self-inflicted — misery.

Chapter 7

Missing Persons: Identity Problems and BPD

. . . .

In This Chapter

▶ Figuring out what identity is

▶ Developing identity in the 21st century

▶ Exploring borderline identities and their effects

. . . .

You've heard about identity theft. You may even be one of the many people who worry about losing their identities to thieves digging through dumpsters, looking for loose credit card receipts. Because so many people do worry about identity theft, personal paper shredder sales have skyrocketed over the past few years.

Some people worry more about losing their identities to theft than about being mugged at gunpoint because the notion of losing one*self* — even just one's financial self — is especially disturbing.

In this chapter, we spend some time illustrating what *identity* actually means, as well as describing its development and evolution over time. We take a look at both the positive and negative aspects of identities. We want you to be familiar with this information before we move on to explain the identity problems people with borderline personality disorder (BPD) often experience. See Chapter 17 for techniques for managing identity problems. (Sorry, we can't help you with identity theft.)

The Concept of Identity

Most people think of themselves as having their own identities. They know what to say when someone asks them to identify themselves. For example, when a police officer asks you who you are, you probably state your name and take out your driver's license. However, personal identity is much more complex than a simple ID card. We look at the concept of identity in this section.

Defining identity

Identity is a theory or concept that someone creates to synthesize information and knowledge about the self. In other words, your identity is your own personal attempt to capture the core elements that make you who you are. Identity evolves over time as it takes on varying areas of emphasis. For example, a 2-month-old baby has no sense of gender, but when that child is 13 years old, she probably thinks a lot about the importance of gender. In grade school, kids don't usually have much of a career identity, but this important sphere takes on great meaning in young adulthood.

Personality, on the other hand, describes broad character traits that *other* people can see (take a look at Chapter 2 for more on personality). Identity is more personal in nature than personality. In other words, identity involves value judgments that people make about themselves, not judgments that other people make about them. For example, wealth has little or nothing to do with personality directly; however, sometimes people tie much of their self-worth and identities to their accumulation — or lack thereof — of money.

Thus, people can have outgoing personalities and be either rich or poor. Their wealth doesn't automatically have a strong effect on their personalities. For instance, some rich people feel like their money has little to do with who they are as people. On the other hand, some wealthy people feel like their identities — who they are and what they value — are wrapped around their possessions.

Like personality, an identity can be healthy or unhealthy. Healthy identities stand on a foundation of sturdy, varied values. They don't center on a single aspect of a person. For example, a healthy identity can encompass multiple sources of self-worth. In contrast, an unhealthy identity has a restricted scope and usually derives worth from only a few elements.

People incorporate just a few or, hopefully, many aspects of their lives in their identities, including the following:

- Artistic talent
- Knowledge
- Wealth
- Gender
- Hobbies
- Accomplishments
- Career
- Relationships
- Status and prestige
- Religion
- Values
- Priorities
- Physical appearance
- Health
- Place of residence
- Cultural affiliation
- Age

To form your identity, you likely look at these various aspects of your life and attempt to describe who you are based on which facets you *value* the most. Personal identity is like a story about your life. For example, someone who values friendships will have a life story, or identity, that emphasizes friendships. For healthy identities, these stories have coherence and some degree of continuity, and, thus, your identities can guide your decisions and choices. However, if your identity is scrambled and lacks continuity, it can't readily guide your life choices.

Terms that many mental health professionals consider similar to identity include self-concept, self-esteem, self-awareness, self-confidence, self-satisfaction, and self-importance. Although a group of psychologists can talk for hours about the nuances that distinguish each term from the others, all the terms capture a similar idea — who you are. We look at developing and defining who you are in the next sections.

Developing identity

Identities develop and change over the course of lifetimes. Identities become more complex and incorporate more aspects of the self with age. Some periods in life present greater challenges to identity development than others. In the following sections, we describe the basic stages of identity development.

Beginning the process of identity formation

Babies begin developing their sense of self early in life. Hopefully, within the first few months, they begin to learn that other people perceive and respond to their discomforts. They slowly differentiate between themselves and their caregivers. As they begin to make these distinctions, interactions between infants and their caregivers are critical in the establishment of identity because, depending on their care, infants learn how what they do affects others in their world.

Identity develops much further as children's worlds expand to include extensive interaction with other kids. A particularly critical time in identity development appears to be between the ages of 4 and 6 when children learn a crucial concept — that other people have thoughts and ideas that are different from their own. Also during this phase, children acquire the ability to understand what other people are likely thinking and feeling in various situations. When either genes or social experiences interfere with this development, children become much more inept at dealing with other people, which may eventually lead to the development of BPD in adulthood.

The core mechanism that allows for self-reflection, identity development, and the ability to relate to others is known as *theory of mind.* Theory of mind is knowing that others think thoughts that may differ from your own and understanding the psychological and emotional states of other people. People with BPD typically don't have a well-developed theory of mind, which leads them to have trouble relating well to others.

Finding identity during middle childhood

From the ages of about 6 to 12, children's identities continue to grow. The ability to regulate emotions, one of the skills that helps foster the development of a healthy identity, usually occurs during this time of life. Other important aspects of positive identity development that often emerge at this time include mastering schoolwork, getting along well with other children, and acquiring basic mental and physical skills. When children fail to acquire the ability to regulate emotions and these other basic skills, they often experience tumultuous adolescent years, which can impair their identity development as adults.

People with BPD may have some highly developed skills (for example, they may be highly intelligent or extremely detail oriented), but they often fail to acquire the ability to moderate their emotions. As a result, roller coaster emotions that skyrocket and plummet at the slightest provocation characterize many people with BPD.

Refining identity in adolescence

Long ago, identity was fairly fixed by the end of middle childhood. After all, parents and teachers pushed kids into predetermined roles. Girls learned homemaking skills in preparation for marriage, and boys learned predetermined trades and apprenticeships.

In the modern world, however, identity has become an especially poignant issue during adolescence. Adolescents try on and experiment with various identities, which psychologists refer to as *possible selves.* Through this experimentation process, they discard some of these possible selves and hold onto others. The downside to all this experimentation is that juggling all these possibilities can be rather stressful. See Chapter 4 for more information about the pressures of modern-day adolescence.

Even people who don't develop BPD find adolescence to be a stressful period of life. So the fact that the major symptoms of BPD start showing up by early adolescence seems only natural. After all, pressures mount to establish a clear sense of self during adolescence, and many people with emerging BPD can't clearly define who they are during adulthood much less during their teenage years.

Anchoring identity in adulthood

Ideally, you manage to get through the challenges of adolescence with a reasonable, balanced sense of self. Your adolescent identity likely has some complexity and includes a variety of elements, but, if it's a healthy identity, it also maintains a coherent set of themes. If one aspect of your identity is threatened, you may need to call on other facets of the self to buffer the emotional distress.

For example, if a father loses his job, he may be able to remind himself that he has many positive attributes, such as his roles as a parent and a husband, his intelligence, his geniality, and his resourcefulness. These qualities not only protect him from a massive assault on his self-esteem — which sudden unemployment often causes — but also give him confidence that another employer is likely to see him as a desirable applicant.

The ability to use different facets of one's identity to help deal with emotional distress is one key element of a healthy identity. People with BPD often struggle to maintain emotional stability when parts of their identities are threatened.

Like many people with BPD, Tyler, a 25-year-old marketing consultant, had an imperfect adolescence. However, the combination of fairly good genes, a few good role models, some decent opportunities, and a lack of serious abuse or trauma allowed him to overcome a less-than-perfect adolescence and form a healthy identity.

> **Tyler** reflects on his life and feels okay about himself. He experienced what he now considers a challenging childhood. His parents divorced when he was 4, and each one found a new partner. Tyler had to move around quite a bit, but his parents did manage to keep him in the same school system. During high school, he did some drugs and abused alcohol. His grades were fair, but he never did much studying. He rebelled against his parents by not caring about school and his future, and he seemed depressed at times. He didn't find real meaning in life until he went to college and discovered a love for traveling and learning. Without the need to rebel, he excelled at school. Eventually, he realized that his life was pretty good and that he was treated fairly well. Now, in adulthood, his emotions are well under control. He still drinks a bit too much, but he enjoys his many friends and interests. Good genes, no extreme abuse, and the ability to delay gratification, which he learned in college, can account for Tyler's relatively good adjustment to life.

Tyler, like many people, had a moderately challenging adolescence. Nevertheless, like most teens, he made it through the difficult years reasonably unscathed. He now has the capacity to further develop his identity in a balanced way as his adulthood unfolds. People who develop BPD experience far more ongoing problems with their personal identities than Tyler did.

Borderline Identity: Unstable and Fragile

People with BPD have identities that differ from those of other people. Their identities show less stability and less coherence. In addition, people with BPD often overreact to minor threats to their frail identities. We discuss these two issues in the next sections.

Waffling identities

Although everyone behaves inconsistently at times, people with BPD exhibit huge fluctuations in attitudes, values, and feelings of identity. The difference between the identities of a person without BPD and a person with BPD is a lot like the difference between a well-edited movie of someone's life and an unorganized box jammed full of photos from that same life. Here are a few contrasting examples:

- A woman *without* BPD values honesty, and as a result, her identity has a stable, coherent sense of basic honesty. Thus, 99 percent of the time, she is quite straightforward with people. She's someone people feel they can count on for the truth. However, at a friend's house for dinner, she compliments the host for the cooking even though she doesn't like the food at all. She maintains her honest identity and accepts the fact that some circumstances call for minor lies. Her life's coherent movie maintains the basic theme of honesty.

- A woman *with* BPD sometimes feels she's an honest person and generally is honest. However, when she lies to her friend about her cooking, she feels a rush of self-loathing and disgust for her dishonest behavior. This situation may lead her to become angry at her friend for "making" her tell a lie. She can't hold onto her basic identity of being honest in the face of a minor indiscretion. In a way, her sense of who she is changes with each photo that's plucked out of her life's box.

- A man *with* BPD may consider himself extremely righteous and devoted to his family. However, he frequently has affairs and loses his temper when his kids fail to meet his expectations in the slightest way. After he flips into these obnoxious episodes, he briefly feels horrible about himself. But within hours or days, he rapidly regains his self-image of being righteous and devoted. His view of himself changes dramatically as each picture is taken from the box.

Lacking a strong, stable sense of their own identities, many people with BPD attempt to adopt whichever identity they believe their current partners or friends want them to have. They believe that doing so can make them very appealing to their potential partners or friends because they may appear like the very personification of their friends' dreams. However, the inherent instability of their personal identities makes maintaining the façades impossible to do. See Chapter 8 for more information about the effects this issue has on the relationships that people with BPD tend to have throughout life.

Responding to worries about identity

When people with BPD have significant worries about their identities and self-worth, one of two situations likely occurs:

- ✔ They desperately attempt to hold onto their fragile sense of self-worth by striking out in rage.
- ✔ Their identity and self-worth crumble, and they fall into a cycle of despair.

Table 7-1 illustrates how some people with BPD use these two strategies in response to various concerns about their identities.

Table 7-1   BPD Responses to Real or Imagined Threats to Identity

Identity Concern	Striking Out at One's Partner	Crumbling Inside
I am a weak person.	"You can't stand up to anyone; you're worthless."	"I can't function in the world. I need someone to take care of me."
I cheated on my husband, which may mean that I'm disloyal.	"It's your fault that I cheated; you never show me any affection."	"I'm a horrible person. I can't even be faithful to my husband!"
I can't control my emotions.	"You make me so mad! No one can take what you dish out without rage."	"I should kill myself. I'm completely out of control."
I'm an inadequate parent.	"When you said that you wish the kids did better in school, you meant that I am a horrible parent. I could do a better job if you weren't so critical."	"I'm so selfish. I should devote far more time to helping my kids with their schoolwork. What's wrong with me?"
I haven't ever accomplished what I should have.	"You don't make enough money! What's wrong with you? We'll always be broke!"	"I'll never get anywhere. I don't have the discipline because of my mental illness. I'm hopeless."

You can imagine what effect these ways of responding to identity concerns have on the people who care about those with BPD. They may feel confused, angry, and mystified by their BPD partner's behaviors because they don't realize the underlying problems with identity that cause the intense reactions. See Chapter 8 for more information about the stormy relationships people with BPD often have.

See Part V for more ideas about how to cope with these identity issues when you care about someone with BPD.

Chapter 8

Perceiving, Understanding, and Relating to Others

. . . .

In This Chapter

▶ Discovering how BPD affects perceptions

▶ Seeing how people with BPD violate other people's boundaries

. . . .

*I*f you're in a relationship with someone who has borderline personality disorder (BPD), you may be confused by the mixed-up communications and unexpected emotional reactions you receive from your lover, colleague, or friend. You may feel misunderstood and puzzled because one day you're wonderful in your friend's eyes and the next you're the worst person in the world. You likely wonder what you can do to make things better.

The first step to improving the situation is becoming more aware of what's going on. People with BPD have serious problems with relationships. Overall, they have more broken relationships, problems getting along at work, and arguments with relatives and friends than most people do. People with BPD marry somewhat less often than other people and usually have fewer children.

In this chapter, we describe the problems people with BPD often have in getting along with others. These problems are the result of their extreme inability to stand back from situations and understand other people's perspectives. The ability to step back requires three different but related skills that people with BPD typically lack:

✔ Ability to understand the needs, feelings, and beliefs of other people

✔ Ability to see how other people perceive them

✔ Ability to see how their own behavior affects others

The problems with understanding other people's needs, feelings, and perspectives lead people with BPD to run over the boundaries of other people. They place excessive demands on people, feel entitled to special treatment, and become enraged when they don't get what they want. We discuss all these issues and more in this chapter.

Standing in Other People's Shoes

Perspective taking involves being able to comprehend the views, feelings, and needs of other people. Having this ability often leads to success in relationships, school performance, and job performance, as well as empathy for others. Good therapists have this skill in abundance. However, this capacity isn't something that everyone shares.

In fact, babies don't come into the world with the ability to understand that other people have views that differ from their own. Instead, this skill evolves through at least young adulthood, if not beyond. Furthermore, in any particular person, the ability to understand other people's perspectives varies over time. For example, someone who normally has good empathy for others can show no understanding of another driver after ice on the road causes that driver to run into him. Life stressors as well as experiences can cause some shift in a person's ability to understand other people.

This section takes a look at how perspective taking affects people with BPD and the ones they love.

Understanding other people

Sometimes people with BPD appear surprisingly able to read cues from other people. They seem almost able to enter other people's psyches and become one and the same. However, most of the time, people with BPD utterly fail to grasp the reasons behind and the implications of what people are thinking and feeling. In other words, they know what others are feeling, but they don't understand why they're feeling that way or what their feelings mean.

The following story about Jasmine, a woman with BPD, and Carlos, her boyfriend, illustrates the skill of picking up cues yet misinterpreting the meaning of those cues.

> **Jasmine** arrives home and sees her boyfriend, Carlos, draped across the couch watching the news. She greets him with a quick kiss and immediately launches into a description of her busy day. Carlos, still immersed in his television show doesn't respond. "Hey baby," she moves closer to him, "you seem out of it. What's wrong?"
>
> Jasmine has correctly discerned that Carlos isn't paying attention to her. Carlos sits up, immediately cautious, "I was just interested in this show; the stock market is down again. I'm sorry, what did you say?"
>
> "Well, obviously nothing important to you," Jasmine retorts. Although she sees something is going on with Carlos, she misinterprets the meaning of his inattentiveness. He was simply absorbed by the stock market, but she assumes he has no interest in her.

Carlos sighs, knowing that he has to be very careful or there will be another fight, something he wants to avoid. "Jasmine, I'm always interested in your day. I'm really sorry that I didn't hear you. Don't make this a big deal; it wasn't to me. Come on, tell me again."

"So now you're telling me that I'm not a big deal. Forget it. Watch your stupid show."

Carlos realizes that he's on a treadmill going nowhere. He sees no way of getting through to Jasmine. Nothing he says at this point will make things okay. So he says nothing, and she leaves the room.

Jasmine was quite accurate in perceiving Carlos's distraction. To that degree, she was able to take his perspective. But she goes awry when she misinterprets his inattentive mood as a personal slight. She proceeds to interpret everything else he has to say in the same way. Her ability to take another person's perspective is impaired.

Therapists who work with people who have BPD often report that their BPD patients have a difficult time seeing things from other perspectives. For example, a therapist may arrive at a session feeling a little tired or distracted. His client with BPD sees the mood alteration and may accuse the therapist of not caring or of being angry.

Being unable to take the perspectives of other people obviously hampers good, long-term relationships. Not surprisingly, this inability can bog down a therapeutic relationship and make intimacy almost impossible. We show you how you can improve your perception skills in Chapter 18.

Seeing yourself through other people's eyes

Taking other people's perspectives includes being able to see yourself as others see you. Unfortunately, most people with BPD have serious deficits in this skill, as well. They engage in a variety of problematic behaviors and emotional outbursts without understanding how other people will see those behaviors. After all, they see their own behaviors as quite rational and reasonable. The behaviors and emotions that they exhibit and that others perceive as outrageous or controlling include the following:

✔ **Jealousy:** Anxiety over the possibility of being abandoned drives many people with BPD to act intensely jealous by calling their partners excessively, seeking constant reassurance, and checking up on their partners' every move. They don't understand that behaviors like these often annoy other people and drive them away.

✔ **Seductiveness:** Often without being aware of how their behaviors appear to other people, many people with BPD engage in sexualized, seductive gestures, facial expressions, and touches that are far from benign or meaningless. They often act surprised or even outraged when others respond with sexual advances of their own. Other times, people with BPD have affairs at the same time that they're jealous of such a possibility in their partners.

✔ **Anger:** People with BPD don't understand why their aggressive outbursts cause others to either avoid them altogether or approach them with trepidation. We discuss this emotion in detail in Chapter 6.

✔ **Hysteria:** People with BPD tend to respond to everyday stressors with excessive emotionality. Whether their irritation turns into rage, their sadness turns into profound dysphoria, their pleasure morphs into ecstasy, or their worry converts into terror, they respond at far higher levels of intensity than most situations warrant.

✔ **Impulsivity:** Whether they take part in self-mutilation, suicide attempts, threats, or out-of-control spending, people with BPD don't know how to put breaks on their behavior. We discuss this symptom of BPD in detail in Chapter 5.

Although you can read about these behaviors in various chapters throughout this book, the point we want to make here is that people with BPD engage in these behaviors with almost no awareness of how their behaviors look to other people. So, when they explode, they don't realize that their anger appears wildly inappropriate to other people. The following story about Karen, Dawn's mother-in-law who has BPD, shows how oblivious people with BPD can be to the impact of their behavior on others.

Dawn is staying with her mother-in-law, **Karen,** while her husband is out of town for a few days. Dawn inadvertently puts a silver-plated butter knife into the dishwasher. Later, Karen unloads the dishwasher and spies the knife. She carries the knife into the living room, where Dawn is reading a novel. Shaking the knife at her, Karen yells, "Are you so utterly stupid that you don't know not to put silver in a dishwasher?"

Dawn replies, "Gosh, I'm sorry. I didn't realize it was silver. I'm really sorry."

"Sorry won't replace the knife. You're just trash; you can't even appreciate fine things. I wish my son could've picked someone more refined."

Dawn blushes and retreats to her bedroom. She calls her husband and asks him what's wrong with his mother. She tells him, "I don't think I can ever trust her about anything."

Her husband sighs and says, "I know; that's my childhood you're looking at. Just talk about the weather or something. I'll be back tomorrow."

Dawn says, "I really don't know if I can ever stay here again."

The next morning Karen greets Dawn with a warm smile and a cup of coffee. She says, "How about we go to the mall today?"

Dawn, now totally confused, says, "Oh, sure." Taking her husband's advice, she adds, "It looks like it'll be a nice day for shopping."

Karen has a rich history of searching for friends and not finding or keeping them. She can't understand why other people remain so aloof. She can't see herself and her actions through their eyes.

Karen believes that after an incident is over, it's over. She fails to understand that Dawn now sees her as a volcano ready to erupt. Karen never comprehends why Dawn seems so distant in the ensuing years. In fact, Karen has no idea how Dawn feels about her.

Causing unintended hurt

Loving someone with BPD isn't easy because people with BPD not only fail to understand how others feel about them, but they also fail to see how they impact others. For those who care about people with BPD, the experience of their relationship can be frightening and hurtful at the same time. However, people with BPD are so focused on their own emotional distress and turmoil that they can't step back and see the pain and suffering they cause others.

The ability to take other people's perspectives is a crucial part of getting along in relationships. Being able to see how other people think and feel enables you to successfully relate to friends, colleagues, and lovers.

People with BPD are truly deficient in understanding the nature of other people's thoughts and feelings. They're not purposely trying to hurt themselves or others.

The following story about Gary, a man who has BPD, and his wife, Denise, depicts Gary's unawareness of how his behavior profoundly affects his wife. Often people with BPD are astonished when their spouses leave them. Outsiders, on the other hand, aren't so surprised.

"Denise, did you get my jeans washed?" **Gary** asks.

"Yep, they should be on top of your dresser with all the other folded clothes for the trip," Denise replies. "By the way, we need to leave for the airport in about 15 minutes. Traffic can be bad at this time of day."

Gary looks at his watch. He knows all about getting stuck in traffic and being late for the airport. Anger pulses through his body. He purposely slows down his pace and starts to stall. As the time they're supposed to leave gets closer, he can see that Denise is ready. She's looking at the boarding passes and making sure that she has both passports. He hates the fact that she's so organized and throws it in his face. His suitcase remains half full on the bed, and it's time to go.

Denise is aware that Gary gets tense before trips. She tries to stay out of his way and be as helpful as she can — unfortunately, it never works. She carries her suitcase out to the car, checks the locks, and leaves on a couple of lights. With no time built in for traffic, Gary rushes out with his suitcase and speeds down the driveway. Neither of them speaks during the tense trip to the airport.

On the plane, Denise orders a drink to calm her nerves. She knows that Gary disapproves, but drinking in front of Gary somehow gives her a sense of control. Gary, full of rage, holds his newspaper so that she can't see his face. Denise settles down with a novel, knowing that this will be another trip of silence. She brushes away a few tears.

Denise knows that Gary suffers from BPD and that he doesn't seem to be able to control his emotional responses. She tries not to take his moodiness personally, but, through the years, she has become more and more withdrawn, afraid, hurt, and angry. One day she will leave him.

Gary's mind is so totally absorbed by his own misery that he simply can't see how hurtful his behavior is to Denise. He has no idea that she will leave him one day even though abandonment is one of his greatest fears.

Busting through Boundaries

Fences set the boundary lines around property, but people have boundaries, too. Personal boundaries set the rules, limits, expectations, and even personal space that people desire. Like different people, different cultures also tend to have somewhat different boundaries.

For example, citizens of the United States usually stand a couple of feet apart when conversing. People in Latin America, France, and the Arab region often prefer to stand somewhat closer, and people from Japan and Germany stand a little farther apart. If you've traveled abroad, you may have felt uncomfortable with the space expectations of the citizens of the country you visited.

Space is only one of many boundaries that people set with the hopes that others will respect them. For example, you probably wouldn't make a social call in the middle of the night because you wouldn't want to greatly annoy your friend. And, you may know that when you call a potential new love interest too often, that person may feel like your crossing an important boundary.

People with BPD don't understand or respect other people's boundaries. Therefore, they often trample on what other people feel are important limits. Brianna's story typifies some of the various ways that someone with BPD may run over other people's boundaries.

> **Brianna** frantically texts her boyfriend, Noah, "Where R U? Thought U were coming at 7. We'll B L8 to the office party."
>
> Noah texts her back, "It's 10 after. On my way. Bad traffic." Noah's having second thoughts about this relationship. He's known Brianna for only a short while. They met at work, and she came on strong. Although they've been dating only about two weeks, she now goes crazy when he's a few minutes late. She talks to him way too much while he's working and gets jealous when he talks to other co-workers about work. He pulls into her driveway, distracted by his concerns.
>
> Brianna stands in the open doorway. She throws her arms around Noah and presses her body close. She says, "Let's make up before we go to the party."
>
> Feeling off balance, Noah says, "Gosh, I'd love to, but not now. Our boss will be mad if we show up much later than we already are."
>
> They arrive at the party and Brianna hugs the boss and tells him, "Noah wouldn't have sex with me before we came. He was so afraid of making you mad. Can you believe that? Do you think I'm cute?"
>
> Both Noah and the boss blush. By the end of the evening, Brianna has had too much to drink and has flirted with most of her male co-workers. Noah tells her, "I'm not so sure we're right for each other."
>
> Although it's 11:30 p.m., Brianna feels upset and calls her therapist for support even though her therapist told her only to call during office hours unless it's an emergency. She tells the therapist, "My boyfriend just dumped me, and I feel awful."
>
> Her therapist asks, "Do you feel like hurting yourself?"
>
> Brianna replies, "Gosh no, I'm just upset and want to talk! Aren't you interested in how I'm feeling? You don't understand me very well, do you? Do you even care about me?

Brianna has breached boundaries in many ways. She flirts and crosses boundaries at work impulsively. She reveals overly intimate information to her boss. And, of course, she crosses her therapist's boundaries by calling at a late hour and asking for special attention. Like many people with BPD, she goes from hot to cold to enraged within minutes. (For more on the explosive emotions that many people with BPD experience, check out Chapter 6.)

Be aware that most therapists have guidelines for after-hours calls. Usually they request that you make such calls only in cases of emergency. Your therapist needs to explain these policies to you, or you need to ask about them, at the initial session.

People with BPD fail to understand and appreciate interpersonal boundaries like the ones we describe in the preceding story. The following sections take a closer look at the problems people with BPD experience with boundaries in various types of relationships.

Disrespecting partners and lovers

People with BPD typically fail to appreciate their partners' and lovers' boundaries. A man with BPD may demand to know where his partner is at all times and subject her to regular inquisitions because he has a deep fear of abandonment. Another man may demand that his partner cut herself off from her friends because of an intense bout of jealousy.

People with BPD frequently attempt to control the lives of their loved ones because of worries about abandonment. Paradoxically, their worries often cause the very thing they're hoping to prevent.

Slighting friends and co-workers

People with BPD always seem to live in the eye of a hurricane, having multiple crises going on in their lives at any given time. During these predicaments, they're likely to push their friends to the point of disgust and practically force them to support their causes. Sometimes they even ask their friends to inappropriately intervene on their behalf. They also may breach boundaries by revealing confidences to other people. And they have a special talent for setting up conflicts among their friends and acquaintances.

In addition, people with BPD make unreasonable demands of their employers, requesting special treatment, hour changes, additional time off, or private meetings. To receive special considerations, they may claim to have esoteric illnesses that they really don't have. They also often spread rumors about their co-workers, igniting the atmosphere at work.

Straining relationships with helpers

Doctors or therapists working with people with BPD notice that their clients make frequent demands that cross professional boundaries. For example, people with BPD are more likely than other clients to do the following:

- ✔ Ask for special appointment times
- ✔ Cancel at the last minute
- ✔ Seem overly friendly and personal

✔ Behave seductively

✔ Call after hours

✔ Make ending a session difficult

✔ Expect discounts or special financial considerations

✔ Expect special help from their providers

✔ Ask inappropriately personal questions

✔ Demand certain medications they think they need

When professionals have a number of people with BPD in their caseloads, they can easily feel overwhelmed by the broad range of demands that their clients and patients make. People in the helping professions sometimes struggle to remain caring and empathetic without losing their professional objectivity. See Chapter 25 for information about how professionals can clarify their own boundaries and maintain their sanity when working through these issues with patients who have BPD.

Riding roughshod over kids

Parents with BPD cross boundaries with their kids in all sorts of ways. Sometimes they worry that their children will stop loving them so they try to become their kids' best friends instead of being the guides or leaders that parents need to be. They often become overly involved in their kids' lives and interfere with normal development by

✔ Doing their kids' homework

✔ Criticizing authority figures when their children run into trouble

✔ Stirring up arguments among their kids' friends and/or parents

✔ Asking their kids to reveal almost every detail of their lives

Mental health professionals call such overinvolvement *enmeshment,* which refers to the difficulty some people have in distinguishing between the lives of others and themselves. As you can imagine, kids with enmeshed parents have a harder time accomplishing the basic tasks of childhood and adolescence, such as forming a clear identity and acquiring the ability to function autonomously.

At other times, parents with BPD fail to set proper boundaries with their kids by withdrawing, retreating, and becoming underinvolved. Such parents fail to set reasonable rules and also neglect to provide love, attention, and support to their children. Kids of parents who can't set reasonable structures often fail to learn critical societal rules and end up vulnerable to various emotional maladies later in life.

Parents with BPD sometimes continue running over their kids' boundaries even after they've grown into adulthood. Sometimes they ask their adult kids for advice about their own strained marriages or relationships. They may go to their kids for support, both financially and emotionally. They may also provide unasked for and unwanted advice to their kids about their relationships, lives, or finances.

Whether people with BPD cross the boundaries set by their lovers, their therapists, or their kids, they do so because they don't understand why their loved ones set boundaries in the first place. All in all, people with BPD have a hard time respecting boundaries because they can't take other people's perspectives.

Chapter 9

BPD and Extreme Thinking

. . . .

. . . .

The behaviors, feelings, and thoughts of people with borderline personality disorder (BPD) generally show up in extreme forms — in other words, not many aspects of the disorder take the middle road. Professionals place part of the blame for the turbulent nature of the lives of people with BPD on what they call *schemas,* or powerful beliefs that people hold about themselves and the world around them. Basically, schemas influence the way people interpret reality and dictate the way they feel.

In this chapter, we elaborate on the nature of schemas and note that people experience a variety of them throughout the course of their lives. We explain where schemas come from. We tackle the difference between healthy, middle ground schemas and unhealthy, disruptive, extreme schemas. Finally, we explore the nature of the problematic schemas that people with BPD commonly experience.

Understanding How You See the World

Schemas dictate how you think and feel about the world around you, as well as how you experience it. Schemas are like pairs of glasses that you use to improve your vision. Sometimes these lenses help you see the world more clearly, but, at other times, they show you a blurred, cracked, or grotesquely distorted vision.

How schemas develop

Schemas start to form during childhood. Your parents and caregivers strongly influence the development of these schemas, but peers, teachers, and relatives play a large role, too. In conjunction with these personal influences, life events, such as illnesses and tragic accidents, and genetic predispositions also help determine the nature of the schemas you develop.

The following examples illustrate how parental figures can cause certain schemas to develop in their children.

Daniel's father routinely criticizes and punishes him severely. When Daniel works beside his dad on a project, his father explodes when Daniel makes the slightest mistake. He yells, "How can you be so stupid and clumsy?"

Daniel grows up believing that he's inherently inadequate to deal with challenges when they arise. He develops a schema of inferiority. Accordingly, he responds to school assignments with little effort because he doesn't believe in his ability to succeed. His schema of inferiority continues to grow as he performs poorly in school.

Anna's father, on the other hand, routinely praises Anna for good work and corrects her without undue harshness. When she asks for help with schoolwork, Anna's father encourages her to find her own answers, but he does patiently explain the difficult concepts. He applauds her tenacity. One day she brings home a B- on a test — well below her usual performance — and he tells her, "You don't have to be perfect all the time. You can learn a lot from Bs. I'm just proud that you worked so hard. Now try to see what you can learn from what you did wrong on that assignment."

Because of the way her father treats her, Anna develops a schema of competence when life's challenges confront her. Thus, when she receives tough school assignments, she has all the motivation she needs to tackle them. Because she tries hard, she succeeds and feels all the more competent. As a result, her schema of competence continues to grow.

When we use the terms parents and parenting, we do so for the sake of simplicity and convenience. We realize that caregivers other than the biological parents may play parenting roles in some children's lives. We don't mean to imply that parents are more important than these other care providers — each family is different.

Although schemas begin to develop in childhood, they continue to grow and adapt to life happenings through adolescence into adulthood.

Types of schemas

Although numerous different schemas exist, most of them involve questioning yourself, others, and the world around you and are characterized accordingly:

✔ **Self-concept schemas:** Who am I? Am I capable? What am I worth?

✔ **Relationship schemas:** Can I trust others or should I avoid them? How do I deserve to be treated, and how should I treat others?

✔ **World schemas:** Is the world safe or dangerous? Predictable or unpredictable?

Most self-concepts and views of the world develop out of appreciation for their opposites. For example, you know what *beautiful* means because you know what *ugly* means. The same premise holds true for other basic concepts, including hot versus cold, short versus tall, sad versus happy, and wet versus dry.

This same fundamental idea applies to schemas. You can think of schemas in terms of opposite extremes, but you also have to remember that schemas, like other basic concepts, have adaptive middle positions, too. After all, water can be hot, cold, or lukewarm. A person can be short, tall, or of average height. The following examples illustrate this concept in relation to schemas:

✔ A woman may hold a belief or schema of incompetence about herself. When faced with a difficulty, she likely feels overwhelmed and incapable of solving the problem.

✔ The opposite schema to incompetence is a schema of omnipotence. A woman with the omnipotence schema impulsively takes on almost any problem and may fail to seek help, even when it's necessary, because she believes she can do anything.

✔ A schema in the middle of these two is competence. A person with the competence schema carefully ponders every situation, considers how to tackle a problem, and seeks help when necessary.

Why schemas are hard to change

After you develop your schemas, you don't change them easily because of four major reasons:

✔ **Schemas act as filters.** Schemas often prevent people from receiving information that contradicts their schemas by focusing their minds only on evidence that confirms the schemas. For example, if you have a schema of inferiority, you likely ignore or discount all evidence, such as a raise at work or a good grade on an exam, that contradicts your belief that you're inferior to the people around you. If you have the schema or belief that the world is a dangerous place, the presence of a policeman in a dark parking lot probably doesn't reassure you.

✔ **Schemas encourage misinterpretation.** Schemas often lead people to change the meaning of events to correspond to the beliefs involved in the schemas. For example, some people have an anxious attachment schema (an intense fear that people they love will leave them). When someone with this schema attends a party at which her partner doesn't remain close to her throughout the whole evening, her anxious attachment schema may cause her to see her partner's actions as evidence that he's looking for someone else.

✔ **Schemas lead to fear.** People are afraid to challenge their schemas because they fear the consequences of doing so. For example, if you have a schema of inferiority, you may not want to put much effort into any task because you're convinced that challenging your inferiority schema in this manner will result in failure. Thus, you don't want to challenge your schema by trying to perform well — at anything. Similarly, if you have the schema of idealizing (in other words, you see another person as absolutely perfect), you may not ask a potential friend or lover many questions because you're afraid of finding out things you don't want to know.

✔ **Schemas are invisible.** People often aren't aware that schemas exist or that these schemas dictate the way they see reality. Not surprisingly, you can't easily change something you don't know exists.

Although schemas don't easily change overnight, they do sometimes change over the course of many years because people are continually having new experiences. They can change even more quickly when a person goes to therapy. See Chapter 19 for some strategies on how you can help reshape schemas.

BPD Schemas: No Middle Ground

Schemas that the BPD mind creates tend to be extreme and maladaptive. In addition, people with BPD frequently flip between opposite schema extremes. For example, a man with BPD typically sees himself as undeserving of the nice things that happen to him. However, when his wife fails to pick up his dry cleaning because she has to pick up the kids from school, he flips into an entitled rage over her lack of care for him.

On the other hand, a man without BPD may respond to the same situation with mild annoyance or even empathetic understanding of his wife's busy schedule. He does so because he has a middle ground schema of deserving, rather than the extreme schemas of undeserving and entitled.

Many people with BPD have difficulty finding a middle ground schema — this difficulty is called *splitting*. In other words, people with BPD struggle to see shades of gray and, instead, see only black and white extremes. No wonder the partners of people with BPD often feel a need to be on high alert — the flipping between extremes can cause emotional whiplash in those who care about people with BPD.

The following sections review some of the most common schemas that plague the BPD mind. We divide these schemas into three basic categories — self-concept schemas, relationship schemas, and world schemas. In each category, we compare the opposite extremes to the more adaptive middle ground views to give you a better understanding of the intense difference between healthy and not-so-healthy schemas. We also take a look at the possible origins of each schema.

Self-concept schemas

All people, including us and you, develop schemas about who they are throughout their lives. These personal schemas are called *self-concept schemas,* and they directly influence how you feel, what you do, and what you expect in life. You develop self-concept schemas through experience and early interactions with caregivers.

Two important self-concept schema dimensions that epitomize the extreme views that people with BPD often have are entitled versus undeserving and inferiority versus superiority.

Entitled versus undeserving

An *entitled schema* describes people who feel they have a right to whatever they want whenever they want it. They expect other people to meet all their needs at the drop of a hat, but, at the same time, they show little to no concern for the needs of others. When they don't get what they want, they feel outrage.

People who have an *undeserving schema,* on the other hand, don't believe they're worthy of getting their needs met by others. These people don't expect any attention or consideration from others, and they don't ask for what they want when they want it. As a result, their needs go unmet.

People with BPD often flip between entitled and undeserving. For example, a woman may cause a scene at a restaurant when she doesn't get immediate service. She takes the slow service personally instead of chalking it up to a busy waitress. She believes that the waitress is insulting her by not meeting her immediate needs. When the waitress profusely apologizes for being slow because she's new on the job, the woman finds herself becoming overwhelmed with shame. She suddenly feels like she's undeserving of kindness because of her uncontrolled outburst.

The middle or more adaptive self-concept schema is *balanced self-worth*. People with this schema expect to get their needs met, but they don't expect to meet their needs at the expense of others or all the time. They balance their own needs with those of others.

Extreme schemas of entitled or undeserving usually develop in childhood because of imbalanced parenting that fails to meet children's needs. In other words, parents who either completely spoil or neglect their children provide fertile soil for these problematic schemas to grow in.

Inferiority versus superiority

People with *inferiority schemas* feel like they're inadequate compared to other people. They lack confidence in their abilities and talents. As a result, they often give up easily, which usually leads to more feelings of incompetence.

In stark contrast, people with *superiority schemas* believe that they're brighter and better than others. They may pursue achievement or status regardless of the cost, and they may thoughtlessly neglect or abuse others because they're so self-absorbed and lofty that other people just don't show up on their radar screen. People often refer to folks with this schema as being *narcissistic,* or extremely self-centered.

The following story about Bernie, a CEO of a corporation, illustrates how someone with a superiority schema may crash and burn because of an unexpected financial blow, which causes him to flip to an inferiority schema.

> **Bernie** is 62 years old and runs a successful auto supply business. His bonus last year was 2.1 million dollars; thus, he enjoys a lavish lifestyle. His business has taken a sharp downturn recently, and the board of directors votes to replace him with a new CEO. Bernie is astonished. He has always seen himself as irreplaceable and totally responsible for his company's success. He assumes that companies will line up in droves to hire him, given his brilliance and superior business acumen. However, several months pass and Bernie begins to see that the rest of the business community doesn't view him the same way. His superior schema disintegrates, and Bernie falls into a major depressive disorder. He acquires an inferiority schema and laments that he may never again work. His wife worries about their finances because Bernie never bothered to invest and save — always assuming bonuses and even a golden parachute would await him in the future.

The more adaptive, middle ground schema, called *self-acceptance,* consists of accurate beliefs about oneself. The self-acceptance schema involves recognizing that people have different sets of skills and talents and that no one person is more important than another. People who achieve this schema can appreciate both their strengths and their weaknesses.

The extreme schemas of inferiority and superiority usually develop as a result of parents who put excessive focus on achievements or failures. Such parents either criticize harshly or pile inordinate, unearned praise on their children. Both of these parenting styles can cause problems as children grow up.

Self-concept schemas in action

The following story illustrates how powerful events in childhood can be in shaping self-concept schemas. Jordan started to develop an entitled schema early in childhood. After his father was sent to prison, however, that schema shattered, leaving him with an undeserving schema. The shame he felt from his father's imprisonment also led him to develop an inferiority schema.

> The last time **Jordan** saw his father was 10 years ago when he was barely 13. Since then, he has received an occasional phone call, usually around his birthday, from the penitentiary. But Jordan never picks up the phone when he sees the prison's name on his caller ID.
>
> Jordan's dad dealt drugs and seemed pretty successful — for awhile. Today Jordan recalls how his father spoiled him with the latest technology, sports equipment, and clothes when he was young. Jordan didn't think things could get any better. He felt on top of the world and boasted shamelessly to his friends about his lavish possessions.
>
> But everything changed when his dad sold drugs to an undercover agent. Jordan's mom did her best and always had food on the table, but the party was over. Jordan's family could no longer afford more than the bare necessities. Jordan tried shoplifting, but he stopped after he almost got caught one day. His friends deserted him after he no longer had the best of everything.
>
> Jordan remains deeply ashamed that his dad sits in prison and, as a result, never talks to anyone about his family. Following these events, Jordan formed an inferiority schema. Although he once felt entitled to the best of everything, Jordan now feels undeserving of anything good that happens to him. He takes a series of call center jobs but can't last at any of them for more than two months.

Early in childhood, events encouraged Jordan to develop entitled and superiority schemas. However, the overly positive, inflated nature of these schemas set Jordan up for the devastating fall into the undeserving and inferiority schemas when his father was arrested. Inflated schemas are easily punctured by negative events, and as a result, people with BPD who have these inflated schemas are at a high risk for emotional upheavals.

Relationship schemas

People develop various schemas that influence how they relate to one another. These schemas either pave the way for or put up serious roadblocks to forming good friendships and relationships.

Two major schema dimensions that strongly influence the nature of relationships that people with BPD have are anxious attachment versus avoidant attachment and idealizing versus demonizing.

Anxious attachment versus avoidant attachment

People who have an *anxious attachment schema* worry greatly that other people will leave them. They fear abandonment and stay on high alert for any sign that someone close to them is thinking of leaving. They're highly sensitive to imagined rejection, and they're often intensely clingy and jealous. Unfortunately, their overly sensitive, jealousy-driven behaviors frequently cause the very abandonment they fear.

On the other hand, people with an *avoidant attachment schema* stay away from other people. They believe that they don't need other people in their lives, often because they assume others will hurt them if they let them in. People with an avoidant attachment schema appear aloof and uninterested in other people.

Many people flip between these two extremes. For example, a woman with BPD may have an anxious attachment schema, which causes her to be overly involved in her adult daughter's life. She calls her daughter several times daily, stops at her house unexpectedly, and shares intimate details of her life. She does all these things to stay connected and reassure herself that her daughter loves her. One day her daughter informs her that she's setting a limit. No longer will she take more than three phone calls from her mother each week, and her mother can no longer drop by the house uninvited. Her mother responds by flipping into an avoidant schema. She rages at her daughter and accuses her of being ungrateful. She avoids calling her daughter for a month.

The middle ground schema in this dimension is called a *secure attachment schema,* and it leads people to form friendships based on mutual caring and respect. People with this schema carefully evaluate new possible relationships without being overly distrusting or naïve, and they don't sabotage their relationships with jealous or clingy behaviors.

As you may expect, parenting practices affect whether or not a child is likely to develop problematic relationship schemas. Parents who either abuse or seriously neglect their kids may set them up for attachment problems. Likewise, parents who become overly enmeshed in their kids' lives, and who try to control and dictate every move, can lead their kids to develop troublesome schemas.

Idealizing versus demonizing

A classic feature of BPD is the tendency to see people as either all good or all bad. This tendency heightens in intimate relationships. People with BPD often see new partners as perfect individuals, having no blemishes of any kind. This tendency is called an *idealizing schema*. People with this schema inflate the images of their partners to such high standards that their partners can't help but disappoint them.

The *demonizing schema*, on the other hand, causes people to view others as malicious and out to get them. They interpret other people's behaviors as hostile and malevolent. Thus, trust is very difficult for them to achieve.

Often people flip between the two extremes. For example, when the partner or friend of someone with the idealizing schema fails to live up to the impossible, idealized standards, the demonizing schema takes hold and drops the partner to demon status. When someone develops the demonizing schema, any flaw or foible in another person simply proves that person's demon status.

The middle ground schema in this dimension is called a *realistic view schema*. When a person develops this schema, she sees other people as neither all good nor all bad. She expects others to have positive attributes but also accepts their negative qualities. Obviously, this schema allows for relationships to endure life's ups and downs more easily than the idealizing or demonizing schemas.

Parents who tell their kids that the world is out to get them and that they should never trust anyone provide fertile ground for the development of a demonizing schema. Similarly, parents who model naiveté and a Pollyanna-style view of others inculcate an idealizing schema. Furthermore, people with BPD tend to see the world in extremes, which means they likely split people into demons and angels.

Relationship schemas in action

The following story about Tara shows you how relationship schemas that are extremely imbalanced interfere with life and relationships. Tara's rocky relationship with her aunt is the result of flipping back and forth between an anxious attachment schema and an avoidant attachment schema. Tara also flips between idealizing and demonizing schemas, which causes additional problems in her relationship with her aunt.

> **Tara** talks to her psychotherapist about a recent argument she had with her aunt. "It all started when my aunt insulted me. I know I'm not perfect, but family is family. We should stick up for each other."
>
> Dr. Feingold asks, "What did she say that insulted you?"
>
> "She basically called me a whore. That's what she did. I hate her. I probably won't ever speak to her again," Tara responds, her face beginning to redden.

"My goodness, you must be upset," Dr. Feingold consoles, "You're so close to your aunt. Help me understand. What happened?"

"My aunt asked whether or not I was bringing anyone to my cousin's wedding next month. I told her that I wasn't dating anyone right now. She said that was unusual for me."

"And . . ." Dr. Feingold waits for Tara to finish.

"Well, what she obviously meant was that I sleep around."

"I'm not sure that I follow you, Tara. Help me understand how her saying that it was unusual for you not to have a date meant that you sleep around," Dr. Feingold responds.

Tara begins to cry. She says, "My aunt was always there for me. She was the mom I never had. When my mom got drunk, my aunt showered me with love and affection. She could do no wrong. Now all she does is talk about my cousin's wedding. My cousin is perfect. She's only had a couple of boyfriends, and you know I've had so many. My cousin does everything right, and I do everything wrong. I hate her, and I hate my aunt."

"Tara, I think I understand what's happening here. Remember when we talked about how sometimes you go from being very insecure and anxious in a relationship to being avoidant and wanting to run away? Your reactions are understandable because you couldn't trust your mother. When she was sober, she cared for you, but, unfortunately, she got abusive when she was drunk. No wonder you bounce around from being insecure to angry. Your mind activates these feelings because you're worried that your aunt may not always be there for you," Dr. Feingold explains.

Tara's upbringing set her up to acquire extreme relationship schemas. At times, she idealizes her aunt and sees her as someone she can count on — someone who can do no wrong. But when her aunt pays attention to Tara's cousin, Tara feels slighted and jealous. She wants to push her aunt away, which indicates a flip to an avoidant attachment schema. Tara also demonizes her aunt without good justification when she does something that Tara believes is wrong. As you can see, Tara's schemas go from one extreme to the other, and they wreak havoc on her relationships.

World schemas

Not only do people form schemas about themselves and others, but they also form them about the world they live in. These schemas strongly influence the way people live and provide a sense of either security or paranoia and fear. Two schema dimensions that often influence how people with BPD feel as they traverse the roads in life are dangerous versus totally safe and unpredictable versus totally predictable.

Dangerous versus totally safe

People who see the world through a *dangerous schema* rarely feel safe. They're hypervigilant and take inordinate precautions whenever they venture outside the relative safety of their homes. They see the world as a jungle and worry constantly about when the next lion will spring from the underbrush. Sometimes their fears grow to such proportions that they rarely leave their houses.

On the other hand, people who see the world through a *totally safe schema* unwittingly take unnecessary risks. Oblivious to the need for being reasonably cautious, they venture forth in life and, not surprisingly, frequently suffer serious consequences for their clueless naiveté.

The middle ground schema in this dimension is called *reasonably safe*. People with a reasonably safe schema manage to reign in extreme paranoia and hold onto appropriate cautions at the same time.

Both the practices a parent uses and the characteristics of a child's neighborhood and school strongly influence the development of these schemas. Abusive parents raise children who may exhibit dangerous schemas because they're used to feeling perpetual fear. On the other hand, parents who overly protect their kids are likely to have children who go into the world with an exaggerated sense of safety because they never let their kids feel fear.

Unpredictable versus totally predictable

People with an *unpredictable schema* see the world as chaotic. They don't attempt to develop a life plan because they don't think plans ever work out. They see themselves as victims to their life happenings. They feel overwhelmed and helpless and, as you may imagine, pessimism rules over optimism in their lives.

In stark contrast, people with a *totally predictable schema* view themselves as the complete masters of their lives. They can't see the possibility of failure because they believe the world will bend to their wills. People with this schema decide on only one plan for their careers, investments, and relationships and don't bother with a Plan B. Unfortunately, when things don't go according to their masterful plan, they tend to fall apart.

The middle ground schema in this dimension is called a *predictable schema* — please note the lack of the word *totally* here. People with the predictable schema realize that the world and the outcomes of their efforts have some predictability but that no one can control all possible eventualities. These people are well prepared for life's curve balls and like to have a Plan A, B, and C. They figure that Plan A will usually work, but they're not devastated when it doesn't.

Both parenting styles and life events shape the world schemas in this dimension. Kids who grow up in families ruled by chaos tend to develop unpredictable schemas. Keep in mind that some childhoods simply have more than their share of unpredictable, uncontrollable events, such as deaths, divorces, job losses, and so on. At the other end of the spectrum, some parents plan every last detail of their children's lives. They schedule every minute of every day, and they dictate precisely what their kids do and with whom they do it. These kids who never have to face an unplanned situation typically end up with totally predictable schemas.

World schemas in action

People's world schemas can pop up anytime and anywhere. The following story about Lily, who doesn't have BPD, and Kaitlyn, who does have BPD, shows how schemas affect everyday occurrences at work. People with BPD tend to have more extreme schemas and, therefore, react to events with greater emotionality and intensity than people who don't have the disorder.

> Lily and **Kaitlyn** are nurses who work the night shift in a big city hospital. Both nurses enjoy the relative quiet and slower pace that the night shift offers. They work on the fourth floor in labor and delivery.

> At 3 a.m. on a slow night, an announcement pierces the quiet atmosphere of the floor, "Paging Dr. Firestone, 5 East." Lily, who is entering notes on a computer, pauses. Kaitlyn, chatting with an expectant father, stops midsentence. The two nurses know that in their hospital, "Paging Dr. Firestone, 5 East" means a fire has broken out in the east wing of the fifth floor. Such incidents are usually trivial and quickly snuffed out.

> Lily has reasonably safe and predictable schemas. She resumes her duties but also keeps an ear out for any further announcements. She's not overly alarmed.

> In contrast, Kaitlyn has BPD, along with dangerous and unpredictable schemas, and immediately feels panic. Unpredictable, traumatic events have marked her life. She gasps and blurts out, "Oh my God, there's a fire in the hospital!" The expectant father she's been talking to turns white and runs to his wife's room to warn her. The word rapidly spreads throughout the floor and patients pour into the hallways.

> Lily quickly calls the fifth floor to confirm that nothing serious is going on. The floor secretary says that a patient lit up in the bathroom and set off a smoke alarm. Lily announces, "Calm down everyone. There is no fire. Repeat, there is no fire. It was a false alarm."

As you can see, Kaitlyn responded to the announcement without waiting to gather more information. Her schemas led her to assume the worst and, more importantly, put her patients at risk. She was lucky that Lily was there to calm everyone down. Otherwise, Kaitlyn may have lost her job.

Chapter 10

Slipping Away from Reality

. . . .

In This Chapter

▶ Sorting out dissociation

▶ Pinpointing paranoia

▶ Dealing with hearing voices

▶ Feeling crazy because of BPD

. . . .

The word *borderline* suggests the edge or boundary between two proper-
ties, conditions, or emotions. Originally, mental health professionals
thought that borderline personality disorder (BPD) sat on the edge between
sane and insane, more technically between neurotic and psychotic (see
Chapter 3 for a discussion of this issue). Although professionals no longer
believe that BPD lies on a clear border between sanity and insanity, many
people who have BPD do report feeling crazy or insane.

Psychosis — the technical term that comes the closest to what people mean
when they say crazy or insane — refers to a loss of contact with reality.
Although people with BPD can experience episodes of psychosis, they do so
only briefly and less profoundly than people with psychotic disorders such
as schizophrenia. See *Schizophrenia For Dummies* by Jerome and Irene Levine
(Wiley) for more information.

In this chapter, we explore the symptoms of leaving reality behind. We begin
by discussing the mildest form of losing contact with reality, which is known
as dissociation. Then we paint a picture of paranoia and describe hallucinations. Finally, we tell you how these symptoms manifest themselves in BPD
and what you can do to deal with them when they occur.

Discovering Dissociation

Dissociation involves the breaking of connections or associations between
aspects of the self that usually go together. These generally connected or
integrated facets of the self can include your body, memories, emotions,

identity, thoughts, and even the connection of yourself to reality. For example, a woman can have a vivid memory of having been raped yet experience no emotions whatsoever in connection with that memory.

Professionals don't consider dissociation to be psychotic even though it can involve some degree of departure from reality. Dissociative experiences are rather common in people with BPD. Many experts believe that dissociation in a person represents a way of coping with some severe trauma and/or stress, which would otherwise emotionally overwhelm the person. Dissociation can occur in the following forms:

- ✔ **Dissociative fugue:** In this state, people may fail to recall major portions of their pasts. They may disconnect from their usual identities and travel away from their homes while adopting new senses of self. People in a fugue state often appear normal to others who don't realize that the person in the dissociative fugue has disconnected from the past.

- ✔ **Dissociative identity disorder:** Professionals once called this problem *multiple personality disorder.* This condition occurs when someone adopts two or more completely different personalities or personas. In fact, people with dissociative identity disorder commonly take on as many as fifteen separate personalities over time. Each personality may represent a strategy for coping with a different type of stressor or problem. The changes from personality to personality can include voice pitch, vocabulary, dialect, and posture. A large percentage of people with this disorder literally change their handedness (in other words, they go from being left-handed to being right-handed) as they move from one personality to another. In addition, each personality likely doesn't have access to memories that occurred when the person was experiencing a different personality.

- ✔ **Dissociative amnesia:** This condition involves a loss of big chunks of memory that are too extensive to be the result of normal forgetfulness. Usually these memories are traumatic in nature. Some people who experience dissociative amnesia attempt to prevent others from knowing about the memory loss. Sometimes they experience a large number of small losses of memory instead of one big loss, but even these small losses are beyond normal forgetfulness.

- ✔ **Depersonalization disorder:** This disorder involves periods of time in which people feel detached from themselves and their experiences. Sometimes people in this state feel like they're detached from their bodies — almost as though they're viewing themselves through a movie camera. As a result, some people say the experience feels like living in a dream or a movie.

Dissociative states are likely the mind's adaptive responses to intolerable situations. They represent the mind's desperate escape strategy. For example, a large percentage of people with BPD report having been seriously abused or traumatized at some point in their lives. Becoming dissociated from their bodies may be their minds' way of dealing with the stress of that abuse. Most people with or without BPD experience at least brief dissociative experiences during or following highly traumatic events.

The following story about Nicole demonstrates how the process of dissociation works.

> **Nicole** hears the door slam; she listens as the footsteps start up the stairs. She feels sick to her stomach and pulls the blanket up to her chin. "Maybe he's too drunk tonight," she prays.
>
> "Nicole, baby, I'm home, baby," her stepfather whispers as he opens the door to her bedroom.
>
> She feels cold hands pulling away the blanket, touching her. She knows what will happen next — it's been happening most nights for the last two years since she was 12 years old. Nicole stays quiet and still and squeezes her eyes shut. She imagines that her body isn't her own, that she's not real. She wills her mind to go somewhere else. She's a butterfly. She flies away.

Nicole was repeatedly sexually abused by her stepfather. Her mind simply couldn't cope with the horror she experienced. As a result, she learned to go into dissociative states — in the form of depersonalization — in which she psychologically left her body during the assaults. Later in life, she will likely find herself going into dissociative states whenever she's reminded of the abuse or, perhaps, even during any time of conflict or stress.

Feeling Paranoid or Delusional

Paranoia involves heightened mistrust and fear. People who suffer from paranoia become preoccupied with imagined plots that others may be hatching against them. They may dwell on unsupported ideas of betrayal by friends, spouses, or acquaintances. They often read unwarranted, threatening meanings into other people's innocent remarks. Such paranoid mistrust and fear commonly accompany BPD.

Paranoia can range from merely heightened distrust to full-blown delusions of a psychotic nature, meaning they have little or no grounding in reality. However, people with BPD don't generally experience extremely intense psychotic delusions. When people with BPD do experience paranoia, their delusions tend to be brief and don't depart severely from reality.

Extreme paranoia: Paranoid schizophrenia

The following story about Joshua demonstrates paranoia that leaves reality far behind.

Joshua works for a government accounting office. He unlocks his file cabinet and reaches for a folder labeled "notes." He glances around to make sure that no co-workers are close by. He opens the folder at his desk and looks at the listed names and comments. Sixteen people are on the list. Joshua looks around once more before he adds another name. Then he writes, "Suspicious behavior in the cafeteria. Subject paying for meal with a large bill. May be collecting money from international terrorists."

Joshua keeps track of his co-workers because he believes that the CIA will soon contact him again for information about spies in his office. He thinks that the CIA communicates to him by sending thought waves to his brain while he sleeps. When he wakes up, he's able to recall his latest assignment.

Although Joshua has worked at this job for many years, he's a loner and doesn't socialize. People know to leave him alone. He manages to get his work done despite his paranoid thinking. Joshua was hospitalized during his late adolescence after he refused to shower for days and started speaking incoherently. However, today he manages to function and earn a living.

Joshua suffers from a condition known as *paranoid schizophrenia*. He doesn't show signs of BPD, and his type of delusions would rarely — if ever — occur in conjunction with BPD.

The following story about Alex, who has BPD, illustrates a type of paranoia that often accompanies BPD.

Alex looks out the window, hoping to see Madeline entering the apartment building. He paces back and forth, his tension rising. He calls her cell for about the 100th time — it goes right to voice mail again. He doesn't leave a message. He says out loud, "Where is she? Who is she with?"

Finally, the buzzer sounds, and a couple of minutes later Madeline opens the door. Alex begins, "Where were you? Why didn't you answer your cell?"

"I was at work. I had my cell phone turned off," Madeline replies.

"You left work early. I called your office. Don't lie to me. I know you're cheating on me. Tell me the truth," Alex's voice is getting louder.

"Geez, Alex, I left early so that I could stop and get my driver's license renewed. I told you last week that it had expired."

"Let me see your new license," Alex demands.

"No, that's ridiculous. I'm not showing you my license. If you don't believe me, that's your problem," Madeline starts to walk past him.

Alex grabs her by the arm and pushes her against the wall. "Don't ever walk away from me. I want the truth. Who are you seeing?"

"Don't touch me. You're way out of control. Let me go!" Madeline screams.

Alex illustrates over-the-top distrust of his girlfriend. However, his somewhat paranoid feelings don't rise to the level of psychotic delusions. The difference between a psychotic delusion and Alex's paranoid distrust is that even though Alex jumps to a conclusion with no real evidence, his girlfriend may be cheating on him — the idea isn't completely unreasonable or unrealistic. Thus, nothing about his jealous thoughts completely departs from reality.

Having Hallucinations

Hallucinations involve perceptions that occur without input from the environment. Thus, people who experience hallucinations hear sounds that aren't there. They see people who aren't present. Smells, temperatures, and tastes emanate from nowhere. Yet, the perceptions have all the qualities of true, real-life events. Furthermore, they occur while people are fully awake and conscious, not while they're in a dream state.

Mild hallucinations are extremely common in many people's lives. You may hear phones ringing when taking a shower or drying your hair, but when you check the caller ID, it shows nothing. Many people with no emotional disorder of any kind report that they sometimes hear faint voices or smell scents with no apparent source. These brief, mild experiences have little meaning, although they may occur more frequently when someone is under stress.

A step up in severity from hearing a brief telephone ring that didn't happen is the experience of hearing very real, distinct sounds and seeing sights that come from nowhere. Thus, someone may report hearing voices that sound sharp, clear, and present even though no one is in the room. However, experts don't consider experiences like this one to be full-blown psychosis as long as people at least maintain awareness that the voices are coming from their own heads.

On the other hand, sometimes people report vivid perceptions of voices, sights, sounds, and smells that no one else can perceive, yet they believe their perceptions are really occurring. They may hear voices telling them to do something and believe that some alien radio source is beaming the voices into their heads. Or, they may see someone standing right in front of them even though no one is there. This type of hallucination is quite rare in people with BPD, and if such hallucinations do occur, they do so only briefly. If such hallucinations occur more often and more severely, the person may have a different type of mental disorder — schizophrenia perhaps.

Hallucinations and schizophrenia

The following story about Mia illustrates some-one who has a more serious loss of contact with reality than what normally occurs with BPD.

The voices tell **Mia** to hurt herself. The chanting gets louder, "Evil devil, you must pay. You must suffer. Mia, Mia, Mia." Mia takes a puff on the cigarette once and then pushes the burning ash into her leg. The searing pain stops the voices. A moment of relief, but the voices return. "Devil, Mia, Mia, you must die. You must kill the devil Mia, Mia, Mia." She takes another drag and then burns her flesh again. It's not enough; she needs to do more to satisfy the voices. She starts to rock back and forth. The intense pain she feels from burning her flesh doesn't distract her from the pain of living.

She can't stand another day of these voices. She goes to the medicine cabinet and finds her medication. Maybe these drugs will stop the voices. She takes a handful of pills

and hopes for oblivion. An hour later, her husband walks in to discover her lying on the bathroom floor, unconscious. He calls the paramedics, who take her to the ER.

The attending physician first diagnoses her with BPD because of the self-mutilation and suicide attempt. However, her husband mentions that she's been hearing voices and having various hallucinations for years. The attending physician makes a wise deci-sion to call for a psychiatric consultation. The psychiatrist accurately diagnoses her with schizophrenia and has her hospitalized to find an appropriate medication to control her psychosis.

Mia's story illustrates that diagnosing disorders like BPD is a complicated and tricky process, even for physicians. If you suspect you have an emotional problem of any sort, seek the ser-vices of a licensed mental health practitioner, and don't attempt to diagnose the problem yourself.

The following story about Eric depicts someone who has BPD and falls apart under stress. Auditory hallucinations like Eric's are the most common type of hallucination that people with BPD experience.

Eric was physically and emotionally abused as a child by his mother and many of the boyfriends she brought into their home. During his teen years, he was in and out of drug treatment facilities and juvenile deten-tion centers. After graduating from high school, he joins the service as a way of getting away from his past and starting over.

Basic training begins. He hates taking orders, and he can barely keep up with the rigorous physical demands. Eric slowly begins to disintegrate. He hears voices telling him that he's stupid and that he'll never amount to anything. These voices seem almost real, but Eric knows they can't be.

Eric's drill sergeant sees that Eric is losing it. He orders Eric to report to the base's mental health center for a checkup. The psychologist at the center interviews Eric and gives him some psychological tests. After reviewing all the information, the psychologist diagnoses Eric with BPD. He doesn't think Eric's hallucinations are full-blown psychotic episodes. Nonetheless, he recommends that Eric receive an honorable discharge because of his mental condition and inability to handle great stress and pressure.

Eric's story shows the kind of brief auditory hallucinations that people with BPD sometimes experience. He hears voices, but he knows they must be coming from his head.

When You Have BPD and Feel Crazy

People with BPD often say they feel crazy because they struggle to control their impulses and emotions. They frequently find themselves acting in reprehensible ways. They also commonly report feeling out of it and dissociative (see the "Discovering Dissociation" section earlier in this chapter for more information). However, these issues aren't what professionals label as psychotically out of touch with reality. You can start to address common BPD symptoms by reading Part IV of this book, which covers everything from dealing with your impulsivity to changing your state of mind.

On rare occasions, people with BPD do experience what professionals call brief psychotic episodes, in which they experience hallucinations or delusions for awhile. When such experiences do occur, professionals can usually easily treat them with a brief regimen of antipsychotic medication. Generally, the people who suffer from these brief psychotic episodes can withdraw the antipsychotic medication after the episodes abate. See Chapter 20 for more information about the medications professionals use to treat BPD and associated symptoms.

Part III
Making the Choice to Change

The 5th Wave   By Rich Tennant

"Smile or lose the 'Life is good' shirt."

In this part . . .

If you have borderline personality disorder (BPD), you may not have already made the decision to seek treatment and make changes in your life. In this part, we describe the various settings in which you may find BPD treatment available. We introduce you to the mental health professionals who provide treatment for BPD and explain what to look for in your individual therapist. We also go through some of the treatments that professionals have found to be helpful in treating BPD — because you need to know what does and what doesn't work. Finally, we help you decide whether treatment is what you really want and then prepare you for fully engaging in that treatment if you decide to seek it out.

Chapter 11

Preparing to Conquer BPD

*B*orderline personality disorder (BPD) consists of a broad constellation of symptoms (see Chapter 3 for more info). The range of problems people with BPD experience makes treatment challenging. For example, some people with BPD have trouble with substance abuse, difficulty keeping a job, tumultuous relationships, or serious problems with mood. Others feel empty inside, worry about being abandoned, or try to physically hurt themselves. Addressing even one of those problems can be extremely difficult, so imagine how hard treating a combination of them can be. Although treatment for BPD takes awhile and can seem overwhelming at first, over time, it usually helps significantly.

Not surprisingly, the wide range of available treatments makes choosing the right treatment challenging for people who have BPD or those people who care for them. If you have BPD, you can choose from an hour a week of individual psychotherapy, day treatment (known as partial hospitalization), full-time inpatient treatment, or group therapy. In this chapter, we help you handle this array of options.

This chapter describes the various treatment options available for people with BPD and explains which ones have been shown to work. We provide a glossary of treatment providers. We spell out what to expect in psychotherapy and, more importantly, show you how to tell whether you've made the right choice. Finally, we discuss how to make realistic goals instead of expecting unlikely miracles.

Exploring BPD Treatment Settings

You can find treatment for BPD in a variety of settings. Each of these settings — whether it's working one-on-one with a therapist, taking part in group therapy, or spending some time in a hospital — has certain pluses and minuses. In the following sections, we describe what to expect from each of these treatment venues.

Working individually with a therapist

Most mental health practitioners practice independently and offer services to individuals, one at a time. Typically, they see each client for fifty minutes either once or twice per week. For people with BPD, especially during times of great upheaval, individual therapy once or twice per week may not suffice. However, many people with BPD do get better with the help of individual psychotherapy. See the "Choosing a Mental Health Professional" section later in this chapter for a list of questions you need to ask your individual therapist before starting therapy.

Giving groups a chance

Group psychotherapy has been around for a long time, but many people shy away from this form of therapy out of fear of confiding personal information to others, especially people they don't know. Sometimes they fear talking in front of a group or believe that other group members will reject them.

However, group therapy can be a very useful part of BPD treatment. Group settings provide an effective way to teach important skills and to provide information about managing BPD. Group therapy is also somewhat more cost effective than individual therapy because the costs are spread among the participants. Furthermore, seeing that you're not the only person who's suffering the way you are can be very reassuring.

If you find the idea of group therapy too intimidating, you may wish to start your treatment with individual therapy. However, we strongly suggest that you talk to your therapist about your concerns regarding group therapy so that the two of you can address these fears. Furthermore, your therapist can tell you whether or not groups specifically designed for BPD are available in your local area.

Spending more time in treatment: Partial hospitalization

Some local hospitals offer programs for BPD treatment in a form called *partial hospitalization*. Partial hospitalization programs usually combine group therapy, individual therapy, medication, and adjunctive therapies, such as art therapy, recreational therapy, and occupational therapy. Although researchers haven't yet studied these adjunctive therapies in relationship to the treatment of BPD, time spent on these activities can have some value for many people, regardless of their disorder. For example, when a conflict arises in a recreational therapy session, a good therapist can use that opportunity to show the patient how to use some basic interpersonal conflict-management skills.

These partial hospitalization programs vary greatly in number of hours per week and may range from a couple of hours two or three days per week to as much as all day most days of the week. To date, no studies have demonstrated exactly how many hours per week are optimal.

Partial hospitalization programs can be difficult to find and rather costly. Insurance often doesn't cover such services. The good news is that most people with BPD don't require partial hospitalization programs, and when they do, they probably don't need them for long periods of time.

Needing more care: Inpatient psychiatric wards

A generation ago, seeing people spend long periods of time confined in so-called mental hospitals for problems, such as BPD and psychotic disorders, was a fairly common occurrence (see Chapters 3 and 10 for more information about psychotic disorders).

Today, however, inpatient psychiatric wards don't serve as mainstays in the treatment of BPD. Mental health professionals use these more intense treatment settings only when people appear to be in imminent danger of causing harm to themselves or other people. When professionals turn to inpatient wards, they usually use them only for a short time (anywhere from a few days to a week or so), mostly for the purpose of stabilizing the person and perhaps regulating the medication regimen.

Some experts in the treatment of BPD warn against using inpatient treatment more than one time for any given patient. They do so because some patients find inpatient settings quite rewarding, supporting, and nurturing compared to the scary world outside the hospital walls. Therefore, these patients may end up seeking hospitalization with increased frequency over time. Many experts think that this pattern of frequent hospitalization ends up causing more harm than good.

Combining and changing treatments

About half the people who seek treatment for BPD receive treatment in more than one format or setting, either at the same time or one after the other. Thus, you may begin with individual therapy and later add group therapy. You may even seek partial hospitalization for a few weeks in addition to your individual and group therapies. You may also go to an inpatient setting, but you probably won't remain in that setting for long or more than once or twice.

You and your primary individual therapist can work together to decide which treatments are best for you at any given time. See the "Choosing a Mental Health Professional" section for help with finding the right therapist for you.

Researching the Treatment Strategies That Work for BPD

If you take a few minutes to call around to different therapists or hospitals or search the Internet, you'll find a kaleidoscope of different types of psychotherapy. You'll find Jungian therapy, primal scream therapy, psychoanalysis (in various forms), cognitive therapy, cognitive behavioral therapy, humanistic therapy, Rogerian therapy, haiku therapy, hakomi therapy, and on and on. Are you confused, yet?

Well, don't be overwhelmed. We're going to make your decision of which therapy to choose a little easier. In actuality, only a handful of psychotherapies have shown significant promise for the treatment of BPD.

You definitely don't want to seek treatment for BPD that isn't specifically designed to treat this diagnosis. Preliminary evidence suggests that non-specific treatment may slow or impede the natural healing that occurs over time.

Research supports the following strategies for treating BPD:

✔ **Dialectical behavior therapy (DBT):** Marsha Linehan developed DBT as the first therapy specifically designed for BPD. Numerous studies have shown that this approach effectively reduces suicidal attempts. Most of these studies have looked at the effects of one year of this kind of therapy. After one year, people show great improvement, but they still generally report significant distress in the quality of their lives. Linehan believes that more substantial improvement is likely after several years of treatment, but, to date, researchers haven't conducted studies looking at this extended time frame.

DBT typically combines individual psychotherapy and group therapy. Group therapy teaches patients how to identify their emotions and then how to apply an array of techniques to help quell out-of-control emotions. The individual therapy works on decreasing self-harming behaviors and removing obstacles to getting better. The DBT approach heavily draws on Buddhist principles, such as acceptance of distress and meditation. DBT also uses elements of cognitive and behavioral therapies, which are designed to improve the way people think and behave.

DBT is truly a breakthrough approach to BPD and the first therapy to generate research to support its effectiveness. However, DBT is a complicated package of strategies, and mental health professionals don't know for sure which techniques are most critical to success. Many of the specific techniques we discuss in Chapters 15 through 20 can be found in DBT.

✔ **Mentalization-based therapy (MBT):** Anthony Bateman and Peter Fonagy pioneered the development of MBT for the treatment of BPD. This treatment is based on the belief that most people with BPD have problems with how they attached to or related with their primary caregivers. As adults, people with BPD continue to have trouble with relationships. MBT attempts to improve the abilities of people with BPD to understand their feelings as well as the feelings and thoughts of other people. MBT also teaches people with BPD how to understand the impact of their behaviors on other people.

Initial studies of MBT have demonstrated encouraging results in people with BPD even eight years after the treatment. Patients had fewer hospitalizations after treatment, reduced their suicidal behaviors, and improved their day-to-day functioning. A number of the techniques in Chapter 18 are consistent with the ideas of MBT.

✔ **Transference-focused psychotherapy (TFP):** TFP is an approach to treating BPD based on the theory that many people with BPD perceive interpersonal interactions in overly rigid, fragmented ways. This treatment attempts to teach people with BPD that they misperceive interactions with their therapists and provides corrective information about those interactions. Early research on TFP is positive, but we can't unequivocally recommend this approach until more studies are conducted.

✔ **Cognitive therapy:** Aaron T. Beck developed cognitive therapy as a therapy for depression, but it has been successfully applied to a surprisingly wide range of emotional problems, including anxiety disorders, obsessive-compulsive disorder, substance abuse, eating disorders, and schizophrenia. Hundreds of studies support its effectiveness for these problems, but much less research has investigated the effectiveness of cognitive therapy on treating BPD. The studies that have been done have found that cognitive therapy shows promise in reducing self-harm and other symptoms of BPD.

Some of the techniques in DBT are based on cognitive therapy. However, studies of cognitive therapy have shown benefits in less than six months, which is a shorter time frame than that of most of the other approaches to treating BPD, including DBT, that we review in this chapter.

Cognitive therapy teaches people to look at the way they think about or interpret the things that happen to them. Generally, people think in distorted ways when they're experiencing emotional problems. Cognitive therapy helps people see those distortions and, thus, their experiences more realistically.

✔ **Schema therapy:** Jeffrey Young originally developed schema therapy as an offshoot of cognitive therapy. This approach focuses on early maladaptive *schemas,* which are broad, deeply held beliefs about oneself and the world that originate in childhood (see Chapter 9 for more information about schemas and Chapter 19 for ideas about how to change maladaptive schemas into more adaptive ones).

Although schema therapy has generated a lot of professional interest, research on its effectiveness is just now emerging. One study in the Netherlands found that two schema therapy sessions per week over three years led to substantial improvement in the quality of life and decreased symptoms in about half the sample patients. Improvements in reported quality of life haven't been typical in most outcome studies for other forms of BPD treatment. Thus, these particular results are highly encouraging, but they beg for replication by other research groups.

✔ **Medication:** Mental health professionals use psychotropic medications to treat most emotional disorders, including depression, anxiety, bipolar disorder, and psychosis. However, medications haven't proven to be especially effective for the treatment of BPD and other personality disorders. Nonetheless, medication sometimes appears useful for treating specific symptoms of BPD. See Chapter 20 for more information about using medication as a part of BPD treatment.

After studying these therapies, we haven't discovered anything that stands out as fundamentally contradictory or incompatible about any one therapy with the major tenets of the others. As of today, no one has studied the effectiveness of combining these strategies, but some experts advocate doing so.

In Chapters 15 through 20, we present an array of techniques that we pull from all the therapies we list here so that you can get a good sense of what you're likely to encounter when you begin treatment for your BPD. Your therapist may primarily use one of these techniques or present you with a treatment that attempts to integrate the best features of each, much like we do in this book. Either approach is likely to be effective.

Choosing a Mental Health Professional

If you have BPD, you need help from others — usually trained mental health professionals. Some treatments involve a team of professionals working together, and others involve only one therapist working one-on-one with you. When you're searching for a mental health professional, you need to ask specifically about her experience and knowledge in treating BPD. You want someone who has experience, especially in providing one or more of the treatments we review in the "Researching the Treatment Strategies That Work for BPD" section. Don't get discouraged if the first provider you contact isn't comfortable treating BPD. Not everyone is, but, if you call around, you'll likely find someone who is.

When you contact a mental health professional, you need to ask that professional a variety of questions, including the following:

✔ **When and how often are you available?** Ask the provider how soon you can make an appointment. Unfortunately, in some areas of the country, providers are so busy that they have waiting lists. Others may have a limited number of appointment times available. Ask about the provider's hours — especially if you need evening or weekend hours. BPD treatment requires regularly scheduled sessions, so make sure you can set up a weekly meeting time that works for both you and the provider.

✔ **Do you offer after-hours and emergency coverage?** Part of the diagnosis of BPD includes risky or self-harming behavior. Ask the therapist what provisions she makes for emergencies. Therapists' policies range from being on call 24/7 with backup when the therapist is out of town to not being available for any reason after hours (in which case the therapist usually gives patients instructions to contact 911 or go to an emergency room in the case of an emergency). To date, no research studies look specifically at how the availability of the therapist helps or hinders treatment of BPD. Both approaches have good reasons behind them. What's important is that your therapist spells out the policies and procedures in advance and you feel comfortable with them.

✔ **What fees do you charge?** Ask the provider what fees she charges for sessions? If your treatment involves multiple sessions a week, are the fees for individual and group therapy different or the same? Will the therapist accept your insurance? Some practitioners don't accept all insurance plans, and others don't accept any insurance plans. Furthermore, some insurance plans don't include mental health. We recommend that you check with your insurance plan, as well as with the therapist. Sometimes providers can convince insurance companies to pay for more than their usual reimbursement when the treatment is a validated treatment for BPD.

Participation isn't optional

If you're seeking help to treat your BPD, the good news is that treatment works and you can expect to feel better. The bad news is that many people never access the kind of help they need.

Quite a few people with BPD make appointments with therapists, but then they cancel. Others make appointments and go to two or three sessions, but then they stop. Do those people receive the help they were looking for when they signed up for therapy? Well, they don't receive much. So, why do so many people stop therapy or never start?

People hesitate to make appointments, cancel them, or quit after a couple of sessions because therapy involves some tough stuff. Some people find admitting that they need help for their emotional problems too embarrassing. Others find talking about feelings and problems overwhelming. And still others are pessimistic and don't believe that talking to someone else will help them with the painful turbulence of their lives.

Imagine that you have a sudden high fever and a sore throat. You miss work and can't get out of bed. After a few days, you still feel horrible. You may call your doctor's office for an appointment or go to an urgent-care facility. You probably don't feel ashamed that this illness requires medical attention. The same should be true when you're suffering from BPD. This disorder is painful and often involves being unable to function, so don't be ashamed to ask for help.

Effective treatments do exist for BPD. The guidance and support of a therapist can be extremely helpful. However, to get better, you have to participate and follow through with the therapy. Remember that *you* are the most important person on your treatment team.

✔ **Do you have a professional license?** Ask whether or not the provider has a license to practice. If not, go elsewhere. The only exception is when graduate students are practicing under the supervision of licensed professionals.

A variety of people with different titles, different levels of education, and different areas of expertise provide mental health services. In the following sections, we provide brief descriptions of the different roles and educational backgrounds mental health professionals can have.

Primary healthcare providers

Whenever you experience significant emotional problems, we recommend that you begin your search for treatment by going to your primary health-care provider — whether that person is a physician, a nurse practitioner, or a physician assistant — for a thorough physical checkup. Various physical issues sometimes cause symptoms that often look like emotional disorders. For example, brain trauma, medications, various hormonal imbalances, dietary supplements, and certain chronic diseases sometimes produce emotional problems, such as anxiety, depression, or agitation.

After your primary healthcare provider rules out physical causes, you should seek the services of a licensed mental health professional for a diagnosis of your specific condition. Primary healthcare providers rarely have sufficient training for understanding the subtle differences in emotional disorders.

Psychologists

Practicing psychologists typically hold a doctoral degree (PhD, PsyD, or EdD) in clinical or counseling psychology. These degrees require at least four years of graduate education. In addition, psychologists generally have to complete a one-year internship and often a one- or two-year postdoctoral fellowship, too. They also must pass a comprehensive examination prior to licensure.

Psychologists usually focus on treatments that have scientific support for their effectiveness. They also use special interview techniques and psychological tests to assist in making accurate diagnoses for emotional disorders. In fact, some psychologists specialize only in assessment and refer people to other practitioners after they've determined the precise diagnosis. In a few states, psychologists go on to complete further training, which enables them to prescribe psychotropic medication — you need to check whether your state allows psychologists to do so.

If you have any doubt about whether your diagnosis is correct, you may want to see a psychologist who specializes in assessment. Getting the right diagnosis makes a big difference when you and your therapist are deciding which treatments to pursue.

Psychiatrists

Psychiatrists have a doctoral degree in medicine (either MD or DO). Board-certified psychiatrists have also completed a four-year residency that specializes in the diagnosis and treatment of mental disorders. In addition, they have passed a rigorous oral and written examination in psychiatry. Most psychiatrists focus on treating emotional disorders through psychotropic medication. They're experts in these medications. However, they vary greatly in their expertise in delivering scientifically validated psychotherapies, so psychiatrists and other mental health professionals often team up in the treatment of emotional disorders.

Physicians who hold an MD can call themselves psychiatrists even if they haven't obtained additional training in psychiatry. This practice is unusual, but you should make sure your psychiatrist has completed at least a four-year residency in psychiatry.

Can I treat BPD on my own?

Generally speaking, self-help isn't enough to treat BPD. But, you can help yourself in many different ways. First, find out all you can about BPD. Find out about the causes, the signs, and the symptoms. Research the most effective treatments.

Take advantage of the treatment you choose for yourself. In other words, go to every session, and carry out suggested assignments between sessions. Dare to be honest with yourself and your therapist. Don't sugarcoat your behavior or hide your true feelings.

You can find many Internet support groups for people with BPD, their friends, and their family members. Some of these groups are extremely helpful and well run. Others can be hurtful. Look for a helpful problem-solving approach to the group's entries. Be wary of groups that focus on complaints and negative comments.

Be careful not to provide too much information online. Unfortunately, some people pose as people with BPD or their family members to take advantage of people who are really suffering and looking for help. Take particular caution before you agree to meet anyone you've only met online.

Counselors

Counselors who are licensed to provide mental health services generally have a two-year master's degree (MA or MEd) in psychology, theology, or counseling. To obtain their license to practice, counselors have to complete varying amounts of supervised practice following the degree (depending on the state) and a written examination. Many counselors also work for a certification from the National Academy of Certified Mental Health Counselors. Although they're not as thoroughly trained as psychologists in the science of human behavior, many qualified counselors have received specialized training in the treatment of BPD, using one of the scientifically supported techniques we review earlier in this chapter (see the "Researching the Treatment Strategies That Work for BPD" section for more info).

Marriage and family therapists

Marriage and family therapists typically have completed a master's degree (MA) in marriage or family therapy, followed by two years or more of supervised practice and a written examination. Some have doctorate degrees from programs in social work, psychology, counseling, theology, or some related field. As a result, their actual training and background varies more from practitioner to practitioner than some of the other mental health professionals. Marriage and family therapists tend to specialize in working with couples and families. Be sure to ask whether your marriage and family therapist has had specialized training in the treatment of BPD with a scientifically based approach.

Psychiatric nurses

The training of psychiatric nurses varies significantly, ranging from an associate's degree in nursing to a doctorate nursing degree. Nurses often act as case managers for people with serious emotional problems. Some of these nurses have sufficient training that enables them to prescribe psychotropic medication. Others focus on providing psychotherapy, although, again, their training varies greatly, so you have to ask what your nurse has been trained to do.

Social workers

Most social workers have a master's degree in social work (MSW), but a small percentage of them have a doctoral degree in social work (DSW). After they attain their degree, social workers have to complete a varying amount of supervised practice before they can take their written examination. Social workers often serve as case managers for people with serious emotional disorders. Depending on their training, many social workers can also provide diagnoses and psychotherapy for people with BPD. Once again, you have to ask about your social worker's specific training.

Other practitioners who claim to be in the so-called healing arts sometimes nail signs to their doors announcing that they provide services for all sorts of ailments, including BPD. No research supports most of what these practitioners do. In fact, you could easily pay a lot of money, waste a lot of time, or even get worse by going to one of these practitioners. So, avoid fortunetellers, crystal gazers, and sellers of snake oil. Make sure your mental health provider is licensed to provide counseling, psychotherapy, and/or medications.

You can obtain referrals to qualified, licensed mental health professionals through your insurance company, your primary healthcare provider, psychology and psychiatry departments at local medical schools and universities, and state associations for each of the mental health professions.

Starting Treatment

Assuming you make the decision to begin treatment for BPD, what should you expect next? First, you need to expect to have to answer quite a few questions. These questions are essential and are designed to help your therapist learn about you and your problems. Be prepared to answer questions about the following issues and concerns:

- ✓ **Symptoms:** Symptoms include anger, rage, sadness, anxiety, impulsive actions, substance abuse, self-harming behaviors, suicidal thoughts or actions, relationship problems, and so on. Your provider will ask you questions about all your symptoms — When did they start? How do they interfere with what you want to do? How frequent are they? What kinds of situations worsen them? How distressed do you feel about them?

- ✓ **Physical health issues:** Your provider will undoubtedly ask you questions about your overall physical health — How is your sleep? How is your appetite? Do you have any physical pain? Have you ever had significant injuries, surgeries, or illnesses? Have you had a physical exam recently? Do you take prescription medications for anything at all? Do you take over-the-counter medications or supplements?

- ✓ **History:** Many factors, including childhood circumstances, contribute to the development of BPD, so your provider will ask you about your history — Have you ever been abused? Have you ever experienced a trauma of any kind? Have you ever been hospitalized? Have you ever thought about or attempted suicide? Have you previously taken medications or received treatment for any emotional problems? What is your educational background? What is your work history? What is your history with relationships?

- ✓ **Family:** Because genetics play a role in the development of BPD, your provider will ask you about your family — Does anyone in your family have emotional problems of any kind? Have any of your relatives received medication or psychotherapy for emotional disorders?

- ✓ **Finances:** Some people express discomfort when discussing financial issues, but your therapist needs to know a few basics — Do you have insurance coverage? Can you afford treatment? Are finances a source of stress for you or your family?

Evaluating your therapy

A core symptom of BPD involves having trouble with relationships. One reason for this difficulty is that people with BPD easily misinterpret the meaning of what other people say to them. So, if at any time you feel criticized, unsupported, or angered by your therapist's words or actions, you need to check out your concerns. Try not to lash out or walk out, but try to find out what led to your reaction. Be open to what your therapist says.

After you've been to a half dozen sessions or so and after you've checked out any concerns you may have, you should typically feel quite comfortable divulging and discussing just about anything with your therapist. You should feel like your therapist listens to you and respects you as a person. Most therapists show reasonable warmth, empathy, and concern. If yours doesn't, discuss your concerns. If you truly feel like you're not connecting with your therapist, get a second opinion by seeking a one-time consultation from another therapist.

Confidentiality concerns

All licensed professionals have ethical codes that require them to keep any information they learn about you, their client, confidential. State laws back up these codes, so you can trust that your therapist won't reveal details about your life to anyone else. A few exceptions to these confidentiality codes and laws include

✔ **Harm to self:** If your therapist feels you're in imminent danger of causing serious harm to yourself, she has to take certain precautions, which can include alerting your family or authorities or even having you hospitalized.

✔ **Harm to others:** If your therapist firmly believes that you're about to cause serious harm to someone else, she has to take action to notify others or to hospitalize you.

✔ **Abuse of children or elders:** If you tell your therapist that you're currently harming a child or elder, your therapist has to inform authorities.

Your therapist should highlight these and any other exceptions to confidentiality that she practices in a written statement that you read and sign at your initial session. Be sure to ask your therapist if you don't understand any of the language that the statement contains.

Remember: Members in group therapy are asked to keep anything they hear during their group sessions confidential. Most members comply with this rule; however, someone may break the rule. Although we generally encourage openness in group therapy, if you have concerns about sharing something with your group, discuss the issue with your individual therapist first.

On the other hand, you can't expect your therapist to become your best friend or your mother. See Chapter 25 for more information about what you can reasonably expect from the therapist/client relationship.

Giving therapy some time

Psychotherapy for BPD takes a little time. Some programs, such as schema therapy (see the "Researching the Treatment Strategies That Work for BPD" section for more info about this particular technique), may take as long as three years, but the results may be worth the wait. Other programs are designed to be much shorter. However, you can expect treatment to take at least several months before you start to feel moderate improvement. Many people with BPD remain in therapy for several years.

Within six months to a year of therapy, you can reasonably expect to reduce and manage your urges to engage in self-harm or suicide. Other goals, such as improved life satisfaction, reduced impulsivity, and better relationships, are likely to require significantly more time. Be patient. You're likely to get better when you give treatment enough time and effort.

Chapter 12

Breaking Through Barriers to Change

● ●

In This Chapter

▶ Taking a look at the fears people have about change

▶ Putting a stop to the blaming game

▶ Seeing the effects of procrastination

▶ Understanding the process of change

● ●

Lonely, empty, sad, angry, bitter, anxious, stressed, and helpless — these are the emotions that many people with borderline personality disorder (BPD) experience every day. No wonder they try to quell their pain with dissociation, thrill seeking, self-harm, or substance abuse. Many people with BPD ache to feel better but struggle to get the treatment they need.

People with BPD, like many others, fear change. They worry that getting help for their problems will be difficult, perhaps embarrassing, and possibly even impossible. So, they ask themselves, if treatment may not be successful, why take a chance in the first place? For many people, not trying at all seems better than trying and failing.

Along with fear, blaming and procrastination also pose barriers to change. Searching for villains or victims shackles people in place, unable to move forward. Ignoring symptoms or putting off treatment impedes progress. This chapter describes the main obstacles that stand in the way of treatment and provides strategies for overcoming them.

If you have BPD, we urge you to either buy a notebook or start an electronic document in which you can take occasional notes, write out your reactions to our ideas, and carry out exercises that seem pertinent to you. Consulting these notes from time to time can greatly facilitate your progress. Ideally, you can share your notes with your therapist as the two of you collaborate on your treatment.

Overcoming the Fear of Change

From time to time, we consult with other mental health professionals about their cases, including ones that involve BPD. Occasionally, our colleagues express concern that their clients with BPD don't really want to change.

You can trust mental health professionals to keep what you tell them confidential. However, sometimes they do seek supervision and consultation from colleagues. Such consultation doesn't violate confidentiality for two reasons. First, professionals don't share names and unrelated details. Second, case consultations are protected by the same rules that protect doctor-patient consultations. Furthermore, consultation enhances your therapist's ability to deliver quality treatment.

In response to our colleagues' concerns about people with BPD, we ask them why they think people with BPD don't want to change. They give us several reasons, such as the following:

✔ Our client never tries any of our suggestions.

✔ Our client gets angry when we tell him to try something different.

✔ Our client says he's hopeless and that no one can help him.

✔ Our client doesn't listen to what we say.

After hearing these explanations, we explain to our colleagues that these patients aren't simply being stubborn, and they certainly don't *want* to have BPD.

So, if stubbornness doesn't explain these patients' blatant resistance to their therapists' best efforts to treat them, what does? Often, the answer is fear, more specifically fear of change. After all, change involves taking a risk and being willing to engage in new behaviors, reactions, and ways of thinking. The following sections lay out the specific risks that people with BPD fear the most.

If you have BPD, you likely have some fears about seeking out treatment and making changes in your life. These fears are normal, acceptable, and expected. If you feel your therapist is pushing you too hard to make changes, discuss your fears openly. The two of you can develop a mutual game plan for dealing with these worries at a pace that works for you.

Losing who you are: It's not going to happen

Most people with BPD struggle with concerns about who they are, what they value, where they belong in the world, and what their long-term goals are all about. Not infrequently, people with BPD embrace only one aspect of themselves in their self-concept — their disorder. They may not like having BPD, but they believe the diagnosis *defines* them.

As a result of this belief, they worry that losing BPD may leave them with no identity at all. Imagine going through each day with no idea who you are or what your life is about — a pretty scary thought, right?

If you have BPD and worry that getting better may leave you with no identity, try to consider the fact that treatment proceeds slowly, one step at a time. As you "try on" new ways of being, you can always let go of the ones you don't like. Furthermore, treatment can help you build a new identity, one that feels real and authentic to you. With treatment, you can be who you really are, not who BPD defines you to be.

Opening up: No need for cold feet

When people with BPD talk about their childhoods, they often recall being scolded frequently by parents or other important people in their lives. These people told them that they shouldn't do, say, or feel what they did, said, and felt. For example, some people recall hearing the following remarks:

- "Stop being so nervous. You drive me crazy."
- "Let me do that; you can't do anything right."
- "That's not true. You should know better."
- "Stop that crying; you're such a baby."
- "You have no right to be angry with your sister."
- "What were you thinking when you did that? Obviously, you weren't."

No wonder many people with BPD hesitate to open up when they begin therapy. They've been told throughout their lives that what they say, do, and feel is wrong.

Therapists aren't there to reenact the role played by people from childhood. Instead, they accept all feelings as valid and legitimate. Therapy can help you manage your feelings and guide you to make changes — and it does so in an atmosphere of acceptance. You can start by saying, "I feel very afraid to reveal the real me to you." Your therapist will likely say something reassuring or accepting in response.

Dreading even more loss: Don't test the ones who want to help

Most people with BPD experienced loss, trauma, abuse, or neglect during childhood. As adults, the unstable moods and impulsivity they developed in childhood may lead to losses of friends, family, and lovers. As a result, they look at new relationships with a combination of fear and hope; they crave closeness yet expect abandonment. Starting treatment involves engaging in a therapeutic relationship with another person, which can be an extremely frightening concept for someone who has been part of countless hurtful relationships.

To protect against feared abandonment, people with BPD often misbehave in social situations. They feel that rejecting is better than being rejected. Therefore, they test the limits and patience of people who try to help them to make sure they do the hurting — not the other way around. People with BPD most often test the relationships they have with significant others and therapists. (See Chapters 21 and 25 for information you need to know if you're the partner or therapist of someone with BPD).

Ask your therapist directly whether he thinks that you engage in testing at particular times. Listen carefully and try to look out for this pattern in future sessions.

Fearing treatment: Don't let therapy myths hold you back

When we meet new people and tell them what we do for a living, we often get a plethora of questions about whether or not we can read minds. Well, unfortunately, we can't — although the idea is sometimes appealing. Mind reading is just one of the many myths about psychology and psychotherapy.

Unfortunately, some of these myths stop people from pursuing therapy. Don't let the following therapy myths stop you from proceeding with treatment:

✔ **Therapy trivializes problems.** Some people believe that therapists make light of deep, complicated issues when they ask their patients to make changes. These people may have experienced horrific abuse or trauma and think that being asked to change trivializes the meaning of these events. If you feel diminished or trivialized in this way, consider telling your therapist how you feel. Good therapists strive to listen and understand the full impact of their patients' painful experiences. They will work with you on a gradual plan for change that enables you to feel appreciated, accepted, and respected.

✔ **Therapy can't give me everything I need.** Actually, this myth isn't a complete myth. Therapy can't give you everything you need. No one person on earth can meet another person's full list of needs. The myth in this belief, however, is in believing that you must have all your needs met all the time. The real role of therapists is to help you find ways to meet your needs more often than you have met them in the past.

✔ **Therapy doesn't work.** Some people buy into this myth because they've been to therapy and haven't experienced success or because they've seen a friend or loved one go to therapy without any obvious benefit. However, hundreds of studies have shown that therapy does work for a wide range of problems, and studies in the past several decades have provided convincing evidence that therapy can reduce BPD symptoms. Keep in mind, however, that not every type of therapy has demonstrated effectiveness for BPD — but a number of them have (see Chapter 11 for information about which kinds of therapy work best for treating BPD).

✔ **Therapists can't possibly understand me.** Some people worry that their problems are so deep and complex that no one can fully understand them. This myth also contains a grain of truth — no one can connect with and appreciate every single facet of your issues 100 percent of the time. However, therapists have spent years in training and practice, listening carefully to people as they explain their feelings, histories, and pain. Your therapist may understand you in a way that you haven't experienced previously.

✔ **Therapists will ask me to do things I can't do.** The fact that therapists do indeed suggest that you attempt various new ways of thinking and behaving fuels this myth. However, if you feel unable to follow a suggestion, talk about it with your therapist — ethical therapists never ask people to do what they're not prepared to do.

If you have BPD, write down any of your concerns about therapy and treatment in your notebook and take them to your therapist to discuss. Try to be open to the idea that your therapist wants to help.

Looking at fears of change in action

The following story about Alexis illustrates how someone with BPD may refuse treatment because of a few misconceptions and fears. Alexis worries about losing her identity, feeling worse as a result of treatment, failing after trying to get better, and opening up to someone new.

Alexis wakes up dizzy, uncomfortable, and groggy. Head pounding, she tries to roll over, but straps tie her wrists and ankles to the hospital bed. "Nurse! Nurse, help me!" she yells. She remembers little of the night before. She had a huge fight with her husband, Aaron, and she thinks she may have taken too much pain medicine.

A woman with a white coat and badge enters the room, "Good morning, Alexis. How are you feeling?"

"Like crap," Alexis replies, "Get these stupid straps off. Who are you?"

"I'm your psychologist while you're here. My name is Dr. Rachel Hunter. Do you remember what happened last night?"

"I know I was furious with my husband, that lazy good-for-nothing piece of trash. He hasn't worked for months; he sits on his butt and watches reality shows on the television while I work extra shifts just to see our credit cards get overdrawn because he's eating popcorn all day," Alexis speaks quickly and continues without pausing, "I stand on my feet all day and they hurt like hell. So I was so mad that I probably took some extra pills to get to sleep. When I get mad at him I get so worked up that I can't sleep. Then I have to get up and go to work and I'm screwed."

"Alexis, you took about ten times the normal dosage of your pain medicine. You were unconscious when your husband found you. When you got to the hospital, you became combative. You were pretty violent. We put the restraints on for your safety," Dr. Hunter explains. "You know, this is your third hospitalization this year for overdosing. The last two times you checked yourself out of the hospital against medical advice. As you know, we believe that you have a disorder called borderline personality disorder. We're very concerned about your going home without getting some help first. Would you consider talking about a program we have here at the hospital? Many people who work through the program feel better and are better able to cope with the world."

"Look doctor, there's nothing wrong with me. I'm mad at my husband, my marriage is a failure, and I work too hard. I've gone to counselors before and nothing changed. I don't think I can change, and I'm not going to waste my time for nothing. I don't need to fail at something else. I just need to get off my butt and lose the loser."

"So, Alexis, it sounds like you're worried that you may not benefit from this program and that to get better, you've just got to leave your husband. No wonder you don't want to stay. Let's keep talking while I get these restraints off. I can tell that you're calm," Dr. Hunter begins to loosen the straps around Alexis' wrists.

"Thanks, that feels better," Alexis shakes her hands. "You know, I have developed a pretty tough exterior to keep myself going. I always go to work. I have to go to work, and I try not to let others see how horrible my life is. So, I worry that if I start some kind of treatment, I'll just melt away and dissolve. I know that sounds crazy, but I'm scared to get help. I think it will make me worse. As much as I hate my husband, I'm afraid of living without him."

Dr. Hunter explains how treatment really works, and she helps Alexis see that a few misconceptions about therapy are stopping her from getting the help she needs.

Alexis's concerns and worries about therapy are legitimate and completely understandable. However, Dr. Hunter helps her decide that treatment is worth the risk. Alexis's therapy will require some time, but it's also likely to teach her how to set better limits with her husband and how to deal with her own emotions in less self-destructive ways.

Taking Charge and Giving Up the Victim Role

People search for answers to why bad things happen to them — they try to discover who or what is to blame. In the same way, many people who have BPD want to know why they have the disorder and whom they can blame for it. Unfortunately, this search for a guilty party usually ends up causing more harm than good. No single cause is responsible for BPD and no one person is to blame (see Chapter 4 for information about the multitude of causes).

In addition, people with traumatic histories often respond to BPD by feeling helpless and hopeless. These feelings lead them to adopt the role of a sick person or a victim. Although these roles have a few advantages, they inevitably handcuff people in their hopeless, helpless states of mind.

Ending the blame game

Most people with BPD can recount numerous negative episodes from their childhoods that caused them pain, distress, disgust, or angst. As they comb through a series of such episodes, sometimes they blame themselves for what happened to them. For example, when children experience abuse, they typically see themselves as deserving the abuse. As a result, their self-esteem disintegrates, and they learn to loathe the very essence of their beings. Unfortunately, many people with BPD cling to this same belief that they somehow caused their own misfortunes and possibly even their BPD.

If you engage in the self-loathing, blaming game, consider reading Chapter 4 to understand the multiple causes of BPD. If a girl tells you she's being abused, what do you tell her? Do you blame and defame her? Probably not. Consider taking the same perspective for yourself. Write your thoughts about how you blame yourself in your notebook, and think about how some of the things you blame yourself for aren't your fault.

On the other hand, many people with BPD blame other people for their current distress. They play and replay scenes in their minds in which others tormented and hurt them. Although much of the blame may be pointed in the right direction, replaying these scenes does little more than re-traumatize.

When you find yourself blaming others for your troubles, try to step back. Remind yourself that blame just digs a hole. Give yourself five minutes each day to blame others, and then focus on something else. If you repeat the five-minute exercise every day for awhile, you'll likely find yourself tiring of the blame game.

One legitimate treatment strategy does involve replaying past traumatic experiences. However, this treatment (often called *imaginal exposure* or *flooding*) needs to occur in conditions carefully controlled by a highly trained therapist. We generally don't recommend attempting this technique on your own.

Thinking like a victim: It doesn't do you any good

When you have a fever, going to bed and resting usually helps your body fight off whatever is causing the illness. If you're sick with something more severe than a low fever, you may have to go to a hospital, where a team of healthcare professionals can take care of you. Because BPD is a kind of emotional illness, part of you probably wants to go to bed and let others take care of you. However, for the most part, treating BPD takes active participation from you, the person who has BPD.

When BPD causes someone to want to hurt himself or others, a hospital setting may indeed be necessary. During situations like these, when someone is at risk of physical injury or death, a team of healthcare professionals may provide the best and most appropriate care.

Thinking like a victim involves believing that you're dependent, sick, and incapable of helping yourself. Victims feel that their problems are especially overwhelming and often complain to others about them. Victims bemoan that their suffering isn't their fault — and, in fact, it isn't! But victims hurt themselves with their own victimhood because feeling like a victim does nothing to inspire positive change.

At first, victims may indeed receive extra attention and help. Other people feel sorry for them and are motivated to try to alleviate their suffering, which is one advantage of taking on the role of victim. However, other people eventually find themselves burning out because they repeatedly try to help but have little to no success. Victims are so entrenched in their helplessness that they can't or won't allow anything or anyone to help them. Over time, thinking like a victim leads to a passive acceptance of BPD for both the helpers and the sufferers. Meaningful change comes when the sufferer finds forgiveness and learns to start coping.

Finding forgiveness and coping

Anger can be a useful emotion. It generates energy and focuses attention. Anger increases the body's ability to respond to danger. However, when you're angry about something in the past, your attention and energy focus solely on the past. As a result, you can't move forward.

When you have experienced trauma, feeling anger at the person or people you believe hurt you is perfectly natural. However, you need to realize that your anger shackles you to your past — you get stuck in the middle of the old trauma. Sometimes people with BPD believe that forgiving somehow means admitting that what happened to them was acceptable. However, learning to let go isn't saying that what happened was okay; it's saying that you're willing to heal.

If you're struggling with BPD, try to understand that although you're not to blame for your BPD, you are responsible for making the changes you want in your life. See Chapters 15 through 20 for lots of ideas about how to make those changes.

Stop Procrastinating

Most people put off doing things they fear or see as especially difficult. Perhaps you have put off looking into therapy for years because you fear that therapy will hurt more than help. Or, you start therapy but can't seem to get anywhere with it. Your brain likely manufactures excuses for not pursuing therapy faster than the United States Mint stamps out coins. The following sections take a look at some of the more problematic excuses and how to beat them back.

Dismantling excuses

People create excuses to avoid addressing problems that seem larger than they can handle. Excuses (some people would call them *lies*) are like stories we create to promote procrastination. Quite often, these stories seem believable. Therefore, before you can move forward, you have to learn how to see through your mind's excuses to recognize the lies behind them. Table 12-1 lists some common excuses and some arguments (also known as *excuse busters*) against them.

Table 12-1	Excavating and Demolishing Excuses
Excuse	**Excuse Buster**
I need to find just the right time for dealing with my issues — then I'll start doing something.	The right time never seems to come. The right time is now.
My case is just too difficult to treat.	I am capable of learning. I survived my childhood and learned to talk, read, and walk. So, I can surely learn a few things in treatment, too.
I need a guarantee that treatment will work before I can invest my time and energy into it.	Nothing in life comes with a guarantee. This kind of thinking just keeps me from doing anything. However, I can use this book to find out what therapists know works for most people with BPD. I can't get a better guarantee than that.
I tried therapy three times before and it didn't work. So I know now that it won't work for me.	I didn't try one of the treatments that has proved to work for BPD. But even if I had, sometimes a person needs to try out several therapists before one clicks.
I'm already overwhelmed. Therapy would just add to my pain.	I can talk to a therapist about my concerns. No one is going to ask more from me than I can give.
I don't have insurance, and I can't afford treatment.	Some universities, medical schools, and nonprofit community mental health centers provide low-cost treatment. And by causing me to lose jobs, my BPD is keeping me from reaching my potential. I need to deal with this issue.
I don't have the time for treatment.	I waste a lot more time with my self-destructive behaviors, such as cutting, drinking too much, and going on spending sprees. I need to make time for treatment.

No doubt your mind can conjure up many creative variations of the excuses in Table 12-1. Consider titling a page of your notebook, "Excavating and Demolishing Excuses." Jot down your mind's reasons why you should put off tackling your problems. Then come up with an argument with a more realistic perspective to demolish your excuses. Here are a few questions you can ask yourself to help develop some excuse busters of your own:

✔ What would I tell a friend who used my excuse?

✔ Will staying where I'm at get me where I want to go?

✔ Is part of my excuse simply not true?

If you have trouble coming up with excuse busters, or if you don't think you're making excuses but you are putting off treatment, you're not a lost cause. Read more of this book and see whether you start feeling a little differently after awhile.

Debating the decision

Another technique that can loosen the hold procrastination has on you is called a *cost-benefit analysis,* a technique psychologists have been using for decades. The beauty of a cost-benefit analysis is that it's fairly easy and straightforward — and also surprisingly effective at the same time. You can use a cost-benefit analysis to tackle almost anything that has you stuck. For this reason, we use this technique in several chapters of this book.

A cost-benefit analysis provides a great way to combat procrastination because procrastination almost always stirs up ambivalent feelings. Part of you sees the advantages or benefits of moving ahead with treatment, while part of you fears the costs or disadvantages of starting treatment. A cost-benefit analysis lets you objectively view these conflicting thoughts and feelings side by side.

The following example of Lucas describes how a cost-benefit analysis can help convince someone that treatment is worth a shot — even when he's been refusing it for years.

> **Lucas** speeds through an intersection well after the yellow light turns red. Horns and squealing brakes accompany the crash. A pickup truck broadsides his car on the passenger's side. His red compact car takes the full impact of the crash and veers into oncoming traffic. A minivan stopped at the light can't get out of the way. Lucas's red car slams into the front of the minivan, triggering its air bags. By this time, the driver of the pickup leaps out of his vehicle, shaking and swearing at Lucas, "What the hell — you ran a red light. What's wrong with you?"
>
> The woman slides out from behind her air bag, screaming that she just dropped off her kids at school. Blood drips from her forehead. Lucas slumps in his totaled car, not speaking. Soon police and paramedics arrive on the scene. Lucas slurs his words and smells like alcohol. He has an open container of beer in the cup holder next to his seat, and the air in the car smells like marijuana. After checking for injuries, the police arrest Lucas. This accident is his third one this year, and this arrest is his fourth one for driving under the influence.

In jail, Lucas reluctantly agrees to a psychological evaluation. He is diagnosed with alcohol dependence, cannabis (marijuana) abuse, and BPD. The judge orders mandated inpatient drug treatment in a secure facility. Lucas is only 20 years old, and the judge wants to give him a chance.

The police transport Lucas from the jail to the rehab site. He refuses to speak to anyone, fights with the staff, and ends up in isolation. After a week or so, a therapist approaches him again. Lucas, bored by his isolation, agrees to meet. They sit together in a small room with a one-way mirror. The therapist asks Lucas whether he is willing to discuss all the reasons why he doesn't want to get treatment. Lucas quickly agrees, eager to show the therapist why he doesn't need to go to therapy. Together, they begin a cost-benefit analysis. This is the first time Lucas takes a reasoned look at the costs and benefits of his treatment avoidance.

Lucas and his therapist talk about the cost-benefit analysis. For the first time, Lucas begins to see where his life may go if he doesn't make some changes. Lucas agrees to start working with an individual therapist, and, after a few sessions, he agrees to begin group therapy. He also agrees to talk to a psychiatrist about medication that may help him with his urges to drink.

This simple technique helps people see what thoughts are preventing them from going forward with treatment. For instance, most of the time people fear failure, embarrassment, and change. Looking at the costs of giving into these fears and staying in one place can be a catalyst for progressing to the next stage.

You can use the following steps to create your own cost-benefit analysis for delaying treatment for your BPD. You can see Lucas's analysis in Table 12-2 for an example.

1. **On a page in your notebook, write down "Cost-Benefit Analysis of Not Seeking Treatment" (or make a copy of the Cost-Benefit Analysis Form in Appendix B).**

2. **Make two columns underneath the title. Label the first one "Benefits" and the second one "Costs."**

3. **In the Benefits column, write down all the reasons why staying the same and not getting treatment are good for you.**

   These reasons can include not having to change what you like about your current situation, not having to experience the pain of change, not having to open up to someone, and not having to pay the costs (personal, financial, and time) of treatment.

4. **In the Costs column, write down all the ways that not getting help and treatment may cost you both in the short run and in the long run.**

   Consider including how BPD is hurting you, how BPD is hurting your family and friends, and how BPD can even hurt innocent bystanders.

5. Write out a few thoughts and reflections about the costs and benefits you've come up with — if you want to.

Think about the relative pluses and minuses of seeking treatment, and, if you're already working with a therapist, discuss your results.

Table 12-2	Cost-Benefit Analysis of Not Seeking Treatment
Benefits	**Costs**
I hate talking about myself to stupid shrinks. If I stay out of treatment, I don't have to talk to anyone.	If I don't start treatment, they might send me to prison.
I can't stand listening to other people whine about their problems. Group therapy is full of whiners.	I'm bored sitting in my room all day.
I like partying and having a good time. Drugs and alcohol are fun.	I shouldn't have crashed my car. Now I don't have wheels. Maybe I can get help so I don't do stupid stuff like this anymore.
Rules are made to be broken. I'm no goody two-shoes.	If I don't start treatment, I'll probably get killed or kill someone else.
I don't trust other people with my problems, and I don't see how talking to people can help me.	I've seen some people get help and stay clean. It'd be nice not to always be in trouble.

Getting Comfortable with the Process of Change

Starting treatment can feel like a tough and risky decision. You don't know what to expect, and you worry that you may not get better. This section takes a look at the process of change and how you can get comfortable with it.

Change takes time, and progress varies. Do you remember learning to ride a bike as a child? You started out with a lot of help. Either training wheels or a person had to hold you up or you fell over. Gradually, you learned to balance on two wheels with support. Then the training wheels came off or the person let go. For a second or two, you were on your own. Balanced for only a short time, the wheels started to wobble and you needed some extra help again.

Learning to ride a bike takes most kids repeated trials and a lot of falls. For some kids, the balancing is too scary and too difficult. They may give up only to try again in a few months or even a year. A few kids have so much trouble that they never learn to ride a bike. But, fortunately, most kids stick with it long enough to learn how to ride without support. The common saying that once you learn how to ride a bike, you never forget, is true. Even so, most adults who haven't been on a bike since childhood start out slowly with a little fear, but they quickly regain their skills.

Getting help for BPD (like most of life's problems) is a lot like learning to ride a bike. At first, you need a lot of support. You may fail and fall quite a bit in the beginning. You may even give up for awhile. But, most people who stick with either bike riding or psychotherapy eventually gain skills and balance. They certainly wobble from time to time and even fall off occasionally, but, with repeated practice, the skills become second nature to them. Like riding a bike, after you learn how to face your problems, you never forget — sure you may be frightened and start out slowly, but with a little support, you can get right back up again.

Chapter 13

Explaining BPD to Others

Afterpeople find out they have borderline personality disorder (BPD) — something they really need to verify with a mental health professional — they often wonder what, when, where, and how to tell other people, not to mention which "other people" to tell in the first place. They typically report feeling ambivalent about whether they should tell anyone at all. They worry about being stigmatized or even discriminated against by others. Should they tell their friends, family, co-workers, bosses, spouses, or others? If they do, will other people understand and express empathy and support, or will they react with criticism and derision?

In this chapter, we help you sort out

✔ Whether to tell anyone at all

✔ Whom you may want to tell

✔ What to say

✔ How to say what you want to say

Don't panic; you don't really *have* to tell anybody. The choice is entirely up to you. This chapter can help you make this decision and know how to tell someone if you decide to do so.

Deciding Whether and Whom to Tell

Before you decide whether to tell anyone you have BPD, verifying that you truly have the disorder is a good idea. Reading the symptom list we give you in Chapter 3 isn't enough. You need a diagnosis from a trained mental health professional who has experience treating this disorder. After you have that diagnosis, you can look at the symptoms in Chapter 3 to see whether you think it fits.

If a professional says you have BPD but your perusal of Chapter 3 doesn't lead you to the same conclusion, consider obtaining a second opinion from another experienced mental health professional.

After you feel certain the diagnosis fits, you have some decisions to make. Here, we take you through the decision-making process — in terms of whether to tell others and whom to tell if you do.

The benefits and costs of telling

We recommend that you carefully assess your reasons for telling someone else about your BPD. Consider why you want to share this information and how you think the other person will react. Working through the following two questions may help you decide whom to tell.

Do you believe that making this revelation will benefit you in some way?

The answer to this question will vary with each person you consider telling about your BPD. For some people, telling a spouse can result in greater empathy if the spouse is reasonably understanding. Telling an abusive spouse, however, isn't likely to result in any benefit.

Besides greater empathy, another benefit you may hope for in telling someone else about your BPD is greater closeness to the person you tell. More often than not, however, this hope is an unwarranted expectation because many people know little about BPD and what they have heard of it often comes with a negative label. Unfortunately, the very term *personality disorder* often carries a highly charged stigma, as if it means something is fundamentally wrong with the person who has the disorder. As a result, people can end up not trusting you or thinking that you're crazy. In turn, they may discriminate against you. As mental health professionals, we know this perspective is wrong, but many people don't.

On the other hand, some folks may be able to help you if you decide to explain your BPD to them (see the "Figuring out whom to tell" section). We simply urge caution in determining whether telling a particular person will help you or hurt you.

Even when you think telling someone will be beneficial to you and that person, you can never know for certain what another person's reaction will be. You need to be prepared for the unexpected. Unfortunately, not everyone will be empathetic.

What negative consequences do you think can happen if you tell someone?

Carefully consider all possible negative reactions you may receive from anyone you decide to tell about your BPD. We discuss the possibility of stigma and discrimination in the preceding section. In addition, some people you tell may feel afraid because of their own ignorance, and, as a result, they may treat you like you have the plague or some other contagious illness. Others may worry that they don't know how to interact with you anymore, and, in turn, they may avoid you. Some may want to help, but they may feel petrified at the thought of doing the wrong thing and making things worse. Still others may view a personality disorder as an excuse for bad behavior, and, thus, they may believe you're using your diagnosis to rationalize your inappropriate actions.

Ava's story demonstrates some of the negative consequences of revealing BPD to the wrong person at the wrong time and place. Unfortunately, she was caught off guard and suffered from her disclosure.

> **Ava** pulls her sweater down over her wrists to cover the bandages. She hopes no one at the bank notices them. She's only had the job for two months and desperately needs to keep it for the healthcare benefits. She's on new-hire probation until she's been there for 90 days, and she's already missed a couple of days of work. She punches in and smiles at her co-workers already gathered in the break room. "Hey, whassup?" she asks Ryan, a teller who usually works beside her.
>
> "Not much," he replies, "did you have a good weekend?"
>
> Ava starts to feel anxious. She wonders why Ryan is asking her about her weekend. She thinks, "He couldn't know that I spent Friday night in the ER after the cuts on my wrists started to bleed too much. But, maybe he was there, too — he has a couple of kids. One of them has asthma. Maybe his kid had an asthma attack, and he had to take him to the ER." Ava's thoughts begin to spin out of control.
>
> Ryan puts his arm on her arm concerned. As she pulls away, her sweater pulls up, revealing her bandage. "Ava, are you okay? Hey, what happened to your wrist?"
>
> "I cut myself shaving," she stammers.
>
> Ryan says, "Come on, Ava. That's a whole lot more than a nick from shaving; besides, you don't shave your wrists do you?"
>
> "Okay, Ryan. Promise not to tell anyone, but I have borderline personality disorder, and sometimes I cut myself to feel better. This time it got out of control. I know it sounds crazy, but . . ."
>
> "Gosh, Ava. I didn't know. I've never heard of that. I'm sorry."
>
> Ryan later asks the branch manager what she knows about BPD and mentions that Ava has it. The manager brings Ava into her office and tells her that she isn't working out. Ava loses her job and takes an overdose of medication that evening in an unsuccessful suicide attempt.

Ava didn't intend to tell people at work about her BPD. When Ryan saw her bandages, she impulsively blurted out the information. That information likely led to her firing, which is why we want you to be prepared for the unexpected and to know what you want to say when someone confronts you about some of your behaviors. See the sections "Deciding What to Tell" and "Telling Your Story Effectively" for more information.

Try to have realistic expectations. Discussing your BPD with others can easily backfire. Nonetheless, sometimes revealing information about your BPD is a good idea. Other times doing so is virtually unavoidable. Never fear — in the next section, we go through the list of people you may be thinking about talking to. Then we tell you what to say and how to say it.

Figuring out whom to tell

Considering the implications of discussing your BPD with others is important. Frequently, people with BPD have trouble putting themselves in other people's shoes and fully understanding what their reactions are likely to be. This is one of the major problems underlying the BPD symptom of interpersonal disturbances (see Chapter 3 for more about the symptoms of BPD). So take your time and go through each of the following sections before you decide whom to tell. We can't make this decision for you, but we can highlight some of the possible reactions.

Telling family

Not all family members should be told the same thing. Some may need a lot of information, others very little, and others none. How much you tell your family members depends a lot on the nature of your relationship with them. But you also need to consider some other factors, such as age, emotional stability, and views about mental illness. Different family members and issues to consider with each include the following:

- ✔ **Partners or spouses:** If you're in a committed relationship, we usually suggest you discuss your BPD diagnosis with your spouse or partner. In fact, many times meeting with your therapist and partner or spouse in an informational session can be helpful. A supportive relationship can be invaluable in your road to recovery. If your spouse understands what's going on, he or she can provide greater empathy and support.

  On the other hand, if your partner is abusive or highly unsupportive, talking about your BPD may not be very useful. In fact, your relationship may even be contributing to your BPD symptoms. Talk this decision over with your therapist.

- ✔ **Children:** Every situation is different. Generally, when children live with a parent who has BPD, they will at some level know that problems exist. You don't want to try and explain BPD to a very young child. However, by the time a child is in elementary school, some limited information is appropriate. For example, you may decide to tell your young, school-aged child that you have a problem controlling your emotions. Even at this age, though, they don't need to hear the diagnosis.

The purpose of talking to children about BPD is mainly to let them know that they didn't do anything wrong. Children need to know that Mom or Dad becomes overly emotional because of an illness — not because they did something that upset their parent. Make sure that the reasons for talking about BPD with children are in their best interest — to obtain support from them isn't a valid reason. You may want to discuss your reasons for telling your kids with your therapist first. The two of you can role-play the discussion to help you figure out just what to say.

✔ **Adolescents and adult children:** Teenagers and adult children may have strong feelings about what being a child of someone with BPD is like. Telling them about BPD can be a way of helping them understand their own feelings. Some adult children of parents with BPD have made a conscious choice to stay away from their BPD parents. If this is the case in your situation, you need to respect this boundary. Talk your concerns over with your therapist.

✔ **Parents:** If you're an adolescent, you may wish to confide in your parents about your concerns that you may have BPD. Ideally, they will respond with empathy and concern — as well as help you seek out professional assistance. On the other hand, they may attempt to minimize your worries by telling you that you're making a mountain out of a molehill. If your parents have typically invalidated you in this manner, they will likely do the same thing here. Some parents may also become defensive, thinking that you're blaming them for your problems.

Generally speaking, we think that having this discussion with your parents is worth the risks involved. Even if their reaction is defensive or dismissive at first, they may come around in time. Besides, they may surprise you.

The major exception to telling your parents about your BPD is if your parents have emotionally or physically abused you. In this kind of case, you may be better off seeing your school counselor, who can help you determine what kind of services you need and where you can get them. A counselor conceivably would even recommend reporting your parents' behavior to authorities if it has been especially outrageous.

Finally, if you're an adult child, you have less risk in telling your parents. You also have a longer history of interacting with your folks, so you have an even better idea of what their reaction is likely to be. We recommend that you confide in them if you feel the chances of a supportive reaction are reasonable.

✔ **Siblings:** Siblings range in closeness from the love of best friends, to outright hate, or even to distant neutrality. Carefully consider your reasons and expectations for divulging your emotional issues with a sibling.

> Under ideal circumstances, siblings can provide much-needed support. However, we recommend talking the idea over with your therapist before going ahead.

✔ **Other relatives:** Distant relatives rarely need to know anything about your BPD. However, some relatives may have been closely involved in your life and are, for that reason, capable of giving you support. They may also have been hurt by your emotional outbursts or other symptoms of BPD, and you may wish to explain your behaviors to them.

Telling friends and acquaintances

Sometimes people with BPD want to tell friends and acquaintances about their diagnosis because they think everyone is interested in their struggles. You have to consider that talking about yourself isn't always in your best interest (see Chapters 8 and 18 for more information about how your words and actions affect other people). Most people in your life don't need to know or want to hear about every detail of your emotional issues. However, a few very close friends will likely want to know so that they can be supportive. Watch how they react when you bring up the subject and stop talking about BPD if they seem disinterested or uncomfortable. Try not to abuse their support by dominating conversations with your troubles.

We recommend not disclosing any information about your BPD to new dating partners unless the relationship has lasted for a number of months and appears to be stable. See Chapter 18 for more information about dealing with close relationships.

BPD drives many people to expect and want relationships to become extremely close very quickly. We recommend proceeding slowly and with caution. Give the relationship time to develop and take your time before disclosing your diagnosis.

Disclosing at work

Typically, you shouldn't tell bosses and co-workers about your BPD. You simply can't expect them to understand and hold sympathetic attitudes. Revealing details about your emotional problems may limit your opportunities for advancement or hinder your searches for a job.

People with BPD often have trouble trusting other people. However, they sometimes invest far more trust in others than their relationships warrant. Generally speaking, we recommend not trusting co-workers and bosses with information about your condition.

On the other hand, if you need reasonable accommodations on your job that directly relate to your BPD, you may decide that the risk of disclosure is worth considering. You have the right to make your disclosure at any time — including after you're on the job. However, disclosing such information won't likely help you if you do so only after you're about to be fired. We urge you to talk with your therapist and/or a vocational counselor about these issues before talking to your boss or co-workers about your condition. Your therapist or counselor will likely discuss the Americans with Disabilities Act (ADA) with you.

The ADA protects people with disabilities from discrimination by employers. The act protects people with both physical and mental disabilities. BPD falls under the ADA's protection; however, the individual with BPD must be qualified and able to do the job with reasonable accommodations.

Despite ADA, an employer can fire a person with a disability for the following three reasons:

✔ The termination doesn't have anything to do with the disability.

✔ The disabled person threatens the safety or health of others.

✔ The employee doesn't meet production standards or requirements of the job despite accommodations.

The courts have ruled that employers shouldn't consider improper behavior to be part of a disability. Employers should also expect people with disabilities to get along with their co-workers and to listen to their supervisors. This expectation is an area that some people with BPD have trouble understanding. Symptoms of BPD include unstable relationships, impulsivity, and emotional dysregulation, all of which often cause the very problems that get people fired from jobs.

If you feel that you've been discriminated against at work for your BPD, go to the U.S. Department of Labor's Web site and search for the Office of Disability Employment Policy (www.dol.gov). This policy spells out what to do and whom to contact.

Revealing to professionals

What you disclose to primary healthcare providers, therapists, and attorneys is held in strict confidence. These professionals often need to know the details of your physical and mental states. Attorneys may not always require as much information, but if they're working for you, an attitude of openness is a good idea.

Deciding What to Tell

If you choose to tell one or more people about your BPD, you then need to figure out exactly what you want to say. Of course, knowing what you're talking about helps. Therefore, we suggest you learn as much as you can about BPD before you share information with others. Then you can decide what specific aspects of your problem you want to disclose.

Educating yourself

Understanding the ins and outs of BPD is like tackling almost any other subject. This book makes a great start because it covers as much information about the disorder as any layperson likely wants to know.

However, we recommend you read additional books, too. Most people comprehend best when they read information from a variety of perspectives. The Internet is also a good source of information, but some sites are far superior to others. (See Appendix A for resources you can trust.) Knowing as much as you can about BPD helps you explain things more clearly to others (to determine whom to tell, see the "Deciding Whether and Whom to Tell" section earlier in this chapter). Furthermore, you'll find treatment easier to understand and benefit from when you have a thorough understanding of BPD.

Deciding how much to say

The amount of information you choose to disclose about your BPD depends on whom you're talking to and why. Some explanations lay out the full story; however, most discussions are more limited. The following descriptions give you ideas about various levels of disclosure.

Giving a complete explanation

You probably want to make a complete disclosure to your therapist and your spouse or partner. On occasion, you may feel that giving a full explanation to an adult child or someone else who is very important to you is a good idea. For these people, you may want to share the following information:

- The symptoms of BPD (see Chapter 3)
- Which BPD symptoms you have
- The causes of BPD (see Chapter 4)
- What treatments are available and how effective they are (see Chapter 11)
- Information about the treatment you're receiving
- Hints about living with someone with BPD (see Part V)
- An apology for how your BPD has affected the person you're talking to

Apologies can be very helpful as part of a complete explanation. However, you need to keep in mind that apologies aren't easy to give and they don't always elicit sympathy and gratitude. Sometimes other people have been sitting on a mound of resentment for years because of how you've treated them. Still, a heartfelt apology can be one of the best ways to improve a relationship. Just remember that the healing process takes time.

The following story about John and Emma illustrates how a father decides to make a fairly complete explanation about his BPD to his adult child. He tells her his diagnosis and a little about the causes, apologizes for his past behavior, and gives her a pamphlet with more information in the hopes that she'll read it.

> Emma agrees to meet her dad, **John,** for coffee. Although she hasn't seen him for a long time, she has mixed feelings. She's both angry and sad. During her childhood, he was unreliable and unstable. He missed countless birthdays and special family events. He didn't even show up for her college graduation last year. When he was in a good mood, her dad could be fun. She remembers the laughter and parties.

> As Emma approaches the café, she notices her dad sitting alone at a table. He looks older than the last time she saw him and kind of sad. "Hey Dad," Emma says. "How are you? Haven't seen you for a long time."

> John looks up at his daughter and says, "Hi Em, it's been about ten months. Too long. You look wonderful. Your mom told me about your new job. I'm so proud of you."

> "I didn't even know you talked to Mom or, for that matter, cared what I was doing," Emma says as she feels the familiar anger rising.

> "Yes, even when I'm not around, I still keep in touch and ask about you. But, I want to talk to you about something today that's pretty hard for me. Let me get you a cup of coffee. Do you want something to eat? I hope you have some time to spend with me," John says.

> "I've got a little time, Dad. I'll have a cup of coffee," she responds.

> "Okay, what I want to tell you is that I was out of town for the past ten months getting treatment for my problems. The first thing I want to do is apologize for all the times I let you down. You know, when you were growing up, I was a pretty horrible dad. I was so focused on my own problems that I wasn't there for you. I'm really sorry."

> "So I'm supposed to forget all the times you exploded and walked out? How about the vacations you never came on with us? Or, how about my birthdays you missed? I'm 23 years old, and you're just now telling me you're sorry? It feels kinda late."

> "I guess I deserve that. You're right. I can't make it up to you; I know that. I just want you to know that these last ten months have really opened my eyes to what I did and why I did it. I don't expect you to understand really. I just want you to know that I am so, so sorry. And I want you to know what it was all about. You see, one thing I learned is that my problem is partly genetic, and it can run in families. I'm pretty sure you don't have it, but you should be aware that your kids could have a little higher risk."

"So, what are you trying to say? That you had some sort of disease that caused you to be a complete jerk?"

"You're not making this easy for me, but I don't blame you. My therapist told me this could be a little rough, and she was right," John sighs and wipes a tear from his eye. "I have something that sounds a little awful. It's called borderline personality disorder. It's a condition that primarily involves huge problems with controlling emotions. My mother had it, and I probably learned it from her in addition to inheriting the tendency. Funny thing, though, she managed to be a whole lot better grandmother to you than she was a mother for me. Again, I'm not trying to make excuses for my outrageous behavior. I brought a pamphlet on this disorder if you'd like to read it. I understand if you don't. I know I rarely ever said this, but I do love you."

Emma chokes up a bit and says, "I don't even know what to say, Dad. I wish we could go back a few years and start over. I'll look at this stuff and maybe we can talk another time. But give me a little time. This is hard for me, too."

As you can see, John's daughter responds with considerable caution. She has been very hurt over the years and fears getting close to her dad. However, she reluctantly agrees to read the information he's given her.

BPD has probably been part of your life for a long time, and, for that reason, the effect on others is likely significant. Give the people you decide to tell about your diagnosis time to hear your apologies. Accompanying your apologies with improved ways of relating to them will likely speed the healing.

Telling part of the story

If you choose to reveal something about your BPD to people other than your therapist or those very close to you, you probably want to limit the discussion. We suggest that you focus on one or two key aspects of your behavior or BPD that seem important to convey to the person you're talking to. Limiting your discussion likely means that you avoid revealing the diagnosis because BPD carries a stigma for too many people. Even the term personality disorder is readily misunderstood and sounds more ominous to other people than it is. Thus, you probably won't go through your entire list of symptoms when you're telling only part of your story.

Instead, you may choose to focus on your difficulty with emotional regulation (in other words, managing your feelings). Perhaps you want to mention that you've been getting some professional help for your difficulty. Again, make sure you have a clear handle on why you're choosing to discuss the issue.

An example of a good reason why you may choose to tell someone who isn't very close to you about your problems is because you've had some trouble at work and you want to provide a brief explanation to your boss. For instance, maybe you've missed more work than you'd have liked to or you've blown up at some co-workers. You probably don't want to tell your boss that you have BPD, but explaining that you're getting help for handling intense emotions may help you keep your job.

Sophie and Adam's story shows you how someone may decide to make a partial disclosure. Sophie has dated Adam for about six weeks and likes him a lot, but she realizes she should focus on treating her BPD before getting serious with someone. Because she hasn't been with him a long time and they haven't gotten that serious, she decides to reveal only a couple of details about her BPD.

> Adam pulls up to the emergency entrance of the hospital. A nurse walks **Sophie,** Adam's girlfriend, out and helps her into the car. "Let me take you home," Adam says when the door closes, "I'm so sorry that I didn't call you last week. You know how much I love you. I want us to work out. I was so scared when you called me. Why did you do it? Why did you cut yourself?"
>
> Sophie glances at Adam. She knows he cares about her and wants her to be stable. She realizes how frightened he was when she called him, drugged and cutting herself. But, she's had a number of long talks with her doctor, and they both finally agreed that she's not ready for a relationship. She must work on her own issues first. "Adam, thanks for coming to get me," she starts, "I really care about you. But, I need to tell you that I have some problems."
>
> "Everyone has problems, Sophie. I can help you. We'll work on this together," Adam offers.
>
> "Adam, I have a lot of trouble staying calm. I need to stay focused on getting myself together. This has nothing to do with you. I've been this way for a long time, and I'm just beginning to understand it myself. So, I'd like you to drop me off at my house and stop calling me for awhile. I need some space."
>
> "Wow, space. I've heard that one before. So I guess this is the end of us," Adam responds.
>
> "Maybe not, Adam. I'll call you in a few months if I'm doing better. I'm so sorry," Sophie grasps her hands together. "This is pretty tough for me."
>
> "Right," Adam stares ahead as he pulls up her drive. "See you around."

Sophie had no compelling reason to tell Adam more about herself and her disorder. Doing so would only risk his telling others about her problems. He knows a lot of her friends and colleagues at work, and he may be tempted to tell them because he feels hurt over the breakup.

Telling Your Story Effectively

Perhaps you've made the decision to tell someone about your BPD, and you've decided what you want to tell that person. We recommend that you ponder how you want to tell your story. Consider the following suggestions:

- ✔ Choose a private place to talk.

- ✔ Allow enough time for your talk.

- ✔ Don't use jargon you learned in therapy.

- ✔ Consider talking during a mildly distracting activity, such as walking, driving, or hiking, to help keep your emotions in check.

- ✔ Practice the talk in your mind or with your therapist. Go over both best- and worst-case scenarios.

- ✔ If you become too emotional, step back. Consider telling the person that you want to talk more but that you need to take a break.

- ✔ If the other person reacts with anger, stop and perhaps try again later.

Talking to others about BPD can be challenging. You don't have to tell every-one everything — and certainly not all at once. Try to be prepared for any reaction you may get. If things get too emotional, stop for the time being and try to resume the talk later.

Chapter 14

Taking Care of Yourself

....

....

*W*hen you feel stressed, depressed, angry, or anxious, your body responds accordingly because the mind and body are so closely related. Unfortunately, when people with BPD have primarily negative emotions, their bodies experience primarily negative effects as a result.

In this chapter, we take a look at the effects of emotional stress on the body. New research comes out all the time showing how the environment, the mind, and the body interact. We also give you some ideas on how to stay healthy — both in your mind and in your body.

Dealing with Stress

People with BPD typically report feeling considerable stress the majority of the time. The body reacts strongly to this stress in a myriad of ways. The purpose behind these strong reactions is to help you deal with threats. For instance, intense bodily responses to danger proved extremely helpful when ancient people had to deal with direct threats to their lives, such as tigers and bears, every day. Fortunately, in the modern world, you don't have to encounter many life-threatening events (like wild animal attacks) on a daily basis. Although the intense threat is gone, the human body still responds to feelings of stress in the same way. This section takes a look at how your mind's stress affects your body's health.

Reviewing how stress affects health

You may be wondering what the body's responses to stress entail and how they affect your overall physical health. Do they cause any serious consequences? Do they affect your ability to deal with stress in the future?

At the first hint of stress, your body gets ready to either stand and fight or run like the dickens. First, your nervous system goes on high alert by releasing stress hormones. These hormones cause your heart to race, your breathing to quicken, and oxygen to pour into the large muscles of your arms and legs. Pupils dilate, digestion slows, and you begin to sweat. All these responses prepare your body for battle. For example, when someone unexpectedly cuts you off in traffic, your body instantly responds with a surge of adrenaline to help you react quickly to avoid a crash. When these stress responses occur on a frequent, chronic basis, they damage the body in more ways than one. Such damage includes

✔ Fatigue

✔ Gastrointestinal problems

✔ Heart disease

✔ High blood pressure

✔ Impaired immune system

✔ Muscle tension leading to severe pain:

- Back pain

- Headaches

- Neck pain

✔ Sexual problems

✔ Weight gain or loss

As physical damage to your body accumulates, your ability to deal with stress decreases further because the mind and body work in concert; impairment to one system harms the other. People with BPD often experience health effects from their chronic levels of stress. Chapter 16 provides you with specific strategies for quelling emotional storms when they hit. Here we tell you how to do everything possible to keep your body healthy and reduce the overall stress levels in your life.

Managing and reducing stress

One of the best ways to manage stress is to reduce the amount of stress you encounter in your daily life. You can accomplish this goal by decluttering your life.

Clutter and disarray usually make people feel out of control. Our office, for example, has a way of making us feel frazzled and frenzied when the piles on our desks reach a certain height. People with BPD tend to overreact to stressful events of all kinds, including clutter. They may go beyond frazzled and react with rage or overwhelming despair.

If such dishevelment stirs up your emotions, we recommend that you commit yourself to managing the mess — no matter how big it has become. Start by making a simple goal, such as

- ✔ Toss out three pieces of paper each day.
- ✔ Spend five minutes a day tossing out junk.
- ✔ Spend five minutes a day rearranging your closets.
- ✔ Try to take one bag of clothes to a charity each week or month.

You can use one or more of the following rules of thumb to help you get started:

- ✔ Toss out clothes you haven't worn in a year or more unless you have a compelling reason to keep a particular item (such as sentiment or an unusually infrequent need to wear certain clothes for a wedding or other dressy occasion).
- ✔ Newspapers and magazines are valuable to recycle, so recycle them; you don't benefit from keeping them.
- ✔ Old books have more value for other people than they do for your bookshelf.

Decisions are much harder to make when you're feeling emotional and overwhelmed, so try to declutter and reorganize when you feel calm (see Chapter 16 for ideas on how to calm your emotions). Also, break the overarching tasks down into smaller pieces so that each piece is easier for you to manage.

After you've made a little progress in the tossing department, consider organizing the items you want to keep. Make a master list of categories; then plan where you want to store items from a given category.

Taking Better Care of Your Body

A healthy body is resilient to stress and, thus, makes you feel better emotionally, as well as physically. In the next sections, we explain how you can work on several major approaches to improving your body's health and various ways to maintain it.

Sometimes people with BPD feel so overwhelmed with life in general that the idea of doing anything besides just living seems to be out of reach. If you feel like this, consider reading the following sections, but don't implement the suggestions into your life until you're ready. You may want to read Part IV about different ways to treat BPD before you begin any of the tasks that follow.

Revising your diet

Good nutrition lays the foundation for good physical health. However, if you faithfully read all the current books and articles about nutrition and try to follow every piece of advice you run into, you may cause yourself more stress than you had before you started because nutritional advice changes almost as often as the weather. One day you may read that you have to avoid carbohydrates like the plague because they seemingly lead people to gain weight. The very next day, you may read that carbohydrates help you lose weight. Trying to keep up with research on nutrition is like trying to track the pea in a carnival shell game.

However, a few nutritional tips are likely to stand the test of time. We recommend that you adhere to the following general ideas about eating instead of worrying about the latest nutritional trends:

- ✔ **Eat unprocessed foods.** Food processing does too much of your digestive system's work, and, as a result, your body absorbs sugars more rapidly than is good for you. Try to eat whole fruits, grains, and vegetables, and avoid processed foods like cookies, chips, and white bread and pastas as much as you can.

- ✔ **Reduce fat.** Most people eat more fat than they should. Of course, you need some fat in your diet to sustain good health, and a little fat also slows your body's absorption of sugar. However, you want to avoid hydrogenated oils, trans fats, and saturated fats as much as possible because they raise your bad cholesterol levels. Check labels to know which foods are high in these dangerous fats.

- ✔ **Control protein.** Generally, you need to eat a little protein with most meals because it keeps muscles healthy. Beans are an especially good source of protein because they also contain fiber, are low in fat, and are absorbed slowly.

- ✔ **Find fiber.** Fiber keeps your intestinal system clean. It also slows down the absorption of sugars which helps prevent unhealthy spikes in insulin levels. Most people don't get enough fiber. Look for fiber in oatmeal, whole grains, beans, and vegetables. Aim to ingest 25 to 30 grams of fiber per day.

Finally, try not to use eating as a stress management technique. Instead, turn to Chapter 16 for numerous ideas on how to calm yourself during times of upheaval. Eating may do the trick, too, but only in the short run. In the long run, overeating causes weight gain and self-recrimination, not overall calmness or high self-esteem.

Energizing with exercise

Another great way to manage stress is to exercise. The benefits of exercise are well known in today's world — it lowers the risks of heart disease, high blood pressure, type 2 diabetes, stroke, and obesity, and it leads to better memory for older adults (which is incentive enough for us!). Exercise also decreases depression, a symptom that frequently accompanies BPD. In addition, exercise is a quick way to burn off excess stress and, thus, often leads to better moods. The two categories of exercise are

- ✔ **Aerobic:** Aerobic exercise involves getting your heart beating and your blood flowing fast. Recent guidelines from the U.S. Department of Health and Human Services advise all healthy adults to participate in 2½ hours of moderate aerobic activity or 75 minutes of intense aerobic activity a week (each episode of exercise being at least 10 minutes long).

- ✔ **Anaerobic:** Anaerobic exercise consists of muscle strengthening activities. The Department of Health and Human Services guidelines also suggest that healthy adults should participate in anaerobic activities that use all muscle groups at least twice a week, though they don't specify the length of time.

For more ideas about exercising, see *Fitness For Dummies*, 3rd Edition, by Suzanne Schlosberg (Wiley), *Workouts For Dummies* by Tamilee Webb and Lori Seeger (Wiley), and the many *For Dummies* exercise DVDs that cover everything from basic yoga to workouts with a fitness ball.

Getting enough sleep

Sleep is another important part of any plan for managing stress. Generally, people need about 7 or 8 hours of sleep to be maximally healthy. Sleep allows the body's cells to repair and helps with memory and concentration. Many emotional disorders, including BPD, disrupt sleep — sometimes causing an excess and often causing a lack of sleep.

Most people suffer from occasional bouts of sleeplessness or interrupted sleep. However, if you're constantly having trouble falling asleep and staying asleep, see your primary care provider. Insomnia may result from a physical malady or a medication you're taking.

Take a list of all your prescribed and over-the-counter medications, as well as dietary supplements or vitamins, with you when you go see your doctor.

We suggest that you try to manage your sleep problems without taking sleeping pills because they can be addictive. Try out some simple techniques to help you sleep before you resort to medication.

The first rule of thumb for getting good sleep is having a routine. Go to bed and get up at about the same time every day. You should spend the last few hours of your evening winding down. During the time before you go to bed,

- ✔ Take a warm bath.
- ✔ Listen to music.
- ✔ Read a book.
- ✔ Watch TV.
- ✔ Have a small snack.
- ✔ Drink warm milk.
- ✔ Don't drink too much alcohol (you may fall asleep, but you'll also wake up early).
- ✔ Don't drink too much of anything (unless you like to get up in the middle of the night).
- ✔ Don't drink anything with caffeine (if caffeine keeps you awake); try decaffeinated tea when you want something warm.
- ✔ Don't engage in arguments.
- ✔ Don't smoke cigarettes before bed.

Make sure that you have comfortable sheets and pillows. To maximize your sleeping ability, try to sleep in a room that's cool, dark, and well ventilated.

During the day, avoid naps and be sure to get some exercise (see the "Energizing with exercise" section earlier in this chapter for ideas about exercise).

Taking healthy actions

Many people with BPD struggle to take adequate care of themselves because they feel overwhelmed by stress and life and often don't feel like they have the energy to devote to their health. And staying healthy does require an active approach. But, it doesn't take a whole lot of time. You just need to use a little common sense and take a few precautions. Try to incorporate the following good habits into your life to help improve and maintain your health:

- ✔ **Wash your hands often, especially during cold season.** Just be sure not to take this advice to the extremes. See our book, *Obsessive-Compulsive Disorder For Dummies* (Wiley), for information about what happens when people gravely fear germs and contamination.

- ✔ **Use sunscreen.** Try not to let yourself get a sunburn, and limit your direct exposure to the sun. Excessive sun exposure may lead to wrinkles, but skin cancer poses a much more serious risk.

✔ **Protect your ears from excessively loud noises.** Over time, subjecting your ears to extremely loud noises can ruin your hearing.

✔ **Take short, frequent breaks at work (as many and as often as you're allowed).** Ideally, get up and walk around a bit every hour or so.

✔ **Know the signs of a stroke or heart attack.** We don't want to scare you, but knowing these signs can save your life (or someone else's).

✔ **Floss your teeth daily.** Spending a few minutes flossing each day not only improves and maintains the health of your teeth and gums, but it may also reduce infections that can contribute to heart disease.

✔ **Listen to a radio health show or podcast regularly.** You can learn many interesting, healthy ways of living by listening to other people.

✔ **Read the labels on food.** You may be shocked to see how much sugar and fat some food contains. Reading the labels can help you make better eating decisions.

✔ **Stay current with your vaccinations.** Your doctor can tell you which ones to get and when to get them.

✔ **Have your blood tested yearly for a range of numbers, including cholesterol, liver and kidney function, and any other tests your doctor recommends.** Talk the results over with your doctor.

✔ **Always use a seatbelt.** Not only does wearing a seatbelt keep you safe when you're driving, but it's also the law in many places.

Incorporating these actions into your daily life doesn't guarantee perfect health, but doing so can help. Furthermore, following these simple tips can help you feel like you're taking care of yourself, which is likely to improve your mood and sense of control over life (both typical concerns of people with BPD).

Finding More Time for Yourself

Improving and recovering from BPD takes time. Time is often in short supply for everyone, not just people with BPD. The first step in finding more time for yourself involves keeping track of what you do every day. For a couple of days, or better yet weeks, try to jot down start and stop times for all your activities. You don't have to write essays or be too specific. Just keeping track of how you spend your days can help you determine whether you need to spend more or less time doing certain activities, such as exercising, reading, reflecting, and so on. For the technologically gifted, use a cell phone or other electronic device to record activities. Be truthful in your records. For example, if you're trying to write a book and every time you sit in front of your computer, you spend 75 percent of your time on Twitter and Google, don't record, "Writing book, 4 hours."

Information is a powerful tool. Take a look at the time you waste on activities that don't help you get where you want to be. After a few days or weeks of recording your daily activities, take some time to reflect on your data. Think about ways in which you can change your activities to be more effective in achieving your goals. Or, plan a meeting with a therapist to discuss some of the changes you may want to make and how to go about making them.

With some effort, you may discover as many as three, four, or maybe even more hours each week that you didn't know you had. You can use this time — the time you once frittered away — on more productive activities. Doing so can help make you feel better about yourself.

Part IV
Treatments for BPD

The 5th Wave   By Rich Tennant

"The good news is, I've curbed my impulsive behavior so I can hold a job. The bad news is, I'd always hoped to work in improvisational theater."

In this part . . .

In this part, we target five major problem areas that most people with borderline personality disorder (BPD) have to deal with. We show you how to borrow strategies from an array of effective treatments to address each of these areas. Although we don't intend these treatments to be standalone means of self-help, you can collaborate with your therapist in the use of these techniques. We also discuss the role that medication may play in the treatment of BPD.

Chapter 15

Inhibiting Impulsivity

· ·

· ·

Impulses are all about feeling an immediate need to get what you want. Throughout life, many people with borderline personality disorder (BPD) listen to other people tell them that what they want or think they need isn't appropriate — that somehow their needs are wrong.

However, that's not true at all. For the most part, people with BPD want the same things that other people do. They want to be happy; they want people to care about them; they want to get rid of bad feelings; they want to experience pleasure. People with BPD generally don't have inappropriate desires, but they do typically want to meet their desires completely and immediately — which leads them down a primrose path that often ends in calamity.

As you probably already know, an *impulse* is a desire, urge, or want, and *impulsivity* describes one way in which people act on impulses. For example, imagine that you stroll into a jewelry store and have an impulse to own a beautiful diamond brooch. If you choose to smash the glass case, grab the brooch, and run, you're experiencing impulsivity. In Chapters 3 and 5, we discuss impulsivity, a common symptom of BPD. People who are impulsive don't take time to think about their actions before they do them, which often leads to all sorts of trouble.

In this chapter, we show you how to increase your awareness of your own impulsivity and the consequences you experience as a result of your impulsive actions. Armed with this awareness, you can step back from your impulsivity and reflect on all your options. We give you tools to help you put the brakes on your impulsivity. Finally, we suggest some healthier ways to meet your needs.

Increasing Your Awareness of Impulsive Behavior

Before you can change something in your life, you first have to be aware that it exists. When people with BPD act impulsively, they often report very little awareness of several critical aspects of their impulsive behavior, including

- ✔ What they did
- ✔ How they felt
- ✔ What their goals were
- ✔ What triggered their impulsivity in the first place

Instead, they report that they have only vague memories of what they did, their feelings at the time, what they wanted to happen, and what led to their behavior. They rarely reflect on these issues and don't ponder whether they met their goals because they usually don't remember what their goals were.

Change begins with monitoring all the aspects of impulsivity that you experience. Awareness alone helps you start putting the brakes on your impulsive behaviors.

We recommend that you read Chapter 5 to understand the full range of impulsive behaviors that people with BPD often engage in. Reading about what others do may help you identify which problems with impulsivity you have. After you recognize which impulsive behaviors you exhibit, you can start to change them.

Write down your impulsive acts

Writing about your impulsivity can help you organize your thoughts and feelings in preparation for change. You can use the blank Impulsive Awareness Form that appears in Appendix B as you work through the steps in this section. The directions for this form follow.

Some of the steps in self-monitoring that we describe next may feel difficult if not impossible for you to do right now. That's okay. Try to do the parts you think you can do. Over time, you can probably go through more and more steps. Also, as with most exercises in this book, you're likely to get more out of them by doing them, or at least discussing them, with a mental health professional.

The following steps can help you monitor — and, thus, increase your awareness of — your own impulsivity:

1. **Describe each time you act impulsively, without thinking.**

   Some examples of common impulsive behaviors include self-harm, spending sprees, gambling, shoplifting, binge eating, reckless driving, reckless sex, and substance abuse. Impulsive behaviors can involve almost anything you do without thinking, especially actions that can result in direct or indirect harm to you or someone else. In your description, include details about what you did.

2. **Recount where you were and what you were doing before you acted impulsively.**

   Were you at work, with a boyfriend, at a party, in a bar, or sitting at home watching television when you had your impulsive urge? This information can help you see what situations trigger your impulsive behavior.

3. **Explain how you felt — before you acted impulsively.**

   Common feelings before exhibiting impulsive behaviors include the following:

   - Bored
   - Anxious
   - Jealous
   - Envious
   - Needy
   - Afraid
   - Angry
   - Vulnerable
   - Upset
   - Sad
   - Excited
   - Sexy
   - Critical
   - Ashamed
   - Guilty
   - Numb
   - Unreal
   - Disconnected
   - Resentful

4. **Write down what you thought or hoped would happen as a result of your impulsive behavior.**

   For example, you may have thought you would feel less bored, more connected, or more real. You may have thought you would feel more in control of a social interaction, less jealous, or less angry. Ask yourself what possible goals you wanted to accomplish through your impulsive behavior.

5. **Express how you felt after the impulsive behavior. Did you achieve your goals?**

   You may find that although you experience a momentary high or rush during your impulsive action, your feelings quickly return to neutral or get worse after you complete the action. Common feelings after impulsive actions include guilt, shame, remorse, regret, self-loathing, and a sense of isolation. Whatever feelings and outcomes you experience, jot them down.

A case study using Impulsivity Awareness Forms

Destiny, a young, married woman with BPD, struggles with impulsivity. The following story takes a look at her experience with impulsivity and depicts several typical impulsive acts and their associated triggers, feelings, and outcomes. At her therapist's suggestion, she fills out several Impulsivity Awareness Forms on the incidents.

Destiny and her husband, Scott, live in a large home nestled in the mountains overlooking Tucson, Arizona. The surrounding community knows well their catered parties with great local entertainment and plenty of alcoholic beverages. The morning after their parties, a few of the guests usually find themselves asleep in guest rooms, on couches, and even sprawled out in sleeping bags. Scott, a retired military officer, likes his guests to have fun but doesn't let them drink and drive.

Destiny has settled down some since her wild years. She likes having a husband even though he's a lot older than she is. She likes not having to worry about money and enjoys the attention Scott lavishes on her.

Tonight they're having their annual summer party. Destiny applies the finishing touches to her makeup and asks Scott to latch her new necklace. "Wow," Scott looks at her appreciatively, "you look really hot. The guys won't be able to take their eyes off you. Do you think that dress may be a little low cut?"

Destiny gives him a full body hug and says, "It's all for you, babe." She can't help but feel excited at the idea of men fawning over her. She hasn't had an affair in over a year and yearns for both the danger and the thrill. After all, she's been feeling a little bored lately.

After the party's underway, Destiny notices Stephen, an old friend, standing with a woman she doesn't recognize. Although she never had a relationship with Stephen, she immediately feels jealous because they're obviously close to each other. She feels an urgent desire to capture Stephen's attention. She strolls over to Stephen and kisses him on the cheek, pressing her breasts into his chest. The kiss lasts a bit too long.

"Who's this?" Destiny asks Stephen, pointing to his guest. "She looks a little bookish to me."

"This is Stacy, my new girlfriend," he responds.

Destiny says, "Hi Stacy, I need to talk to Stephen for a moment. It's personal. You're not the jealous type, are you?"

Stacy stammers, "Uh, no. That's fine, of course. I see someone I know across the room."

After she's alone with Stephen, Destiny says, "How about you lose her and we go upstairs for awhile? My husband is busy and drunk; he won't notice. And your Stacy looks boring anyway."

Stephen, looking shocked, says, "Destiny, no. You're an attractive woman, but I can't do something like that. What's gotten into you? You're married. I went to your wedding."

Destiny, now furious, storms into the kitchen and starts drinking Scotch. After tossing down a tumbler full of the whisky, she looks for another male target. The first guy she finds is as drunk as she is and readily accepts her invitation for a quick encounter upstairs. Afterward, she feels horrible and retreats to her own bathroom. Crying, she sits on the edge of the tub and slices her thighs with a razor blade.

Destiny has an appointment with her therapist two days later. She feels horrible and ashamed. Her therapist suggests that she fill out four separate Impulsive Awareness Forms to help them identify and study her impulsive behaviors. Table 15-1 shows what they come up with on the first form.

Table 15-1   Destiny's Impulsive Awareness Form: Seduction

1. Describe each time you act impulsively, without thinking.

I tried to seduce an old friend. I just went right up to him and his girlfriend and took him away.

2. Recount where you were and what you were doing before you acted impulsively.

I was at home. I had a drink or two before the guests started arriving at the party. Parties always make me feel excited.

3. Explain how you felt — before you acted impulsively.

I was feeling bored before the party. But then I felt jealous when Stephen came in with a new girlfriend.

4. Write down what you thought or hoped would happen as a result of your impulsive behavior.

I thought seducing a guy would make me feel alive again and relieve some of the boredom I'd been feeling lately.

5. Express how you felt after the impulsive behavior. Did you achieve your goals?

I was angry. I couldn't believe he turned me down. He ticked me off so much that I started drinking. So, no, I guess I didn't achieve my goals.

From this first form, Destiny discovers that parties, boredom, and even a little alcohol can all trigger her impulsive behavior. She also sees that she didn't feel better afterward; in fact, she felt angry. Her next Impulsive Awareness Form, shown in Table 15-2, helps her understand her impulsivity even more.

Table 15-2	Destiny's Impulsive Awareness Form: Drinking
1. Describe each time you act impulsively, without thinking.	
I started downing Scotch straight up.	
2. Recount where you were and what you were doing before you acted impulsively.	
I was rejected by someone in my own house. I was surrounded by a party atmosphere and a lot of alcohol.	
3. Explain how you felt — before you acted impulsively.	
I was totally ticked off and angry. I also felt hurt.	
4. Write down what you thought or hoped would happen as a result of your impulsive behavior.	
I just thought some Scotch would make me feel better — less angry and hurt. I didn't have any other goals.	
5. Express how you felt after the impulsive behavior. Did you achieve your goals?	
The drinking made me want to have sex even more. After I had enough Scotch, I threw myself at someone I knew I could snare. In that respect, I think drinking did help me achieve my goals — I got laid.	

Destiny and her therapist talk about how impulsive drinking leads to even more impulsive behavior. Destiny initially felt that the drinking helped her achieve her goals, and, in actuality, it did for a short while. But, drinking also led to a much darker outcome — sex with a virtual stranger. Table 15-3 shows what she discovers about her next impulsive action.

Table 15-3	Destiny's Impulsive Awareness Form: Sex
1. Describe each time you act impulsively, without thinking.	
I threw myself at a guy and had sex with him. I don't even remember his name.	
2. Recount where you were and what you were doing before you acted impulsively.	
I was in the kitchen drinking like a fish. Then I dragged that guy upstairs and had sex with him.	
3. Explain how you felt — before you acted impulsively.	
I felt drunk. I could barely stand up. Scotch and sex felt good, though.	
4. Write down what you thought or hoped would happen as a result of your impulsive behavior.	
I hoped it would take away my feelings of rejection, hurt, and anger.	

5. Express how you felt after the impulsive behavior. Did you achieve your goals?

I felt horrible and disgusted with myself. I felt like a total slut, completely ashamed. I also felt guilty about what I did to my husband. I can't believe he didn't find out, but he could next time. I didn't get anything out of the experience. I don't even remember what the sex was like.

Destiny sobs as she goes over her third form with her therapist. She can see that her momentary impulses lead her to feel worse about herself and that, in the long run, they don't help her get anything she wants. For the first time, she confesses to her therapist that she cuts herself when she feels shame. See Table 15-4 for Destiny's final Impulsive Awareness Form.

Table 15-4	Destiny's Impulsive Awareness Form: Cutting

1. Describe each time you act impulsively, without thinking.

I cut my thighs with a razor blade again.

2. Recount where you were and what you were doing before you acted impulsively.

I was in bed having sex with a man I'd never even met before.

3. Explain how you felt — before you acted impulsively.

I felt horribly ashamed of myself. I felt nauseous and guilty. I was worried my husband would catch me. It was horrible.

4. Write down what you thought or hoped would happen as a result of your impulsive behavior.

I wanted to punish myself. I thought I'd feel better if I did that.

5. Express how you felt after the impulsive behavior. Did you achieve your goals?

After I cut myself, I did calm down some. However, now I feel such shame over all the scars I have. Hurting myself certainly isn't getting me what I want.

Destiny's evening went from bad to worse — thanks to her long string of impulsive behaviors. Some very short-term benefits, such as brief relief from upsetting feelings, may occur as a result of impulsive behavior, but the gains are fleeting and usually just lead to more impulsive behavior.

Impulsivity starts in the brain

Think of your brain as being a system of many interconnected areas. To effectively plan ahead and prevent impulsivity, your brain has to put the brakes on all these areas so that you don't act before you think. For example, one area in your brain keeps track of memories of the past. Another area of your brain deals with thoughts about the future, and another area processes what's going on in the present moment. Finally, a fourth area considers and integrates the implications of the past, present, and future — and then makes a decision. Managing all these areas is a difficult task for many people to handle, not just folks with BPD.

For example, a small, turtle-paced town outside of Albuquerque, New Mexico, called Corrales, contains only one long road that winds through the centuries-old business district. Galleries, antique stores, restaurants, and professional offices fill the town. Small streets (some dirt, some paved) intersect the main street and take residents to their homes. On these side streets, the speed limit ranges from 15 mph (miles per hour) to a brisk 25 mph. Numerous dedicated police officers in patrol cars park under and behind huge cottonwood trees along the small streets. The crime rate is fairly low in Corrales, so these officers monitor car speeds to pass the time. As a result, most residents have learned to drive slowly and enjoy the sunshine.

You may wonder what this small town has to do with impulsivity. Well, people in Corrales usually think about past tickets and their repercussions, ponder the future effects of increased car insurance rates, notice the abundance of police cars as they drive, and adjust accordingly. However, from time to time, some nonresidents, as well as a few impulsive residents, can't resist the urge to zip along the little winding roads. They aren't stupid; their brains simply don't put the brakes on their actions by reflecting on the past, present, and future implications of speeding.

Putting the Brakes on Impulsivity

People with BPD who experience the symptom of impulsivity find themselves getting into trouble. This trouble can range from having minor arguments with partners to ending up handcuffed in the back of a police car. Thus, for many people with BPD, part of their recovery must focus on slowing down their impulsivity. In this section, we offer the following four strategies to help you or someone you love control impulses:

- Putting time on your side
- Putting your impulses off
- Doing something different
- Fire drilling

Putting time on your side

People with BPD who act impulsively often regret their actions — eventually. Affairs, substance abuse, self-harm, and other risky behaviors usually have negative outcomes. But remorse comes the morning after, or at times, even later.

The following strategy takes advantage of these feelings of regret by bringing them to the surface *before* the impulsive action takes place. If you figure out how to slow down and consider the consequences of your impulsivity, you won't find yourself sliding down the slippery slope as often. We start by providing the instructions for how to use your regret to help manage your impulsivity, and then we give you a real-life example to clarify the technique.

Taking a moment to ask yourself some questions before you act is one way to help you bridle your emotional impulses. Write out the following questions on a piece of paper or small calendar, or input them into your cellphone or personal digital assistant (PDA). When you have a strong desire to engage in impulsive behavior, take a minute to look at these questions and think about your responses:

✔ How important is doing this action to me?

✔ If I go ahead and do this action now, how will I feel about it tomorrow?

✔ What are the long-term consequences if I continue this action?

✔ How will I feel tomorrow if I *don't* carry out this impulse right now?

This question-response strategy isn't always easy to implement. Obviously, impulsivity involves acting without thinking — and, not surprisingly, these questions require thinking. If you take the time to think before you act, many times you won't do something that can lead to long-term trouble. However, don't expect that the questions will just pop into your mind — we encourage you to write them down for a reason. If you have a habit of impulsivity, you need time and effort to break this habit.

The following story about Justin illustrates how asking these four questions helps him consider the consequences of his impulsive behavior. He isn't quite ready to commit to never smoking marijuana again, but the strategy plants the seed in his mind.

> **Justin**, a young adult with BPD, abuses marijuana. He often smokes in his garage after work. He is a licensed electrician and makes good money. He has a juvenile record for drug possession, but he's never been caught as an adult. He believes the marijuana helps him stay calm and control his anger. His employer conducts random drug tests, and Justin knows that

he can lose his job if he fails the drug test. He started therapy a couple of months ago after his boyfriend left him. His therapist suggests that he try answering some questions the next time he feels an urge to light up. The following answers are what he comes up with:

How important is doing this action to me?

Well, it feels important because it's something I want to do, and I'm not sure what else to do to stay calm if I don't smoke. But, I guess in terms of my life as a whole, it isn't all that important.

If I go ahead and do this action now, how will I feel about it tomorrow?

I know the answer to this one. I try not to think about tomorrow, but I know that every time I smoke, I feel guilty and stupid for having spent the money and taken the risks.

What are the long-term consequences if I continue this action?

I can lose my electrician's license in the blink of an eye. I can even go to jail. Ugh.

How will I feel tomorrow if I *don't* carry out this impulse right now?

That's an interesting question. I admit the few times I stopped myself, I felt pretty darn proud of myself. I didn't actually feel more tense or angry without the marijuana.

As Justin discusses these responses with his therapist, he expresses some interest in quitting marijuana for the first time. He tells his therapist that he appreciates her for not telling him to quit smoking and, instead, helping him see the problems smoking can and does cause in his life. Later he says he's interested in changing some of his other impulsive behaviors, too.

If you engage in impulsive behaviors, consider writing answers to these four questions about your own specific impulses. We aren't trying to make you quit, but you may find that discussing your answers with a therapist makes you think twice about giving in to every impulse.

Putting off your impulses

You may feel that you're not ready to stop your impulsive behaviors after trying the preceding strategy. Or, you may not be convinced that you can actually stop even if you do want to. No problem. We offer a second strategy for you to try out here.

This strategy involves experimenting with your impulsive behaviors. When you feel an urge to do something impulsive, such as shoplift or cut yourself, see what happens when you *delay* going through with the urge (see Chapter 5 for a full list of impulsive behaviors). For example, if you have an urge to drive recklessly, try to drive like everyone else for fifteen minutes first, and then see how you feel. Or, if you have an impulse to gamble, try waiting for a half hour or more before you go to a casino. Over time, lengthen these delays to an hour or even a day or two. Doing so can help you build up your ability to tolerate frustration and delay gratification — both of which are key elements of a healthy personality (see Chapter 2 for more on healthy versus unhealthy personalities). After some practice with delaying your impulses, you may discover that you don't miss your impulsivity as much as you thought you would.

Just because we don't tell you to stop engaging in potentially destructive behaviors immediately doesn't mean we give you permission or encourage you to continue to do them. We simply recognize that some people aren't ready or willing to stop these actions. In these cases, starting with delay tactics often helps bring people to the realization that stopping their impulsive behaviors is within their reach.

Doing something different

When you feel a strong desire to do something without thinking, doing something completely different from what your impulse tells you to do can help quell the urge. The best way to use distraction as a strategy is to plan ahead. What are some activities you like to do that keep your mind focused? Taking part in these activities can help prevent you from doing the impulsive act.

Everyone has a different list of distracting activities they enjoy. Here are a few examples of activities that can help focus your attention away from the impulsive act:

- Going for a walk or jog
- Watching a movie
- Knitting or crocheting
- Making a collage of how you're feeling (have some old magazines on hand)
- Going to the gym or exercising at home
- Reading a good novel
- Calling a friend
- Twittering or surfing the Internet
- Taking a hot bath
- Getting a massage at a spa
- Cleaning the house

Take some time to think about what activities you find interesting and attention grabbing. Be sure to include some activities that you can do on the spur of a moment. The most important aspect of this technique is to plan ahead so that you're ready with an alternative activity when your body tells you it's ready for an impulsive behavior.

Fire drilling

Fire drilling is a technique you can use to handle the emotional spikes that precede impulsive behavior. These upticks in emotions aren't always highly negative, and they're not always extremely intense. For instance, when you're experiencing boredom, you may impulsively seek excitement through sexual seduction, risky driving, or spending sprees. Other times, a positive event, such as receiving an unexpected bonus or a compliment from a friend, can trigger the desire for even more positive feelings and, in turn, can lead to the impulsive behaviors you think are necessary to obtain them.

 If extremely powerful and negative emotional outbursts typically trigger your impulsivity, we suggest that you take a look at Chapter 16 for ideas on how to deal with explosive emotions. After doing so, you can return to this chapter to find out more about inhibiting your impulses.

Fire drilling consists of taking the following steps:

1. **Make a list of coping self-statements that you can say to yourself instead of acting on your impulses (we discuss these statements in detail right after these steps).**

2. **Imagine situations that tend to trigger your impulses (see the "Increasing Your Awareness of Impulsive Behavior" section earlier in this chapter), and picture yourself using the coping self-statements rather than indulging in your impulses.**

3. **Replay these scenes in your mind over and over again.**

4. **Finish the scenes with some sort of self-congratulatory gesture, such as telling yourself what a great job you did.**

So, what is a *coping self-statement*? Coping self-statements are what you say to yourself to help you deal with emotions like boredom, cravings for excitement, or anxiety. Often these statements help remind you of the reasons you want to control your impulses rather than act on them. Here are a few examples of coping self-statements:

- ✔ I can always indulge in this impulse later, so why don't I delay it for awhile first?

- ✔ I may not like these urges, but they do go down when I give them enough time.

✔ I realize that my impulsiveness is hurting me; I just need to come up with a distraction (see the "Doing something different" section for some distracting activities).

✔ Each time I hold my impulses at bay, I am increasing my resolve and strength.

✔ I want to feel proud of my efforts instead of constantly feeling like I've messed up.

✔ Feelings don't have to be acted on.

✔ What feels good in the short run often feels terrible over the long haul.

✔ Just because I want something doesn't mean that I need it.

Go through this list and pick a coping self-statement or two that you think may help you increase your resolve. Or, make up one or more similar statements that have more meaning for you. Consider writing these statements down in a notebook or computer file for easy reference. Make a point at least three or four times each day to practice imagining yourself in a situation that makes you want to be impulsive and that allows you to use one of your coping self-statements.

Refer to the "Increasing Your Awareness of Impulsive Behavior" section earlier in this chapter to find out what situations trigger your impulsiveness. You can use those triggers in conjunction with the fire drilling technique to better prepare yourself to deal with your impulses.

When you imagine these triggering situations, make sure you also picture yourself using your coping self-statements over and over again. You may wish to use several of them at one time. Let your mind conjure up a scene of success in which you inhibit your impulse with one of your statements. Then tell yourself what a terrific job you did. Repeated practice of such scenes will likely enhance your self-control in the long run.

Seeking Healthier Alternatives

Risky and impulsive behaviors are often attempts to satisfy a need for excitement. That need, which psychologists call *sensation seeking,* is partly the result of a genetic predisposition. Some people are born with a strong desire for stimulation and thrills, while others prefer tamer and safer activities.

You may have heard the term *adrenaline junky* to describe a person with this tendency for excitement. People with BPD are much more likely than people without the disorder to exhibit this need for excitement, which is rooted in their genes and biology. So it makes sense that the impulsive behaviors most associated with BPD involve risk and sometimes danger.

If you experience this intense need for excitement, you may engage in activities that get you in trouble from time to time. You may also enjoy some of these activities so much that you don't want to give them up. The thought of boredom is worse than the risk you take to pursue the activity. Well, we're not asking you to lead a life of complete safety and dullness; we're simply asking you to look for ways to achieve excitement that don't involve risking your life or the lives of others.

Seeking healthier alternatives involves acknowledging the need for excitement and finding activities that satisfy this need. These healthier alternatives are different from your impulsive behaviors because they won't lead to jail time or trouble with others. These healthier sensation-seeking activities can involve playing on a softball team or hang gliding. Here are a few other examples of healthy alternatives to impulsive behavior:

✔ Rock climbing	✔ Rodeo riding
✔ Bungee jumping	✔ Following high-rope courses
✔ Sky diving	✔ Car racing
✔ White-water rafting	✔ Taking part in equestrian competitions
✔ Scuba diving	✔ Heli-skiing
✔ Backpacking	✔ Mountain climbing
✔ Mountain bike riding	✔ Participating in extreme sports
✔ Hot air ballooning	✔ Skateboarding
✔ Taking flying lessons	✔ Competing in adult sports teams
✔ Kayaking	✔ Adventure traveling
✔ Skiing	

Some of these activities are indeed a bit dangerous. Approach them with as much care and training as possible. Indulge in such endeavors using common sense. Hopefully, these activities can provide you a healthier outlet for your need for sensation and stimulation. Oh yeah, and how about wearing a helmet, too?

Not all people who crave excitement need to compete in sports or perform difficult physical feats to attain the sensation they're looking for. Some people find excitement in changing jobs or occupations, tackling a difficult project at home, playing competitive poker or bridge, debating politics with friends, watching the stock market go up and down, exploring unusual foods and spices, completing advanced degrees, day trading on the stock exchange, or even writing *For Dummies* books (did we really say that?). The point is you can find stimulation in many activities that aren't self-destructive.

Your sensation-seeking need isn't all bad — if you temper your need, you can appreciate it as a quality that makes you interesting.

Chapter 16

Calming the Storms Within

In This Chapter

▶ Taking a look at how feelings and thoughts relate to each other

▶ Discovering the truth about feelings

▶ Learning to relax using a variety of techniques

▶ Mastering meditation

▶ Accepting where you are and then moving on

Look up and imagine a colorful kite flying in the sky on a windy day. Blue sky, a few wisps of clouds, everything is peaceful and quiet, but suddenly a wind gust captures the kite. The kite twists out of control and crashes to the ground. The emotional lives of people with borderline personality disorder (BPD) look much like kites. At times, they soar high, but like a kite, they easily spin out of control and crash.

In this chapter, we tell you how to identify emotions and explore some myths about what they mean. After all, acknowledging and labeling emotions is the first step in quelling them. We present a few specific techniques you can use to contain and quell emotional storms. As with the other strategies we give you in this book, we recommend that people with BPD work with a mental health professional to carry them out.

Putting a Name Tag on Feelings

Many people have trouble identifying and owning up to their feelings. However, not noticing your emotional state at every moment is perfectly normal. Most of the time you don't actively think about how you feel unless you're extremely sad, angry, fearful, or happy. For example, has anyone ever said to you, "Why are you in a bad mood today?" and you respond, "I'm not in a bad mood," without really thinking?

Then a few minutes later, you realize you actually have been feeling irritable and a bit crabby (not that you'd admit it). Even so, your response wasn't a lie or an attempt to hide your feelings. You automatically denied the feeling because you weren't consciously aware of your bad mood.

Understanding the thought-feeling connection

So what's the big deal if you're not thinking about what you're feeling? Feelings are profound tools of communication — they keep people connected to each other, and this connection breeds life and love. Feelings provide motivation and advise caution. In essence, they tell us how to behave. For example,

- When people grieve, they tend to retreat.
- When people are afraid, they defend or run.
- When people are angry, they attack.
- When people are curious, they explore.
- When people are joyful, they celebrate.

Yet, although feelings do impact how you behave, they can also become overwhelming and unhelpful when they aren't balanced by your thoughts. Both thoughts and feelings should play a role in your behaviors because thoughts help modify feelings. When your feelings determine your actions without any input from your thoughts, your actions are unmodified by wisdom and may lead you into trouble.

Allison has BPD, but she has benefited greatly from a year of therapy. She has figured out how to identify her feelings and put a hold on her typical, reflexive tendency to let her feelings control her actions. The following story shows how Allison can now acknowledge her feelings without acting on them:

> Walking home from a restaurant at night, **Allison** sees a group of loud teenagers standing on the corner smoking and laughing. Her immediate emotional reaction is fear. Last year someone broke into her house, and she felt extremely vulnerable and violated. But Allison decides that acting confident is a better way to get by the kids. So she calmly and quickly walks by them, not making eye contact. She doesn't turn her head when one of the teens says something derogatory. Furious that she can't walk a few blocks home from a restaurant without being harassed, she really wants to turn around and yell at the teens. Even though she feels intense anger, she chooses to keep walking. Instead of letting her emotions control her, she uses her rational thoughts and common sense to avoid potential danger.

Allison experiences fear, but she doesn't act afraid. She believes that showing fear will encourage the teens to intensify their harassment of her. She feels anger, but she walks away, knowing that a confrontation won't change the situation and may be dangerous. What Allison demonstrates is called *emotional regulation*. She chooses how to express her emotions based on rational thought, not feelings.

Practicing emotional regulation

The ability to control feelings and change behaviors grows over time. For example, a toddler acts according to his feelings, not his thoughts. When a toddler is upset, he cries; when he's happy, he laughs; when he's angry, he throws a tantrum. As he matures, his emotional expressions become more complex — he doesn't cry every time he's upset — and he may whine or ask for help from his parents instead. He realizes that he has other options for displaying his feelings. If he develops normally, by the time he's in elementary school, he begins to think about how he feels and how to express himself. So, he may get angry at a playmate on the playground but refrain from hitting him. Or, he may feel hurt by someone's teasing, but he doesn't burst into tears.

Even as time passes, however, people with BPD generally don't master the art of emotional regulation. To find out more about the biological, psychological, and social reasons for this deficit, head to Chapter 4. Basically, emotions take charge and dictate the behavior of people with BPD because they have no idea how to modify feelings with thoughts. Emotions and thoughts aren't connected for them, and this disconnection interferes with their ability to temper feelings and control outbursts. Understandably, the emotional lives of most people with BPD are fraught with instability.

Feelings can be positive like happiness or negative like grief or a mixture of both, but they're not inherently good or bad from a moral standpoint.

If you have trouble noticing and describing what and how you feel, keep a daily log for a couple of weeks. Take a few moments three to five times a day to write down how you're feeling at that particular time. Notice the body sensations that accompany your feelings. Jot down your feelings, your physical sensations, the situation at the time of your note taking, and any thoughts you may have. Don't worry about your punctuation and grammar. Write quickly without thinking too much. If you're in therapy, discuss your results with your therapist.

You may also want to review Chapter 6 for more information about the relationship between emotions and BPD. We also provide various terms and words for describing your emotions in that chapter. Feel free to use those terms when you're jotting down your feelings.

Allowing Feelings to Trump Thoughts

Some people with BPD stay acutely tuned in to their feelings. Their attention is so focused on feelings that they may ignore or refute facts. They operate on the belief that feelings accurately indicate reality and must be true. So, under this premise, when you're angry, there must be something to be mad about. When you're jealous, your partner must be cheating on you. When you're afraid, something must be scary.

The problem with this way of thinking is that emotions and feelings often portray reality inaccurately. For people with BPD, negative feelings — whether the feelings are memories of abuse or feelings of emptiness — often spring from somewhere inside. These strong feelings distort the here and now. The following story about Jack demonstrates how intense feelings can cloud reality.

> **Jack** watches his wife, Sara, cut the red peppers for the salad. Their company will be arriving soon. Jack gets nervous whenever they have people over for dinner. He's starting to feel irritated with the way Sara's cutting the peppers. "Here, let me do that," he says as he brusquely takes the knife from her hand.
>
> Sara knows how Jack gets. She tries to avoid any conflict. "Go ahead," she says as she backs away, "I'll set the table."
>
> Jack begins to slash violently at the peppers. He misses and the knife gouges the countertop. Sara asks him whether he's okay. Saying nothing, Jack puts down the knife and leaves the room. Sara knows that he may not come down for dinner when their guests arrive.
>
> Jack doesn't know why he gets so upset whenever they have company. He feels incredibly anxious and irritated. He often retreats and leaves Sara to make excuses. Over the course of their marriage, Sara finds that having people over isn't worth the emotional cost.
>
> Jack's father was emotionally abusive. Growing up, every dinner included brutal humiliation and cruel criticism. Jack doesn't yet understand that his feelings about present-day meals reflect the terror he has of his own father.

Jack experienced repeated emotional abuse as a child. His strong emotions are understandable. However, because his negative feelings spill over into the present, they're confusing to other people. Without help, Jack will likely lose the people he cares about the most.

Just because you feel a certain way doesn't make that feeling true. Reality and feelings don't always match up. If you have BPD, you probably have intense emotions that confuse and distort the truth. The next sections offer strategies that can help you control these intense emotions.

Relaxing and Practicing

Frequent, intensely negative emotions take a toll on your body because each time you feel a strong negative emotion, your body prepares for danger and gets ready to run or fight. People with BPD report more negative emotions and fewer positive emotions than most other people do (see Chapter 6 for more information about these negative emotions). These highly negative emotions are stressful and increase the risks for the following health issues:

- ✔ High blood pressure
- ✔ Chronic headaches
- ✔ Muscle aches
- ✔ Type 2 diabetes
- ✔ Back pain
- ✔ Irritable bowel syndrome
- ✔ Acid reflux
- ✔ Depressed immune system
- ✔ Heart disease
- ✔ Stroke

The simple motivation behind controlling emotions by discovering how to relax is based on a biological truth: You can't be both relaxed and frantic at the same time. When you're in a state of relaxation, your body slows down, your heart rate decreases, your muscles relax, and you have time to reflect. Therefore, relaxation helps people gain control over their emotions. In the next sections, we describe several ideas and methods for relaxation.

Making muscles relax

Progressive muscle relaxation has been around since the late 1930s when physician Edmund Jacobsen first wrote about the procedure. Basically, the technique involves tightening a group of muscles and then letting go of the tension. You're supposed to pay attention to the group of muscles you're tensing and then notice how they feel when you release the tension. Almost anyone can benefit from this simple technique. Of course, if you have back problems, arthritis, muscular pain, or have been injured, check with your medical provider before attempting this technique.

Getting ready to relax

If you're considering this muscle relaxation technique, keep the following tips in mind:

- ✔ Find a quiet place and turn off your cellphone.
- ✔ Don't use mind-altering substances.
- ✔ Don't have a full stomach.
- ✔ Wear loose-fitting clothing.
- ✔ Wear socks if your feet tend to get cold.
- ✔ Try to consciously keep your face relaxed.
- ✔ If you experience pain when you tense your muscles, stop.
- ✔ When you release your muscles, focus on the relaxed feeling.
- ✔ If you feel very anxious during this exercise, stop.
- ✔ Don't worry if you fall asleep; just resume when you wake up.
- ✔ Don't expect to be perfect; after all, this technique is supposed to be relaxing.
- ✔ Expect the process to take some time to master.

Full progressive muscle relaxation

You can begin with full progressive muscle relaxation. Although you don't need to follow the directions in this section exactly, they can help you get started. After you practice a few times, you'll be able to use progressive muscle relaxation without a script.

If you choose to use this technique to help you gain control of your strong emotions, you should practice it every day for at least a week or more. After you've practiced several times, you can work on a shorter version; and eventually you'll be able to relax your muscles willfully without any formal procedures at all.

To begin full progressive muscle relaxation, follow these steps:

1. **Get comfortable and take a few breaths. Inhale deeply through your nose. Hold your breath for a few seconds; then slowly exhale.**

   Each time we suggest tensing your muscles, hold the tension for 10 seconds or so. When we suggest letting go of the tension and relaxing, focus on the relaxation for 10 or 15 seconds. But don't get uptight about the exact time, and don't use a stopwatch!

2. **Start with your feet. Curl your toes; tense all the muscles in your feet. Now relax. Concentrate on the feeling of relaxation in your feet.**

3. Moving up, tighten your calves by pushing down on your heels and pointing your toes up to your face. Watch out for muscle cramps, and stop if you experience any pain. Release; feel the tension from your calves flow out.

4. Squeeze your thighs. Hold and release.

5. Tighten up the buttocks. Stay focused. Relax and notice the relief.

6. Pull in your abdomen. Imagine your belly button touching your spine. Tighten; then release. Feel the tension flow away.

7. Make fists and squeeze. Release. Notice the feeling.

8. Tighten your arm muscles. Push your upper arms close to your body. Hold your forearms out as though you're holding something in front of you. Use all your strength; now let your arms collapse, releasing stress.

9. To relax your shoulders, you need to use two separate movements. First, raise your shoulders up and try to touch your ears. Hold and release. Next pull your shoulder blades back and stick out your chest. Think about your shoulders meeting behind you. Then relax.

10. Be careful with your neck, don't push too hard and don't try this if you have whiplash or any type of neck injury. Push your neck down to your chest. Hold and relax. Now take it to one side. Tilt your ear toward one shoulder; hold and release. Now follow the same movement on the other side — ear to shoulder. Finally, gently pull your head back toward your back, and then release.

11. Now for the face. Scrunch up — squeeze your forehead, mouth, tongue, and lips. Relax.

12. With your eyes closed, imagine going through an inventory of your muscles. If you still feel tension in any area, repeat the muscle tension-and-release cycle. Spend a few minutes breathing and feeling relaxed.

 Many people feel tension in their shoulders, back, or neck. Feel free to modify or increase the number of times you tense and release those areas. You may also want to tense and relax an area in your body several times a day as an instant stress reducer.

Shortened muscle relaxation

After you've practiced the muscle relaxation as depicted in the preceding section, try putting groups of muscles together. See whether you can achieve relaxation by using the following technique.

1. Get comfortable and take a few deep breaths.

2. Tighten all the muscles from your waist down. Squeeze your buttocks, curl your toes, and tighten your thighs. Hold that tension for about ten seconds; then relax.

3. **Pull in your abdomen and try to push your back into the floor (or chair). Hold and then release, feeling the tension flow away from you.**

4. **Press your arms into your body, squeeze your hands, and push your shoulders up to your ears. When you relax, imagine waves of warm water gently washing over you.**

5. **Squeeze the muscles in your face — grin, grimace, and squint. Keep the muscles tight and then relax.**

6. **Stay focused on your body. Are there areas of tension? If so, tense and release the muscles in those areas. Breathe and enjoy. Notice how your body feels.**

If you achieve a relaxed state using the shortened relaxation technique, you may be ready to imagine your body relaxing without actually tensing any muscles. The idea is to practice the longer versions of muscle relaxation until you're pretty familiar with how being physically relaxed feels. Your body remembers the experience of being relaxed, and, with enough practice, this memory can enable you to relax at will.

A more mental kind of muscle relaxation

When you're ready to move on to relaxing your muscles without physically tensing them up, try the following technique. These steps can help your muscles stay loose and relaxed:

1. **Close your eyes and take a long deep breath.**

2. **Attend to the top of your head. Relax and let all the tension go from your mind.**

3. **Slowly move your attention down your body, through your head. Think about your neck and shoulders. Relax the muscles.**

4. **Move down through your arms and your abdomen. Breath and relax.**

5. **Now continue down. Release any tension.**

6. **Decide to be calm and quiet.**

Hypnotizing yourself into relaxation

You can use your mind to relax your body, too. And you don't need to pay for a hypnotist to achieve this state. Instead, you can use the *autogenic* method (which means produced from within). This method is based on the power of suggestion and was developed by German neuropsychiatrist Johannes Shultz in the 1930s. Like progressive muscle relaxation, which we describe in the preceding section, this technique has many renditions.

First, you need a quiet place in which to practice this technique. Most people use the autogenic method lying down. However, if you have a really comfortable chair, you can use it. Make sure that you're wearing loose-fitting clothing and that you won't be interrupted. We recommend that you practice this exercise about three times a day for a week or two.

Don't try too hard to relax. Too much effort defeats the purpose. Let yourself experience the soothing suggestions of autogenic training. Try to feel warm and quiet, and follow these steps:

1. **Start by making sure that you're in a comfortable position. Take a few slow, deep breaths.**

2. **Imagine that your arms and legs are starting to feel heavy.**

   They're getting so heavy that you can't move them. Your arms are heavy; now your hands are heavy. Your legs feel like they may sink into the ground. Your feet are getting heavy, too. The heaviness is beginning to pull away all the stress from your body. The words keep coming . . . heavy . . . heavy . . . heavy. Your arms and hands are heavy. Your legs and feet are heavy. You are still. Keep focusing on how heavy you feel. You are calm. As you remain still, the worries are slipping away from your body.

3. **Imagine that the sun is shining brightly and warming your body.**

   Your arms are getting pleasantly warm. Your hands begin to feel warm. A warm blanket surrounds you. Your legs are starting to feel warm. Now imagine a pond with warm water. You decide to sink into the water. The gentle current brushes against you. The water is warm and melts away the tensions in your body. You are warm and still. The water swirls and warms your body. You feel slow and steady, peaceful and calm. Relaxed. Feel the comfort of the sun and the warm, gentle water. No need to move, nothing to do — except to enjoy the feeling.

4. **Place a hand over your heart.**

   Your heart beats strong and steady. You have nothing to do. Your heart beat is regular, beating steady. Nothing to do. Your heart beats like a steady, regular drum. Strong . . . steady . . . strong . . . steady . . . feel yourself relax. Tension fades . . . let go of worries . . . warm, secure, calm, peaceful.

5. **Now relax. Close your eyes. Think about your breathing.**

   Don't use any effort. Just let yourself breathe. Allow your body to take charge. Breathe slow and steady. Enjoy the feeling of quiet. Serene, calm, easy. In and out, slow and steady, smooth. Each breath brings peace and calm. In and out, slow and easy.

You can change autogenic training to fit your own imagination. For example, you can take yourself on an imaginary journey to the beach or a quiet mountain setting rather than into a warm pond. Keep in mind that the basic principles are focusing on feeling heavy and warm and concentrating on slow and steady breathing.

Soothing through the senses

Listening to classical music soothes and relaxes some people. Others, on the other hand, find sitting through a symphony torturous. A hot bath for some brings peace and calm; others find sitting in the bathtub boring. Although aromatherapy makes some people sneeze, others feel calmed by certain smells.

We encourage you to sort through the following activities to find a few that you can use to relax. If you have BPD, make a list of five to ten activities that you can easily do to help you calm down. Having a list will help you remember to do one of your soothing activities when you find yourself overwhelmed by emotions.

Write your list on a few index cards. Post one card at home in a place where you will notice it (on your bathroom mirror, for example), another in your car, and another at work. Try to pick at least one activity that you can do in most of the places you find yourself in. For instance, you probably can't sit in a hot tub while driving, but you can have a CD of calming music in your car. You probably can't start a campfire at work, but maybe you can have a cup of tea. Here are some of our suggestions for relaxing activities (but don't limit yourself to our ideas — feel free to come up with some of your own):

- ✔ **Sound:** Whether you choose jazz, classical, rock and roll, or hip hop, pick a music that often puts you in a better place. You can also try out recordings of nature sounds or quiet music. For example, you may enjoy the sound of water flowing. To use that sound to calm you down, you can find a CD with water sounds on it, or you can buy or even make a personal indoor fountain. Sound machines can also be soothing. Depending on where you live, you may enjoy going outside and listening to the wind, traffic, birds, or the ocean.

- ✔ **Sight:** Look outside, find a park, watch animals play, go to a museum, look at a beloved photo album, look at an aquarium, watch a waterfall, watch a campfire or fireplace, look at the ocean or a lake. If you don't live near the ocean or a waterfall or any other part of nature that soothes you, buy a book with pictures of that piece of nature and look through it when you feel overwhelmed with emotions.

✔ **Smell:** Light a candle, bake some cookies, smell flowers, burn incense, try aromatherapy, put on a little perfume, or take a walk in the mall near the cinnamon buns shop.

✔ **Taste:** Savor a hot cup of coffee, a small piece of chocolate, a cold glass of ice water, a piece of toast with jelly, some green chili stew (the hotter, the better), a cup of chicken noodle soup, or a bowl of ice cream. Sip a glass of wine, milk, or chamomile tea — whatever calms you.

If you have any issues with substance abuse, a glass of wine is a very bad strategy for relaxing. A single glass of wine is fine, but if having one glass leads you to want more, don't go there. The same principle applies to ice cream if you have an eating disorder.

✔ **Touch:** Get a massage or a hug from someone you care about, pet your dog or cat, sit in a hot tub, wear your favorite sweats, crawl into bed and pull all the covers up.

You can also calm your emotional state by radically changing your body temperature. You can accomplish this change with a hot bath or a sauna. Or, you can do so in a very surprising way — by immersing your face in a sink of ice water! Yes, you read that correctly. Dipping your face into ice water while you hold your breath for 15 or 20 seconds triggers your body to change its metabolic rate, which causes your mood to shift along with it. This technique is especially effective for severe emotional distress, and it isn't nearly as unpleasant as you may think. We've even tried it ourselves. You may need to immerse your face two or three times to get the full effect of this strategy.

After you make your list of relaxing activities, don't wait for overwhelming emotions to try one out. Like the Boy Scouts say, be prepared. Practicing relaxation now can help you get ready for times when you truly are stressed. Practice provides you with the knowledge of what your body feels like when it's relaxed. And knowing what being relaxed feels like can help you calm your body and mind down when you feel tense.

Discovering Meditation

Like an untethered kite caught by a sudden shift of wind, your emotions likely swing widely with little provocation if you have BPD. Your emotions soar sky-high quickly and crash unexpectedly. The idea of controlling emotions through meditation may seem difficult, if not impossible, but don't shut the book just yet.

Meditation helps quell emotional storms. With practice, the mind can become a place of peace and contentment. A balanced mind is steady and able to accept daily challenges. Meditation helps stabilize the unbalanced mind.

For meditation to work, frequent practice is necessary. No set rules or guidelines exist for how many times you should meditate, but once a day for about five minutes is a good start. The goal is to become regular about meditation. After you start practicing meditation, extending the five minutes is a good idea. How much time you devote, though, is up to you. Many people discover that they really enjoy meditating for 30 minutes to an hour every day. Here are a few hints for acquiring the meditation habit:

- ✔ **Wear comfortable, loose clothing.** No special attire is necessary (just don't wear skintight jeans).

- ✔ **Turn off your cellphones, pagers, telephones, and so on.** Don't watch TV or use your computer — doing so just won't do. You can listen to quiet music if you want to.

- ✔ **Meditate wherever you want to.** Outside is great (although perhaps not so easily done in the middle of Fifth Avenue in New York City). If you want, set up a special place in your home; you may want to have a candle, a special picture, a painting, some objects with spiritual significance, or a photograph to look at.

- ✔ **Sit on a mat — called a *zabuton* — or a pillow.** Some people also use wood bricks, blankets, or a small pillow called a *zafu* to make sitting more comfortable. You can also sit on a chair or couch. The important part is to sit up straight.

- ✔ **Sit still.** You can sit in several different positions. For example, you can sit with your legs crossed and your hands resting on your knees, palms up. Or, you can sit with your heels pressed against each other. You can also just sit comfortably the way you usually do. At first, maintaining one position for a long time may be hard for you to do, which is why practice helps. Also, consider taking a class in either meditation or yoga for help in finding the right position for you.

- ✔ **Start by noticing your breathing.** You can close your eyes or leave them open. Try not to focus on anything but your breathing. Let thoughts come and go.

You have many forms of meditation to choose from. We briefly discuss breathing meditation, walking meditation, guided meditation, and candle meditation here.

- ✔ **Breathing meditation:** Be still — keep your eyes partially opened or closed. Direct your attention to your breathing. As you breathe in through your nose, be aware of the flow of air. The air flows softly through your nostrils into your lungs, then deeper until the air pushes out the abdomen. Place one hand on the abdomen to feel the air fill it up; then pull those muscles tighter to push the air out. Breathe deeply, and concentrate on the sensation of breathing. Focus on the air going in and the air going out. If your mind begins to wander, bring it back to your breathing. Stay with this meditation until your mind quiets.

✔ **Walking meditation:** Take a slow walk on a nice day. Don't go to a crowded mall. Take a few deep breaths before you start. Notice your body moving. Focus on your legs. How do the muscles in your calves, ankles, and thighs move so effectively to propel your body through space. Think of the magic of movement. Stay focused on your legs, body, and feet. If other thoughts come to your mind, let them go. Return to thinking about walking. Concentrate on the pace of your stride, the rhythm of your breathing. Focus on the noise of your feet falling. Keep a steady and focused walk. Pay attention to the feelings in your body — the temperature, your breathing, your muscles. Walk like this for ten minutes or more.

✔ **Guided meditation:** This type of meditation involves imagination or the use of words or phrases to transform and heal. You can choose from many varieties of guided meditation. You can download scripts for free from various Web sites on the Internet. (For example, www.how-to-meditate.org, www.wikihow.com/meditate, and www.meditate.com provide a lot of insight into this type of meditation.) Or, you can make up your own guided meditation. Here are a couple of suggestions:

  • Breathing in, I calm my body; breathing out, I relax.

  • Feeling peace, I breathe in; feeling joy, I breathe out.

✔ **Candle meditation:** Watching the flame of a candle while breathing deeply is another form of meditation. Sit quietly and focus all your attention on the flame. See the different colors of the fire; watch the flame twist and turn. Stay focused for five or ten minutes.

Experiment with various meditation practices. Don't expect a quick result. The benefits of meditation may not be obvious for some time. But, the subtle changes in your mind, emotions, and body can be very healing. The following story about Grace, who uses meditation to help her maintain emotional balance, depicts how healing this practice can be.

Grace wanders into the lunch room at work. A couple of her co-workers are sitting at another table laughing. When Grace walks in, they notice her and stop laughing. Grace asks, "Did I interrupt a private conversation?"

"No, we were gossiping and laughing about you," one of the women jokes. Grace feels her face flush and starts to get angry. "Just kidding, Grace," says one of her co-workers. "We weren't talking about you at all. You take everything so personally. Get over it."

Grace turns and leaves the lunch room. She goes back to her office and closes the door. Grace has been in therapy for about six months because of BPD. Learning to control her anger has been a focus of her work in therapy. She feels pretty good that she walked away from the lunch room. She realizes that even a couple of months ago she would've reacted to those women with an explosive tirade. Now, she sits at her desk and closes her eyes. She takes a few deep breaths and starts to feel her body relax. After a couple of minutes, she feels a deep peace and joy. Grace returns to the lunch room and apologizes to her co-workers.

Grace's story typifies most people's experience with meditation. Meditation is neither magic nor a quickly acquired skill. However, with practice, it can help you gain a measure of control over your emotions that you didn't have before. And there's no real limit to how far meditation can take you. Grace may eventually become so skilled at meditation that she's able to cut her reflexive anger off before it even hits her. Check out *Meditation For Dummies,* 2nd Edition, by Stephan Bodian and Dean Ornish (Wiley), for more information.

Acquiring Acceptance

What we're about to tell you may sound a little strange, but bear with us. If you have BPD, you've probably spent a lot of time fighting against what your BPD drives you to do, such as your

- ✔ Emotional outbursts
- ✔ Impulses
- ✔ Temper
- ✔ Desire to drink or take drugs

Indeed, you likely view your BPD symptoms as completely abhorrent and unacceptable. Yet, in spite of your best efforts, you feel trapped by the stranglehold these problems have on you.

What you probably don't realize is that you've been fighting too hard. What? Are we suggesting that you give up your struggles and simply accept all your problems? Not exactly.

Consider that your experience with BPD is much like getting caught in a riptide. Riptides are narrow bands of water that generally flow powerfully away from where you want to be (the safety of the shore). Even accomplished swimmers who attempt to swim against a riptide can drown. Experts strongly advise people who get caught in riptides not to swim directly against the flow of the tide. Rather, they recommend that swimmers in this predicament "accept" that they're ensnared by the riptide and swim parallel to the currents until they abate. After the flow subsides, they can safely swim to shore.

Similarly, escaping the currents of your BPD requires that you first accept where you're at — which means you need to stop impugning, punishing, and pummeling yourself simply because you have BPD. No one asks to have disorders like BPD, and many forces outside of your control contribute to your acquiring this disorder (see Chapter 4 for examples). As you gradually accept where you are now, you can find more energy for moving to a better place.

We offer you two major strategies for finding an accepting state of mind. As you practice the following two skills, you're likely to find yourself swimming slowly toward the shore, away from where BPD wants to take you:

✔ Discovering your observant mind

✔ Playing with your judgmental mind

Discovering your observant mind

The human brain is a remarkable organ. Humans have used their brains to create language and explore the mysteries of the universe from the level of the cosmos to that of the subatomic. The brain also evaluates and judges most everything it perceives.

All too often, those evaluations are negative, disturbing, and upsetting. In truth, most people probably engage in such harsh judging more than necessary, but people with BPD take this habit to extremes.

People with BPD are no less intelligent than other people. But they do make excessive use of the judging, evaluative part of their brains, which increases their negative thoughts. For example, a brilliant physician with BPD cares deeply about the health of his patients, but he judges them harshly for their unhealthy lifestyles. If he didn't judge and evaluate so much, he could more successfully influence his patients with gentle understanding.

One way out of this dilemma is to foster awareness and development of what is called the *observant mind.* To find your own observant mind, close your eyes for a few minutes. While your eyes are closed, notice when a thought enters your mind. It may take a few seconds or a few minutes, but we're pretty sure a thought will come in — even if the thought is simply, "I wonder when a thought is going to come into my mind" or "This feels stupid and boring."

After you notice the thought, open your eyes. Ask yourself who noticed the thought. Clearly, you are not your thoughts. Rather, an observant part of your mind notices what's going on inside of you without offering up a judgment or evaluation. Your thought may have entailed a judgment, but your *observation* of the thought was merely that — an observation.

When we travel, we enjoy combining a little work with leisure. We lug our computers around and dedicate portions of our trip to writing. Writing away from home gives us a different perspective — and at times, it can be surprisingly productive. Today is a writing day. We took a long walk and asked that the maids at our hotel clean our room while we were out. But, when we came back, the maids were still in our room.

So as not to waste a single moment, allow us to show you the difference between the evaluative or critical mind and the observant mind in terms of our experience at the hotel.

✔ **Critical mind:** We're forced to wait outside because the hotel didn't get someone to clean our room the minute we asked. Our computers are locked up in the room. We have nothing to do. It feels a little too warm out here. Trains and traffic are rumbling obnoxiously in the distance. You can barely hear the ocean. How are we ever going to get this book done on time? This is awful. Yellow leaves are on the vines, and dead leaves lie scattered around the patio. Disgustingly skinny people swimming in the pool remind us of the French fries we ate at lunch.

✔ **Observant mind:** We're sitting outside. The temperature is about 75 degrees Fahrenheit. The sun is shining, and the sky is bright blue. You can see the ocean across the lawn. Purple, red, pink, white, and blue flowers surround us. A trellis supports a green vine with some yellow leaves. The breeze blows a few dead leaves across the patio. Hotel maintenance workers rumble by with their carts clattering on the cobblestones. A train whistle pierces the quiet. In the distance, a few cars go by.

We're cheating a bit. We happen to be in Santa Barbara, California, in the middle of winter. We could easily have made the observant mind's scene idyllic because the setting in Santa Barbara is so strikingly beautiful. However, the observant mind merely describes what is. By contrast, the critical mind judges and typically does so harshly. When we rely solely on our critical minds, we can make ourselves miserable just about anywhere — even in Santa Barbara!

The observant mind accepts whatever is around you and merely describes what's there. The more you use your observant mind and accept what's going on around you and inside of you, the less distressed you're likely to be.

Try thinking back on a time when you felt upset. Write down all the critical, evaluative thoughts that generated your distress. Then, rewrite your story while refraining from making any judgments whatsoever. Focus on describing events and scenes from a detached, neutral perspective.

To give you an idea of the disparity between these two parts of your mind, notice the difference between the following critical mind–generated thoughts versus the observant mind's descriptions of the same scenes in Sharon's story.

The bank teller returns the check to **Sharon** and says, "I'm sorry, Miss. This check is from an out-of-state bank. We can deposit it, but the funds won't be available for five business days."

Sharon, who has been banking at this branch for six years, asks the teller, "Would you check that out with your manager? I've cashed checks in this amount from this bank before."

Sharon's critical mind: That little twit, how dare she! I can't believe this is happening to me. What does she think? That I'm trying to steal money from this frigging bank? I can't believe she has the nerve. That's it, I'm going to take my money and find a bank that will respect me.

Sharon's observant mind: Well, this has never happened before. I wonder whether my bank implemented a new policy. Perhaps the manager that I know is working today. I'm sure that I can show someone that I have enough in my account to cover the check. If not, I suppose I can wait a few days for the money.

How does Sharon feel when she's using her critical mind? Probably quite angry. However, when she stays in her observant mind, she remains calm for the most part. Perhaps she feels a tad inconvenienced but certainly not full of rage.

Having an observant mind doesn't rid you of all distressing feelings. However, it does help you reduce the stranglehold those feelings have on you by allowing you to accept what is rather than making things worse by judging your feelings. Paradoxically, giving yourself permission to have negative feelings softens their overall impact.

Playing with your judgmental mind

Yet another strategy for dealing with your mind's tendency to generate harsh, judgmental thoughts is to take a playful approach. Psychologists know that completely stopping negative thoughts is almost impossible. In fact, research shows that when you try to suppress such thinking, the negative thoughts boomerang on you and increase in intensity.

However, you can make great headway in reducing the emotional impact of your self-denigrating thoughts by figuring out how to relate to them differently. We recommend that you try two strategies for taking your negative thinking less seriously — thanking your mind and putting your thoughts to music.

Thanking your mind

Thanking your mind entails using the power of sarcasm to diffuse the emotional turmoil that negative thinking causes. When you hear harsh, critical thoughts running through your mind, you literally thank your mind for being so helpful. Here are some examples of negative thoughts and ways you can respond to thank your mind for producing them:

> **Negative thought:** I'm hopeless.
>
> **Sarcastic, thankful thought:** Thank you, mind; that was such a helpful thought.
>
> **Negative thought:** I'm a mean, hateful person.
>
> **Sarcastic, thankful thought:** That was a creative thing to say. Thanks so much for the help, mind.
>
> **Negative thought:** I'll never be happy.
>
> **Sarcastic, thankful thought:** What a fantastic prediction for my future! How can I ever thank you enough, mind?

The thanking-your-mind technique may seem a little silly at first. But, in a way, silliness is the point. Using this strategy can help you relate to your thoughts differently. With practice, you'll see that thoughts are truly just thoughts and don't reflect reality straight up. Thanking your mind is yet another way of cooling the emotional fires caused by hot thoughts.

Putting your thoughts to music

The next time you find yourself ruminating about how awful you are, how your life sucks, or how poorly people treat you, try singing your thoughts to the tune of a song. Almost any song will do so long as it doesn't have a down-cast spirit. We find nursery rhymes, Christmas carols, and pop hits especially useful. Singing your thoughts out loud to upbeat tunes changes the meaning of your thoughts.

Chapter 17

Creating an Identity

. . . .

In This Chapter

▶ Discovering your values

▶ Developing a personal mission statement

▶ Appreciating forgiveness of yourself and others

. . . .

People with borderline personality disorder (BPD) wake up one morning and find themselves intensely enthusiastic about a person, a job, a political idea, a project, or a religion. Their passion is contagious, and others often join in with eagerness. Then, without warning, they reject or lose interest in their previous passions. Their fleeting interests and fickle loyalties leave them feeling fragmented and disjointed, and they confuse the people around them, especially those who shared their passions.

When pressed to think about their values, goals, and beliefs, people with BPD often become uneasy and disoriented. They can't put their ideals or principles into words. The slightest nudge by a new person or a new idea can shift their focus completely. Thus, they may have trouble developing a consistent identity or sense of who they are. Their lives are often full of discarded friends, relationships, and interests.

In Chapter 7, we describe in greater detail the problems with unstable identities that people with BPD often experience. In this chapter, we give you ideas about how to work on obtaining a more stable sense of self. We provide strategies for identifying your values and then show you how to use those values to write a life mission statement. To facilitate this process of living by a new life mission, we lay out a plan for letting go of blame and rage and finding forgiveness.

Clarifying What's Important in Your Life

Remember when you were a child and it seemed like forever until summer vacation or your birthday or the next holiday? If you're like most people, the older you get the faster time seems to speed by. You probably don't have a lot of extra time to reflect on life's purpose — after all, most people struggle just to go about the daily business of living.

However, taking a bit of time to step back and think about what your life is about and how you want to live it can be useful and, occasionally, life changing. Whether you have BPD or not, figuring out what's most important can help you form goals for the future, which, in turn, can help you stop struggling from moment to moment.

Thinking about the big picture can be fairly overwhelming to people with BPD, so we encourage people with BPD to work on the exercises we present in this section with a therapist — and to do so gradually over time.

Finding your personal priorities

To clarify what you value, you must think about what you want out of your life. You have several big matters to consider. Some of the topics we describe in this section may not interest you, and others may not be relevant or possible in your life. You don't have to answer all the questions we ask here, but the list of personal priorities following our numbered instructions gives you some subjects to think about.

Consider writing out your thoughts and answers to our questions in a notebook or computer file. Writing down your thoughts helps clarify thinking and will be useful when you want to develop your personal mission statement. If you're working with a therapist, having a document to refer back to in later sessions can be helpful. The following steps can help you start looking at what's most important in your life:

1. **Write each bold word or phrase from the following list of personal priorities in your notebook.**

2. **Ponder the questions that follow each bold word or phrase.**

3. **Write down your answers. If a specific category is unimportant or irrelevant to you, skip it or write N/A for not applicable.**

4. **Circle the five values that you feel are most important to you.**

5. **Then pare your choices down to the three values you want to focus on first. Underline them.**

Here's the list of personal priorities to choose from:

✔ **Charity:** What does charity mean to you? Is charity a part of your life? How do you want to change your life in relation to charity? Do you spend as much time helping others as you'd like? How can you be more charitable with yourself?

✔ **Environment:** Do you value conservation? Do you want to leave the world a better place than when you found it by minimizing your carbon footstep? Do you recycle? Do you take time to appreciate and enjoy nature? How do you see yourself in relation to living creatures and plants?

✔ **Work:** How do you define work? Does work give you meaning? What can you do to change your work life? Are you satisfied at work? Do you support yourself? Is your work helping others?

✔ **Spirituality:** What, if any, are your spiritual beliefs? Do these beliefs give you comfort? How do these beliefs impact the way you live your life? Are you living a life that is compatible with your spirituality? What changes do you want to make to your life to make it more compatible with your spiritual beliefs? How can you make those changes?

✔ **Community:** Who are the people in your community? Do you contribute to your community? Do you take away from your community? What does being a member of your community mean? Do you think taking part in politics is important? Do you want to make changes based on these thoughts?

✔ **Intimate relationships:** Whom are you close to? Have you lost relationships because of BPD? How do you show concern for the people you care about? Do your close relationships help you or hurt you?

✔ **Family:** Define family for yourself. Who is your family? Are you holding onto anger about your childhood? What does being a family member mean to you?

✔ **Friends:** Do you have friends? Do you value friendship? What changes do you want to make in your life when you think about your friendships?

✔ **Creativity:** What is creativity to you? Do you have ways in which you can express your creative power? Are you satisfied with the place creativity has in your life?

✔ **Intellectual goals:** What value do you place on life-long learning? Are you giving yourself credit for learning to help yourself with BPD? Are you taking advantage of opportunities that evolve? What do you want to do differently now that you've thought about learning?

✔ **Recreation and entertainment:** What do you like to do for fun? Do you spend enough time doing things you enjoy? Are hobbies important to you? Do you value recreation for the positive effects it can have on your mood and your life?

✔ **Possessions:** Are possessions important to you? Do you have all you want? Do you have all you need?

✔ **Finances:** Are you comfortable with your finances? Do you have problems with overspending? Are you saving for the future? Do you have needs that aren't being met financially? Can you do something now or in the near future to help your situation?

✔ **Health:** How is your health? Is it important to you? Do you spend time fostering good health? Do you exercise and eat right?

✔ **Appearance:** Do you like the way you look? How important is appearance to you? Is the appearance of your friends important to you?

✔ **You:** What do you like about yourself? Do you want to accept yourself? Do you value honesty? What do you dislike about yourself? Do you blame yourself for all your problems and struggles? Is recognition or success critical to your happiness? Do you feel being right is important?

Try not to beat yourself up if you notice that you're not living in a way that matches what you value most. Whether you have BPD or not, only a few saints live fully and always in ways consistent with their values.

After you've reviewed your values and decided which three feel the most important to you, you're ready for the next step — writing out a personal life mission statement.

Creating a personal life mission statement

Businesses create mission statements to capture the essence of their organizations' purposes, goals, and directions. Doing so helps executives keep track of whether their company is staying on the right path or deviating from its primary mission. A mission statement also helps consumers understand the purpose and values of a particular business and its products.

Creating a personal life mission statement accomplishes similar goals for you in your life. Having such a statement can help you know whether you're going where you want to go or investing considerable time in activities that deviate from your priorities.

Preparing to create your statement

Here are some tips to keep in mind when you're preparing to create your life mission statement:

✔ **Think small, not globally.** For example, you don't want to promise to eliminate global hunger. Nice thought, perhaps, but it's pretty hard for one person to do in a lifetime! Instead, you can consider volunteering at a food bank once a week.

✔ **Try to include ideas that you can enact in small ways most days.** For example, you may have identified a value of being more charitable. You can include in your mission statement that you want to contribute a small amount of time most days to either doing nice things for people or helping others in some manner.

✔ **Focus on specific, positive actions instead of saying what you won't do.** For example, you don't want to say that you'll never rage again. Instead, vow to compliment others and practice emotional regulation skills (see Chapter 16 for ways to regulate your emotions).

✔ **Make your mission statement short and doable.** Usually a paragraph or so in length is dandy. Try not to cover too much ground; remember that you can always revise and add items over the years.

✔ **Focus on changes you'd like to make in your life.** These changes typically involve things you'd like to do more of.

✔ **Change your mission statement if and when it doesn't quite feel right.** With the passage of time, you may have something you wish to add to or remove from your list. After all, values can and do change.

Putting your statement on paper

You can't write your life mission statement without thought, effort, and time. You may write several drafts before you're happy with your statement. Feel free to ask for feedback from your therapist or a close, trusted friend you've known for quite awhile. To put your mission statement on paper, follow these steps:

1. **Start by reviewing your three most highly rated core values.**

2. **Consider filling in the blanks for statements similar to the ones in the following list to create your life mission statement:**

   Because I value _____, I plan to _____.

   I will _____ in order to _____.

   I will become more _____ by _____.

   I will improve _____ by _____.

   I commit to strengthening _____ by _____.

   I dedicate my life to _____ by _____.

3. **Be sure to cover each of your three core values in some way, but keep the actions small and achievable.**

Sampling two life mission statements

When you're designing a life mission statement, seeing what other people have done helps. The following story about Diana demonstrates how an initial mission statement can reflect values that are in a state of flux.

Diana, a talented dancer in her mid-twenties, loses her job at a local musical theater. Her boss fires her because she missed too much work and argued incessantly with other cast members. She's briefly hospitalized after an overdose of prescription medicine. While in the hospital, she's diagnosed with BPD and is referred to a partial hospitalization program (see Chapter 11 for information about the different treatment options for BPD).

As part of her treatment, Diana works on exploring and identifying her core values. She chooses three areas that she wants to concentrate on: friends, work, and appearance. Here's the mission statement she comes up with:

Diana's first life mission statement: Because friends are important to me, I will work on controlling my emotions and remaining calmer around my friends. Because I know I'm lucky to work as a dancer, I will appreciate the privilege by being more reliable. I value my appearance and it's critical for my job, so I will keep up with dieting and exercising to stay healthy.

Over the course of two years of inconsistently going to therapy, Diana suffers several relapses. Her good intentions don't prevent her from getting fired two more times from theater jobs. The pressure of performing on stage seems too emotionally charged. She finds herself unemployed, dependent on her parents for support, and without friends. Frustrated and lonely, Diana seeks help. Her therapist asks Diana to look again at how she's living her life. Diana revisits her mission statement. "These values seem superficial to me now," she tells her therapist, "I sound like a teenager. I was focused on how good I looked and how to please my friends. Now, I just want to feel like a good person and keep a job."

Diana decides that her values have changed. She now wants to find a work situation she can handle. She understands that she needs a more structured and less demanding job. She sees her appearance as much less important than she did before. After reanalyzing her values, Diana determines three new areas she wants to focus on — improving her own mental health, finding a stable, low-stress job, and giving to others by volunteering at the National Alliance for the Mentally Ill (NAMI). She develops the following new life mission statement:

Diana's second life mission statement: I commit to staying in treatment to take better care of myself. Because I value financial independence, I plan to find a job I'm capable of sticking with. Because I'm grateful for the help I've received, I want to commit to helping others by connecting with something like NAMI.

Notice that Diana's first mission statement didn't contain statements about what she wouldn't do, such as raging, but focused instead on making positive efforts to remain calm. She discovered that she wasn't quite ready to control her emotions but figured out that controlling where she worked might help. When she reanalyzed her values after two years of living, she recommitted to therapy and decided she wanted to help others. She felt that her values had evolved in a positive way.

The following story about John highlights someone who is failing to live according to his value system because he's caught up in anger.

> **John,** an attorney, enters treatment for BPD after his third divorce. John works long hours but is financially unstable. He spends too much money, and his divorces have cost him plenty. His physician tells him that he has to learn how to control his anger or he'll end up having a heart attack.
>
> John decides to see a psychologist to work on his issues. His psychologist wants John to look at his life and his values. John realizes that he has spent much of his life being angry at how unfair the world is. He recalls that in his youth he imagined making a difference in the world. He decides that the three core values that are most important to him are intellectual goals, commitment to community, and financial stability. With those values in mind, he develops the following mission statement:
>
> **John's life mission statement:** I commit myself to spending time pursuing my interest in politics. I will attend local political meetings and learn about how I can participate in my community as a leader. I vow to put 15 percent of my income into a retirement account to rebuild my finances.

John found that his life mission statement helped him clarify who he was and where he wanted to go in life. He realized that much of his behavior and focus took him away from his real goals and values. After writing his mission statement, he developed a deeper understanding of his identity and what his life is about.

The value of work

In our practice, we've found that work (paid or volunteer) is a crucial part of therapy for most people with BPD. Joel Paris, a renowned expert in the treatment of BPD, finds that helping people return to school or go to work takes priority over working on intimate relationships. Work brings you into a social network where you can practice what you're learning in therapy. Work also reduces the time that you may otherwise spend ruminating about your problems. Work or school builds feelings of competence and independence. Success at work breeds hope.

One caution: Work can be stressful. So make sure that you evaluate any job carefully in terms of pressures for productivity as well as long hours or potential emotional conflicts. We encourage our clients to consider part-time work or school if they've been out of the workforce for a long time.

You may also want to consider going to your state's department of vocational rehabilitation or an occupational therapist if you haven't done well in previous work placements. An occupational therapist can evaluate your skills and guide you in a better direction.

Finally, Finding Forgiveness

You'll likely succeed in implementing your new life mission statement with time, patience, and persistence. However, how bogged down you are by rage at other people, or even yourself, can hamper and stymie your ability to progress. Rage consumes huge amounts of emotional resources. Even a small fraction of the energy you currently devote to rage can take you a long way toward positively implementing your life mission.

However, learning to let go or find forgiveness can be a disturbingly difficult task — especially when you have good reasons for feeling enraged. But, we do believe that forgiveness is worth the effort. As you begin to consider forgiveness as a step toward implementing your life mission, you need to think about the two types of forgiveness: forgiveness of yourself and forgiveness of others.

Forgiving yourself first

Many, perhaps most, people with BPD spend a lot of time feeling down about themselves. They usually know when their behaviors have been inappropriate or have caused unnecessary harm to others or themselves. With that realization about their actions, they feel self-loathing and despair. Typical thoughts at such times include

✔ I'm a worthless human being.

✔ I'm hopeless.

✔ I don't deserve to live.

✔ What's wrong with me?

If you ever think the preceding thoughts, we want to remind you of an important concept we cover in Chapter 16: Just because you feel or think something doesn't make it true. Consider the following steps the next time you start beating up on yourself:

1. **Start by acknowledging and accepting responsibility for actions you now deem hurtful and/or regrettable toward others or yourself.**

   If possible, apologize or make amends if your actions involved someone else. If your actions harmed only you, apologize to yourself.

2. **Appreciate the fact that you didn't cause or ask for your BPD.**

   Your BPD is the result of a series of complicated, interacting factors, which we talk about in Chapter 4. No one wants to have BPD.

3. **Realize that you can't change the past. Nothing you do now will undo your past actions.**

   Focusing on past regrets absolutely prevents you from moving forward. Self-abuse virtually morphs into self-indulgence when it prevents you from making positive changes. In other words, when you stay stuck in self-abuse and wallow in self-loathing, you accomplish very little, and all you do is focus on your own issues.

4. **Repeat the following to yourself over and over again, "I'm at where I'm at. All I can do is make positive steps now to get to a better place."**

Forgiving yourself is a long-term process. It's not something you just decide to do once and then you're done. You're bound to fall down on this job many times on the way toward forgiveness. But after you begin to forgive yourself, you want to work on forgiving others, too.

Fumbling to forgive others

Many of our clients over the years, and especially those with BPD, have related stories of horrific abuse, times of unimaginable hurt, and shockingly difficult life circumstances involving losses, financial setbacks, and unexpected disappointments. Many of these events have been inflicted by cruel, hateful parents, family members, or peers. Are we seriously suggesting that you forgive these people?

We are, in fact, recommending that you do so. However, please realize that forgiving doesn't mean that you're declaring the grievous acts perpetrated against you acceptable. Nor does the act of forgiveness mean that you must discount the importance of what happened to you. Rather, forgiveness involves letting go of the rage, hatred, and/or desire for revenge that you carry around with you like a 200-pound knapsack strapped to your back every day of your life.

Studies have shown that coming to terms with the past through forgiveness allows people to lead happier, more satisfying lives. After they're freed from the burdens of rage, they can move forward once again.

You may wonder how you can ever let go like we are suggesting you do. Well, forgiveness is a process that takes a lot of work. Here are the steps we recommend you take on your path to forgiveness:

1. **Bring the memory of the offense that someone perpetrated against you into your mind.**

   However, when you do, try looking at the event from a little distance. Imagine that the event is occurring on a screen, as though you're watching a movie about the event. Look at the offense as objectively and impartially as you possibly can.

2. **Take away the perpetrator's power.**

   By letting go of your rage and forgiving, you drain the power away from the person or persons who wronged you. Imagine the perpetrator becoming weak. Do not, however, imagine inflicting revenge on the perpetrator.

3. **Imagine yourself as a coper and no longer as a victim.**

   You accomplish this task by picturing yourself as newly empowered and strong as opposed to helpless and weak. Copers have dealt with equally difficult circumstances, too, but eventually they let go of their rage and move on.

4. **Forgive.**

   Again, when you forgive, you don't declare that the perpetrator's actions were right, acceptable, or okay. Instead, you decide to let go. Give yourself the right to seek the life you would've had if the event had never occurred.

Chapter 18

Putting Yourself in Other People's Shoes

• •

In This Chapter

▶ Empathizing with other people

▶ Understanding how your words and actions affect others

▶ Overriding defensiveness

▶ Practicing positive actions

• •

*I*f you have BPD, your relationships with friends have probably been tumultuous, chaotic, and unsatisfying. Intimate relationships have likely been downright disastrous. Chapter 8 reviews some of the core reasons lying behind these difficulties. We encourage you to read that chapter before this one if you feel ready to work on improving your relationships.

Good relationships have countless benefits for people, in general. Research shows that people with supportive social networks have better physical and mental health, as well as longer lives. In fact, having people to talk to also seems to protect against early memory loss. With so many natural benefits, building better relationships should be an important part of your plan to overcome BPD.

In this chapter, we detail the foundational importance of understanding the perspectives of other people, and we show you how to do so using a few key strategies. We also show you how to better understand how your emotions and behaviors affect other people. Then we discuss how to recognize and minimize defensiveness when relating with others. Finally, we introduce you to a few of our favorite interpersonal skills that can help you create better relationships with friends, family, co-workers, and even strangers.

Understanding Others' Points of View

The most pivotal interpersonal skill of all is the ability to understand that although other people, like you, do have thoughts, opinions, and emotions, those thoughts, opinions, and emotions aren't always concordant with yours. When you fail to grasp where others are coming from, you run a high risk of offending, disrespecting, hurting, or annoying them. You may also bore people by running on about your own issues and failing to notice the cues that tell you it's time to connect with whomever you're talking to.

This interpersonal skill involves both understanding that other people have independent thoughts and feelings and appreciating that other people have various motivations and intentions that they don't always state openly and explicitly. Being able to understand the perspectives and mindsets of other people allows you to do the following:

- ✔ Empathize with other people
- ✔ Make sense of what others do
- ✔ Change your behavior in response to how others respond
- ✔ Predict how other people are likely to respond to you
- ✔ Understand nuances in conversations, such as sarcasm, humor, and teasing
- ✔ Adjust what you say in accordance to feedback from others

Sympathy and *empathy* are often used interchangeably, but they have very different meanings. Sympathy occurs when you share a feeling of caring or concern for an individual or even a group of people. For example, you may sympathize with the plight of the homeless. Empathy, on the other hand, involves being able to imagine yourself in another person's situation. You may be empathetic because you experienced a similar event at some point in your life, or because you can truly put yourself in someone else's shoes. Empathy appears to be an advanced thinking skill that varies among people — some people simply seem to be naturally more empathetic than others.

Projecting: Thinking others feel what you feel

People who have BPD develop strategies of coping that can turn out to be quite self-defeating in the long run. One of these coping methods involves taking their own painful, negative feelings or qualities and *projecting* them onto someone else. In doing so, they hope to avoid their bad feelings by giving them to another person.

A few examples of projecting

To clarify the concept of projecting, here are a few examples of how people with BPD use projection as a way to cope with the pain of negative feelings:

Connor believes that he's horribly out of shape and will never be fit enough. The thought of not having a good body terrifies him. He constantly nags his wife that she's out of shape and too fat. He yells at her when she buys occasional cookies for their kids. He uses projection to defend himself against his own painful body image.

Kaylee is overwhelmed with rage after an argument with a co-worker. She arrives home and tells her roommate what happened. Her roommate asks Kaylee if maybe she's overreacting a little. Kaylee tells her roommate to stay out of her business if all she can do is get angry and criticize. Kaylee misinterprets her roommate's question and sees it as criticism because of her own anger about the situation.

Olivia's mother is frightened and worried when she stays out all night. One morning when Olivia comes home, her mother is sitting in the kitchen and asks Olivia, "Where have you been? I was frantic with worry." Olivia screams at her mother, "Every time I stay out, you treat me like I'm a slut." Olivia sees her mother's sincere concern as highly judgmental and critical because she's ashamed of her own behavior.

Connor, Kaylee, and Olivia feel bad about one of their personal qualities — poor body image, overreacting rage, and sexual looseness, respectively. Yet, all three of them criticize others so that they don't have to deal with their own distress and shame. In doing so, people in relationships with them feel unfairly maligned and don't understand why they're always on the receiving end of critical barrages.

Reducing occurrences of projecting

If you have a tendency to project your own emotions onto other people, you can reduce it with practice. However, you should combine your own efforts with work in therapy for maximum effectiveness.

The process of decreasing projection begins with increasing your *self-awareness,* or honest observation and appraisal of your emotions. Look back at your past, rocky interactions with others. Ask yourself whether you were accusing others of having feelings that mirrored how you were feeling about yourself? If so, you want to prevent this pattern from ruining or interfering with your current and future relationships.

In addition, you want to tune into your emotions, especially anger and rage. Try to notice your body's reactions (such as muscle tension in your chest, shoulders, or jaw, rapid heart rate, flushing, and sweating) that occur before you say something critical or before you attack someone else. When those physical feelings hit you, delay saying anything at all costs! Delaying your initial reaction may help you take a couple of slow, deep breaths instead of lashing out.

After you delay your reaction, ask yourself a few questions:

- Could I be feeling upset with *myself?*
- Did something make me feel ashamed recently?
- Am I feeling afraid of something?
- Am I worried that someone is going to abandon me?

If you answer yes to any of these questions, your anger is probably more about your own worries than the other person. Try to make one of the following alternative statements, or less-provoking statements, instead of lashing out:

- I'm feeling emotional right now; I need to get back to you on this.
- Before we go further with this, I need to take a break.
- I've got some things to think about before I comment on this.
- I hear you, and I promise I'll discuss it with you when I'm feeling better.

 Getting angry with others because of your own feelings of shame and rage at yourself is a long-standing habit. Changing such enduring patterns takes a lot of time and practice — not to mention effort. Give yourself some time and don't expect instant results.

Practicing perspective taking

Although not assuming that other people feel what you feel about yourself is an important skill to master, perspective taking also requires you to know how to understand other people's states of minds — in other words, their thoughts and feelings. In the following sections, we take a look at a few strategies for working on this skill.

Taking turns

When emotions run hot, the intensity of distress tends to consume all your focus and attention. And, unfortunately, emotions frequently run hot in people with BPD. Think of the brain as having only so much room — when filled with emotion, thinking skills are overwhelmed.

At such times, the temptation to talk on and on to whomever will listen about whatever you're feeling is hard to fight. But if you give into that temptation, you likely miss seeing that the person you're talking to is becoming restless, bored, and/or burned out.

One way to fight this temptation is to work on forcing yourself to "take turns" in most, if not all, of your conversations. Just as parents teach their kids to share and take turns, you need to teach yourself to take turns when you converse with other people. In the process, you're likely to learn a lot about what the person you're talking to is thinking and feeling.

A good rule of thumb is to try to take up half of the conversation time and to let the person you're conversing with take up the other half. Asking a lot of questions can help you accomplish this goal, and we cover this strategy in the next section.

Asking questions

When you show interest in other people, they're much more likely to feel interested in you. Not only do questions keep conversations flowing, but they also help you show the person you're talking to that you're interested in him and the topic at hand. You can then use the answers to your questions to infer what the other person may be thinking.

When you ask questions, try to listen carefully to the answers. Consider following up the answer with another question related to what you heard. Again, doing so keeps the conversation going and maintains interest in both parties. See the "Listening" section later in this chapter for more thoughts about this issue.

When people answer your questions, try not to see their intentions as malicious, and do your best to hold back your defensive responses. Check out the "Decreasing Defensiveness" section for more information about this issue.

Perhaps you're wondering what kinds of questions to ask people you're talking to. Although almost any question can be helpful, we realize that you may want a few examples to build on. The following list, though far from exhaustive, is applicable to many different situations:

- ✔ Can you tell me more about that? (Shrinks love asking this one.)
- ✔ How did you learn about that?
- ✔ Is this something you feel strongly about?
- ✔ How do you feel about this issue?
- ✔ Tell me something about yourself. (Okay, this one isn't exactly a question, but it accomplishes the same goal.)
- ✔ Have you ever run into something like this in your life?
- ✔ How do you handle this kind of thing?

Work hard to ask your questions in a gentle, inquisitive tone. Avoid any hint of sarcasm or accusatory slant. Failing to do so can defeat the purpose of helping you develop and maintain relationships.

Considering alternative meanings and motivations

People with BPD tend to misconstrue the meanings and intentions of other people's words. All too often they infer malicious, attacking intentions from the words of others. This misinterpretation is known as the *malicious assumption*. After you make a malicious assumption, a counterattack is virtually inevitable.

Work with your therapist to review some of your past conversations that turned out badly. Your therapist can help you develop less malicious and judgmental interpretations that are, as a matter of fact, more likely to be correct.

The following examples in Table 18-1 show how someone with BPD can easily make malicious assumptions about other people's relatively neutral statements. The table also shows examples of nonjudgmental interpretations of the same neutral statements.

Table 18-1	Assumptions about Neutral Statements	
Neutral Statement	**Malicious Assumption**	**Nonjudgmental Assumption**
Did you get the mail today?	He's saying that I never do anything without being reminded first.	He's just curious about the mail.
How are you feeling today?	He's saying that I look sick and old.	He truly wants to know how I feel.
Gosh, getting to the store is taking a long time.	He's saying that I don't drive fast enough.	He's right. Traffic is really bad today.

If you find yourself making malicious assumptions, you're likely to have a lot of negative interactions. These assumptions not only make you unhappy, but they also add to the stress in your life. In addition, malicious assumptions take a toll on the quality of all your relationships.

Occasionally, malicious assumptions prove to be true. In other words, sometimes people really are expressing hostility. However, you have nothing to lose by believing in the nonjudgmental assumptions. More often than not, your nonjudgmental assumption is right, and by holding back your malicious assumption — thus avoiding a counterattack — you avoid turning an innocent conversation into an argumentative debacle. Not to mention, you can maintain or improve your relationships, too.

Bridget's story illustrates the reflexive tendency many people with BPD have to make malicious assumptions about other people's motivations. If you tend to make malicious assumptions, taking some time to think through your past heated conversations (like Bridget does with her therapist) can help you identify more realistic and positive, nonjudgmental assumptions.

Bridget sees Dr. Rodriguez twice a week for therapy. She's currently working on improving her ability to understand other people. She tells Dr. Rodriguez about an incident she had with a friend last week.

"So, my friend calls me and asks me if I want to go shopping," Bridget explains, "I tell her yeah, but not today. And my friend says that she'll go without me. So, that made me mad, like if I don't do what she wants when she wants, she's just going to dump me. I told her fine — find another friend to go shopping with. Then she seemed surprised that I got mad and asked me what was wrong with me. So, not only does she dump me, but she tells me I'm crazy, too. I don't get it. Why are people so mean to me?"

"Bridget, let's use what you just told me to practice taking another person's point of view. First, your friend asked you to go shopping. Tell me what she may have meant by that," Dr Rodriguez gently inquires.

"Well, that's easy — she wanted someone to go shopping with her," Bridget responds.

"What did that invitation tell you about how she feels about you?"

"I guess that meant she wanted me to go shopping."

Dr. Rodriquez probes further, "Do you think she was saying that she wants your company? Does she like you?"

Bridget replies, "Yeah, she wanted to spend time with me. And I suppose that means she likes me. I never really thought about that."

"So next you tell her that you can't go, and she says that she'll go without you. What did that mean?"

"That meant that she didn't care about me," Bridget responds.

"Really? Is there any other reason why she may have said that?" Dr. Rodriguez asks.

"I don't know. I guess she could've meant that she needed to go shopping that day. Right, like you have pointed out a million times before, maybe it didn't have anything to do with not liking me. But she had no right to call me crazy."

Dr. Rodriguez says, "I'm not sure I heard when she said you're crazy. You said she asked what was wrong with you. Could she have been trying to convey any other meaning?"

"None that I can think of. She was being really rude."

"Well," Dr. Rodriguez continues, "Is it possible that she was expressing frustration with you? In other words, could she have been flustered and upset by your anger and simply didn't know what to make of it? Was she necessarily saying that you're *crazy*?"

Bridget hesitates and says, "Hmm, I suppose that's possible. You have pointed out that I tend to see the worst possible meaning in what people say. You really think she was just frustrated with me?"

"Yes, I really do. You went from a conversation about shopping to accusing her of abandoning you over nothing. This assumption makes perfect sense to you because being abandoned is one of your core fears. But other people don't understand how sensitive that issue is for you."

Bridget reflects a moment and says, "Wow, you've given me a lot to think about."

Bridget misinterpreted her friend's meaning, and this misinterpretation led her to accuse her friend of wanting to end their relationship. When her friend asked Bridget, "What's wrong?" she believed her friend was calling her crazy. Her therapist helps her see the other, more realistic ways she could've interpreted the conversation.

Like Bridget, people with BPD are often reasonably good at reading others, but they greatly magnify the negativity in most conversations. If a statement *can* be taken negatively, they take it that way. People with BPD see even neutral comments as being tinged with hostility.

Feelings, even strong, negative feelings are neither good nor bad. You have the right to feel what you feel. What matters is how you act on your feelings.

Noticing Your Impact on Others

People with BPD commonly don't fully appreciate or even recognize how their behavior affects the people who care about them. Because their own overwhelming emotions consume their attention, they don't attend carefully to other people's reactions. These communication breakdowns are part of the *expression–disconnection–rejection cycle,* which starts when people with BPD overly focus on expressing their own emotions and concerns. As their conversations wear on, other people feel a lack of connection with them, and as a result, they may ultimately reject the people with BPD.

Indeed, if you have BPD, you run a high risk of rejection from other people. We won't pull any punches here. However, the reason for this rejection isn't because you're an awful person. It's because you may not understand how your behavior or words affect other people.

One way to start understanding your impact on other people is to start looking at people's faces. Practice noticing different expressions. See whether or not you can figure out the difference in facial expressions when people are tired, bored, irritated, enthusiastic, sad, neutral, happy, and *truly* angry. Also pay attention to other people's voice tones and gestures. Begin this practice with people who are talking to other people, and then apply your skills to people who are talking to you.

Although realizing your impact on other people is an important step in achieving your overall goal of better understanding other people, you also need to work on reducing defensiveness. If you're not sure what defensiveness means, read the next section.

Decreasing Defensiveness

Defensiveness refers to the habit of warding off perceived attacks, assaults, and criticisms with retaliatory statements. We aren't talking about physical attacks here. Rather, we're talking about the times when you perceive other people as being critical of you. People with BPD often react to these imagined assaults by counterattacking, which can include blaming others or turning up the heat on the conversation by lacing your words with sarcasm or hostility.

Remember that anybody who's feeling intense anger is far less able to think or perceive interactions accurately than someone who's feeling calm and relaxed. The responses of people who are intensely angry are inappropriate 99.2 percent of the time — well, we made that number up, but you get the point. When you're mad, your thinking skills just aren't at full capacity. The following three strategies can help you combat defensiveness.

Taking the "I" out of interactions

Defensive people focus their attention on themselves. They don't necessarily believe they're better or more important than others, but they do believe, in a sense, that the world revolves around them. In other words, they're constantly in the spotlight — but that spotlight can shine much too brightly. Consider that when everything in life has personal significance, all the good and bad things that happen affect your feelings and moods.

Taking things too personally is a common communication problem, especially for people with personality disorders, including BPD. Here are a few examples of this problem in action:

✔ A patron at a restaurant becomes furious when she has to wait for service because a couple of the wait staff called in sick and there aren't enough waiters available for the crowd. She's so rude to her waiter that others at her table are embarrassed. The waiter apologizes and explains that they're short staffed, but the patron refuses to accept the apology. Instead, she feels that the restaurant is somehow singling her out for bad treatment.

✔ A driver becomes infuriated when a train crossing delays his commute to work. His blood pressure rises as he watches the train pass by in front of him. He wonders why trains always seem to interrupt his commute when he's already late.

✔ An ER physician calls a neurologist to schedule a consultation with him and becomes sarcastic and enraged when the neurologist asks a few questions about the patient before scheduling the meeting. The ER doctor feels personally insulted by the neurologist's failure to jump into his car and come to the ER without questioning the doctor's judgment.

✔ A man becomes enraged after his computer keyboard stops working. After getting a replacement, his anger interferes with his ability to get back to work. He believes that computer problems happen to him far more often than they should.

The key problem in all four examples is that each person believes that the incident somehow has a negative, personal meaning. Even random events like computer breakdowns and train crossings become personal. If you tend to personalize events like the people in these examples do, it's time to work on this issue. The following steps can help:

1. **Slow down and take two or three slow, deep breaths.**

2. **Ask yourself whether the irritating event is truly centered on you or whether it's possibly just circumstances or bad luck.**

3. **Ask yourself whether getting upset and angry will have some benefit for you.**

4. **Ponder whether your anger could hurt someone around you or yourself, for that matter.**

5. **Consider telling yourself, "Stuff happens — not everything is about me."**

Putting a friend on your side

Some of our patients over the years have found our second technique to be surprisingly useful in defeating defensiveness. This technique asks you to imagine an *objective observer* sitting on your shoulder to provide you with sage advice and guidance in a clutch. Your observer's task is to notice when you're feeling irritated, angry, or threatened. At those times, your observer should offer you some helpful advice, such as the following:

- ✔ Slow down. You're going to make things much worse if you speak right now.

- ✔ What do you have to lose by assuming that he's not attacking you?

- ✔ Let's try something different from the usual blow up this time, okay?

- ✔ I'm here to help, remember? Say something positive instead.

- ✔ How many times has exploding helped the situation?

- ✔ What is he going to think and feel if you say this? How would you feel if someone said that to you?

- ✔ How about you actually try complimenting him instead of ripping him apart like you want to?

After listening to your objective observer's advice, work hard to follow it! This technique can really help you if you practice it. It's not likely to work well the first few times you try it, but over time, you'll hear these calming words coming from the observer more and more often.

Some people jot down the preceding phrases on an index card and read them every day to remind their objective observer to use them when things start to deteriorate.

Musing over defusing

A great alternative to becoming defensive is called *defusing*. When you perceive someone as being critical of you, defusing can keep things calm instead of encouraging escalation. Defusing involves doing the opposite of what you feel like doing: Instead of counterattacking, you try to find some sliver of truth in what the other person has just said to you. When you express actual agreement of a small part (sometimes even all) of what someone has said, you keep the dialogue going and gradually let out the steam from the conversational pressure cooker that may have been ready to explode.

To clarify, defusing doesn't mean capitulating or lying to the person you're talking with. Instead, defusing represents an honest attempt to find something about the other person's perspective that you can truly endorse. Table 18-2 shows you how you can use defusing in response to various types of criticisms. For these examples, we use situations that sound clearly critical even to us. However, you can also use defusing when you're not certain your perception is correct.

Table 18-2	Defusing Defensiveness
Criticism	*Defusing Response*
You're yelling at the kids too much.	Sometimes I do yell. That's one reason I'm in therapy. I get frustrated too easily. But try to tell me more gently if you can.
You're spending way too much money on junk.	That's something I do need to watch, and I'm trying. I'm hoping that using the computer to track my expenses will help me.
I can't believe you got another speeding ticket.	You're right, I did. However, that's the first one in a year; that's a big improvement for me.
You always leave dirty, smelly dishes in the sink.	I understand that you feel upset. However, I don't care quite as much as you do about a few dishes. Can we work out a compromise on this?

Defusing isn't the way to deal with clear-cut, egregious verbal or physical abuse. If you're in that kind of situation, you need to seek help from your therapist, a shelter for domestic violence, or, in violent situations, from the police. Sometimes people don't know for sure whether they're being abused. If that situation fits you, a trip to a mental health professional can help you sort it out.

Getting Along Better

People with BPD often lack sufficient social skills to maintain and nourish good interpersonal relationships. Loss and conflict often characterize their romantic lives. This section describes some basic ways to improve social interactions.

If you have BPD, we recommend that you practice the following skills with acquaintances or friends. Try to increase your interpersonal skills with people you don't have intense relationships with before you attempt to work

on more intimate relationships. Expect that these strategies will feel somewhat awkward and uncomfortable at first. However, with a little practice,
you'll likely find that they become second nature.

Listening

Listening to others not only conveys interest, but also helps develop your
perspective-taking skills. Listening is both a skill and a habit that you have
to nurture. With practice, listening becomes natural. You may think you're
already a good listener. If so, you may not need to work on this issue. But
before you make that decision, consider asking some people whether they
think you could improve your listening skills. If they say yes, try to avoid
becoming defensive!

Giving compliments

Giving compliments not only makes other people feel better, but also
increases your own self-confidence. You will gain confidence when people
respond positively to your efforts. Make it a goal to give out at least two
compliments each day. We predict that you'll find this practice fulfilling and
worthwhile. Follow these guidelines when giving compliments:

✔ **Be specific.** Don't make grand, global statements like, "You're the best
person in the whole world," because most people won't believe you.
Instead, find something smaller and more concrete like, "I loved the way
you handled that sales meeting," or "This dinner is delicious."

✔ **Don't throw in negatives with the positives.** For example, don't say, "I
loved the way you handled that sales meeting, especially after the horrible job you did last week," or "This dinner is delicious. I wish you could
cook like this every night."

If you haven't given compliments in a while, other people may react strangely
at first. They may wonder what you're up to and perhaps even become a little
sarcastic. However, we recommend that you keep trying. Over time, they'll
get used to the new you, and they'll likely respond quite well to the change.

Pillowing rather than pillorying

People with BPD often report difficulty in getting their needs met by other
people. They complain that others don't hear them or that they don't feel

comfortable asking directly for what they want. We have a strategy that may make getting your needs met a little easier. This technique is called *pillowing* — as opposed to pillorying. When you *pillory* someone, you dish out abuse, contempt, and ridicule. How likely are other people to listen and do what you want when you resort to pillorying? Not very.

With pillowing, however, you soften the blow as much as you can, while still clearly stating what you want. You can accomplish pillowing by using some simple phrases. These phrases can help you point out that you're not the one and only owner of truth and wisdom in the world. In other words, they help you acknowledge that your point of view may be somewhat flawed. And, in truth, it always is — for all people, whether they have BPD or not.

Here are some sample statements that can help you develop your pillowing technique. They can be very useful when you're trying to fill your needs or requests of other people. The pillowing phrase is in boldface:

- ✔ **I could be off base, but I was wondering** whether what you said was intended to hurt me?

- ✔ **Maybe I'm being overly sensitive,** but I can't hear you when you use that tone of voice.

- ✔ **I realize that this could be an annoying request,** but I'm feeling so over-whelmed; would you mind taking over for a little while?

- ✔ **I could be wrong,** but it feels like you're upset with me.

You don't want to make excessive use of pillowing, because, if you do, others will find it a bit contrived. But the technique does make expressing your needs easier to do. Statements like the preceding examples also help you feel like you're being less demanding of people. Furthermore, the technique makes hearing you an easier task for other people to accomplish. Of course, *we could be wrong* about that!

Chapter 19

Finding Shades of Gray: Changing Problematic Core Beliefs

. . . .

In This Chapter

▶ Using different strategies to monitor your schemas

▶ Living with new, more adaptive schemas

. . . .

*I*n Chapter 9, we discuss how the way you perceive or interpret events can greatly influence your feelings about what's going on around you. In a very real sense, your emotional reactions come at least as much from your interpretations as from the events themselves.

For example, if a friend tells you, "You're usually pretty fun to be around," your feelings about the statement will spring from the meaning you give to it. If you believe your friend's comment is a compliment, you probably feel quite pleased. On the other hand, if you believe that people almost always reject you, you probably zero in on the word *usually*. Thus, you may conclude that your friend is really saying that you come up short in the fun category. As a result, you likely feel distraught. *Schemas*, or the core beliefs that you hold about yourself, the world around you, and the people you relate to, are responsible for how you habitually interpret events.

In this chapter, we focus on how to change the schemas that keep you from seeing your life clearly. We provide a range of strategies you can use to start challenging your schemas. Then we guide you through techniques for acquiring new, more adaptive schemas that can help you feel better about your life.

Schema Busting Strategies

Before you can change your problematic schemas, you have to fully understand what those schemas are and where they come from. Please realize that countless problematic schemas are possible and that no matter how hard you look, you won't find a definitive list. Any broad, problematic and long-standing belief that you hold about yourself or the world may be a schema worthy of your attention.

Chapter 9 covers schemas in detail, including what schemas are, where they come from, how they work, and which ones you likely have. Table 19-1 provides a brief summary so that you don't have to flip back and forth.

Table 19-1	Schema Recap	
Self-Concept Schemas		
Problematic Schema	*Opposite Problematic Schema*	*Adaptive Schema*
Entitlement: Believing you have the right to anything you want and feeling outraged when you don't get it	**Undeserving:** Believing you're not worthy of having your needs met	**Balanced self-worth:** Believing your needs deserve to be met, but not always, and not at someone else's expense
Superiority: Seeing yourself as being better than other people	**Inferiority:** Believing you're not as capable or as good as other people	**Self-acceptance:** Appreciating both your strengths and your weaknesses without being overly concerned about them
Relationship Schemas		
Problematic Schema	*Opposite Problematic Schema*	*Adaptive Schema*
Avoidant attachment: Believing you don't need other people and, thus, keeping others at a distance	**Anxious attachment:** Believing that others are highly likely to abandon or leave you and being overly clingy and jealous as a result	**Secure attachment:** Believing that friendships and intimacy are possible and likely, yet being aware that some people can't be trusted
Idealizing: Seeing new partners and friends as being perfect and without flaws	**Demonizing:** Believing that your partner or friend is almost totally flawed (often occurring when the idealizing schema proves to be false)	**Realistic view of others:** Believing that everyone has both positive and negative qualities and tolerating a reasonable degree of flaws

World Schemas		
Problematic Schema	**Opposite Problematic Schema**	**Adaptive Schema**
Totally safe: Believing that you don't need to take reasonable precautions and exhibiting a blasé naiveté	**Dangerous:** Believing that the world is highly dangerous and worrying greatly about your safety	**Reasonable safety:** Understanding that you need to be cautious in this world but also not allowing fear to dictate your life
Totally predictable: Believing that you're completely in charge of how things turn out in your life and, thus, thinking that you'll succeed at anything you attempt (usually being devastated when failure does occur)	**Unpredictable:** Seeing the world as being totally chaotic and unpredictable and, as a result, believing that you're powerlessly at the mercy of random events	**Predictable:** Appreciating that the world has a reasonable degree of predictability but that random events can upset the apple cart and, as a result, preparing for an array of possibilities and believing that things typically work out

People sometimes flip from one problematic schema to its opposite. Other times, folks may experience a problematic schema, its opposite, and occasionally its adaptive counterpart. The key is to know which problematic schemas you experience frequently and then to work on weakening those particular schemas. Later in this chapter, we show you how to strengthen adaptive schemas.

Don't beat yourself up if you see that you frequently experience a variety of problematic schemas, or even all of the ones we mention in the previous table. As you work on one or two problematic schemas, others sometimes begin to lessen their influence over your life, too. With time and diligence, you can change your schemas for the better. The sections that follow show you some ways to start this process of change.

Recognizing the effects of schemas on your feelings

One of the best ways to reduce the influence that schemas have on your life is to shine a light on them and track where and when they occur. Schemas are sort of like cockroaches; they prefer to operate in the dark nooks and crannies of your mind. As you observe your schemas at work, you'll come to understand that your emotional reactions aren't an inherent part of who you are — they stem directly from your schemas. And you're not the same thing as your schemas.

See Chapter 16 for a discussion about how you can observe or monitor your mind and emotions. In this section, we ask you to call on that part of you to look at your own schemas and the effects they have on your feelings.

If you start to observe your own schemas day to day, you're bound to understand more fully why you think and feel the way you do. In addition, as you realize that your schemas — not you — are flawed, your schemas are likely to exert less influence on you and your feelings. Observing your schemas just takes practice. See Appendix B for a blank Schema Monitoring Form. We recommend that you fill out this form every week for several months. Here are the steps you take to fill out each form:

1. **When you feel distressed, try to figure out what event seemed to trigger your feeling.**

   Jot down at the top of the form what that event was. The event can be something that actually happened to you or an image that came into your mind. Describe the event clearly.

2. **Jot down in the middle column what thoughts, perceptions, interpretations, or meanings the event had for you.**

   In other words, make note of what thoughts were going through your head when the event actually occurred.

3. **In the right-hand column, make note of how you feel about the event.**

   If you have trouble labeling your feelings, consider reading Chapter 6, which explains bodily sensations and words that describe feelings.

4. **Go through Table 19-1 to discover whether one of your problematic schemas is related to your thoughts and feelings.**

   If so, make note of that schema and the related feeling. You may conclude that more than one schema seems to apply, which is okay. Jot down however many schemas seem to be involved. Briefly describe your schema based on our definition, or individualize how that schema seems to apply to you.

Monitoring your schemas is like exposing a vampire to sunlight. Keep observing them over and over again, and, as you do, they begin to wither.

The difference between thoughts and schemas is that schemas are general, broad beliefs that continue from event to event. Thoughts, on the other hand, are specific to a given event. The following examples of Melissa, Amanda, and Caleb show you how three people can experience the exact same event yet react with completely different thoughts and feelings because each of them carries around different schemas.

Melissa, **Amanda**, and **Caleb** all like to eat out at restaurants when their budgets allow them to, and, on occasion, the service is poor. These three individuals have completely different responses and feelings to poor service because each one of them has a different primary schema: Melissa views the event through an undeserving schema, Amanda views the event through a dangerous schema, and Caleb views the event through an entitlement schema. Tables 19-2, 19-3, and 19-4 show what each person thinks and feels when a restaurant's server fails to take drink orders after 20 minutes.

Table 19-2	Schema Monitoring: Melissa	
Schema and Definition	*Thoughts*	*Feelings*
Undeserving: I don't expect my needs to be met, and I'm not worthy of people's attention.	No one ever pays attention to me; why should this waiter be any different? I guess I'll just go home in another ten minutes or so.	I feel despondent and gloomy.

Table 19-3	Schema Monitoring: Amanda	
Schema and Definition	*Thoughts*	*Feelings*
Dangerous: I worry all the time about my safety.	I wonder if this long wait means they leave food lying around until it spoils. If they have service this bad, maybe their food is ill-prepared and I could get sick by eating it.	I feel anxious and full of dread.

Table 19-4	Schema Monitoring: Caleb	
Schema and Definition	*Thoughts*	*Feelings*
Entitlement: I deserve the best of everything, and people better give me what I want or else they'll get a piece of my mind.	I can't believe they're so negligent and sloppy in their service here. I'm going to complain to the management, and I may even write a letter to the editor of our newspaper. There's no excuse for something like this.	I feel outraged, scornful, and tense.

The examples of Melissa, Amanda, and Caleb illustrate how powerfully your schemas affect your thoughts and feelings when things happen to you. Note that all three people experienced the same event, but their schemas led them to profoundly different reactions.

Exorcising problematic childhood schemas

People acquire their schemas in childhood. At that time, schemas often make a lot of sense because schemas represent your mind's attempt to figure out your world. Thus, most people's schemas represent their way of interpreting how their parents raised them, as well as how their teachers, friends, and relatives treated them. So what's the problem with schemas if they're simply the brain's way of making sense of the world?

Your schemas aren't problematic if the world of your childhood was healthy, balanced, and reasonably predictable. Unfortunately, this description doesn't fit with the way most people with BPD describe their childhoods. Often, the childhood worlds of people with BPD were chaotic, unpredictable, and riddled with extreme parenting messages — both overly harsh, demanding messages (such as "You're a pathetic, clumsy oaf!") and unrealistically positive messages (such as "You're the best kid in the entire world; there's nothing you can't do!").

Not surprisingly, the schemas of people with BPD tend to be extreme and often lead to overwhelming emotions. Given the world their schemas evolved in, these tendencies are reasonable and, well, rather normal. But the world usually changes as people grow up. In the adult world, most people don't treat one another in the same extreme ways that the parents of people with BPD treated them.

Don't despair. You can use the Then and Now Form in Appendix B to help you see that the events that trigger your schemas today typically pale in comparison to the events that created them in your childhood. Feel free to make as many copies of this form as you need for your personal use. Here's how you use the form:

1. **Write down your problematic schema in the left-hand column (see Table 19-1 for examples of problematic schemas).**

Describe how this particular schema plays out in your life. You can either use the definition we provide in Table 19-1 or individualize your definition, using your own words. Don't forget that some people experience opposite schemas in various situations. Include both opposites if you experience them.

2. **Jot down one or more recollections from your childhood that may have helped create this schema.**

3. **Write down the events or happenings that tend to trigger this schema for you in your current life.**

Notice how old you feel when an event triggers your schema.

4. **Remind yourself that you're older today, that the current triggering events aren't usually as significant as the events that created your schemas, and that, with time, your mind will see the difference between the events of your childhood and those of the present.**

Be patient; fully distinguishing between then and now takes time.

Jennifer's story demonstrates how someone with BPD can use the Then and Now Form to help the mind break the connection between the triggers that set certain problematic schemas off today and the events that created them during childhood. Jennifer's form appears in Table 19-5.

Jennifer is a 38-year-old real estate agent who has been in therapy for a couple of months. She has an interesting pattern of problematic schemas that includes the dangerous schema, the anxious attachment schema, and flipping inordinately between the entitlement and undeserving schemas. Her psychologist recommends that she fill out a Then and Now Form to help her see that events triggering her problematic schemas today are relatively mild compared to her childhood experiences.

Jennifer fills out her Then and Now Form regularly each week for about two months. She constantly compares and contrasts the events that helped shape her problematic schemas in her childhood with happenings that trigger them in her world today. She sees that relatively trivial events trigger these schemas now, whereas the events that shaped them in her childhood had far greater significance, at least to a child. This realization helps Jennifer forgive herself for having these schemas and also allows her to view present-day realities in a more realistic way.

Table 19-5	Jennifer's Then and Now Form	
Problematic Schema	Image(s) of Childhood Origins	Current Triggers
Dangerous: I panic and worry constantly about my safety.	Our neighborhood was horrible. We had gangs and even an occasional drive-by shooting. My mother used to warn me constantly about criminals and other dangers in the world.	Whenever I have to leave the house for more than an hour, whether I'm going shopping or just running an errand, I feel a sense of dread. If someone says hi to me, I freak out.
Anxious attachment: I get so jealous and clingy all the time. I can't stand the idea of being abandoned, but I always seem to be abandoned anyway.	In spite of all her warnings about dangers in the world, my mother got really angry with me whenever I messed up. Then she stomped out of the house and left me alone in the house by myself for several hours. I was only 8 years old, and I was scared to death.	Even the slightest criticism or negative word out of a boyfriend makes me feel like I'm 8 years old again. I panic inside, and my stomach does flip-flops. My panic causes me to cling. Also, whenever a boyfriend is a few minutes late, I accuse him of seeing someone else.
Entitlement and undeserving: I usually feel totally undeserving and unworthy of having my needs met. But, on rare occasions when someone denies me what I want, I explode with rage as though I'm the most entitled person in the world.	My parents both viewed children as something to be seen and not heard. They rarely showed regard for us. Whenever I asked if I could go play at another kid's house, my mother would say she didn't have time to drag me around.	If I have a favor I want to ask someone for, I can rarely do so. I feel so incredibly undeserving. But, whenever I do ask for something and get turned down, I feel abused. At those times, I feel like the little kid again and like people don't respect my basic needs.

Tabulating a cost-benefit analysis

Changing schemas can be a daunting task because your mind so fervently believes in the truth of your schemas and sees them as being beneficial. The idea that your mind actually thinks your schemas help you may seem counterintuitive to you. How does someone see a dangerous schema as useful? Perhaps a few examples can help you better understand this concept. In the following list, we describe a few of the benefits people may see in keeping their problematic schemas. These benefits usually come in the form of fears about what would happen if people let go of their schemas.

- ✔ **Dangerous:** If a woman with this schema chooses to no longer believe in this schema, she gravely fears that she'll put herself in needless danger because she'll no longer be hypervigilant about her safety.

- ✔ **Inferiority:** If a man with this problematic schema decides he's not going to believe in his inferiority anymore, he knows that he may be inclined to try giving public speeches (something he's avoided his entire life). However, he doesn't challenge his schema by making speeches because he so strongly believes in his inferiority and "knows" that he will surely fail if he tries.

- ✔ **Entitlement:** A woman may hold this problematic schema because she's terribly worried that her needs must be met all the time. She fears that if she becomes less demanding, people will walk all over her.

Fortunately, you can find a way out of this schema dilemma — it's called a *cost-benefit analysis*. A cost-benefit analysis can help you scrutinize your problematic schemas and determine whether they're as beneficial as you think or they're causing you far more harm than you realize.

Here are the specific steps you want to take in conducting a cost-benefit analysis of your problematic schemas. You can find a blank Cost-Benefit Analysis Form for your use in Appendix B.

1. **Jot down one of your problematic schemas that seems to get in your way, along with its definition (see Table 19-1 for examples of problematic schemas).**

   Feel free to individualize the definition to make it describe the way this schema works in your life.

2. **Write down any and all conceivable ways in which your schema seems to benefit you or protect you from harm. Take your time.**

3. **Jot down any ways in which you can imagine that your problematic schema costs you something.**

   Sometimes you can start by reviewing the benefits and writing out how they may not actually be true. For example, if you have a dangerous schema and believe that one benefit is that the schema keeps you safe from all danger, you can question whether attempting to avoid all risks can ever really work for anyone. In other words, is there truly a way to avoid lightening strikes, natural disasters, or other random accidents? The answer is no. So your dangerous schema really just prevents you from taking part in everyday life.

4. Carefully mull over your cost-benefit analysis.

Decide whether your schema provides more costs or benefits to your life. Discuss your results with your therapist.

A cost-benefit analysis is a good tool, but it's only one of many ways to work on your problematic schemas. This kind of work takes time. Be patient with yourself.

Shannon's story demonstrates how someone can use a cost-benefit analysis to help her see that a couple of her problematic schemas are doing more to get in the way of her life than to help her.

> **Shannon** has worked as a retail clerk at a department store for the past year. She has held this job longer than any other over the past fifteen years since she graduated from high school. She has BPD and began psychotherapy about three months ago. She and her psychologist, Dr. Bashan, have identified one schema that gets in her way more than any other — anxious attachment. Although her therapist has suggested a variety of ways to start dismantling this schema, she has resisted making the attempt.
>
> At one of their appointments, Dr. Bashan says, "Shannon, I can see that you're pretty reluctant to tackle your anxious attachment schema."
>
> Shannon replies, "Yes, I know what you say makes sense, but I just can't seem to get myself to try the things you've suggested."
>
> "Actually, I think you've struggled for very good reasons," Dr. Bashan continues, "I think I've been suggesting that you take action against this schema before you're ready."
>
> "How is that, doctor? I thought you knew everything and had all the answers."
>
> Dr. Bashan raises his eyebrows and says, "If only that were true. I think I goofed up in this case. I've been recommending that you try to change something that your mind assumes is beneficial. I think we need to examine that assumption with a cost-benefit analysis. Let's write down every conceivable way that your schemas may benefit you. Then we can look at how those same schemas may cost you something, too."
>
> Shannon says, "I thought problematic schemas were always bad and hurt you. What are you saying?"
>
> "Well, at the end of the day, they probably do hurt you, but you wouldn't hold onto your schemas if they didn't at least feel like they held some benefits. How about we try to look at the costs and benefits of your schemas?" Dr. Bashan gently suggests.
>
> Table 19-6 shows what Shannon comes up with in terms of the benefits of her anxious attachment schema.

Table 19-6	Shannon's Cost-Benefit Analysis of the Anxious Attachment Schema: The Benefits	
Schema: Anxious Attachment — I'm absolutely convinced that anyone important to me will eventually abandon me.		
Benefits		**Costs**
This belief helps me be on the alert for any early warning sign that a new person is losing interest. I don't get caught by surprise that way.		
I won't be hurt so badly if I'm aware of what's coming.		
This schema makes me very good about staying in close touch with anyone who matters to me.		
People think I'm great at being thoughtful.		

Now Shannon sees why she's been reluctant to give up this schema. It seems to have some terrific benefits for her. However, Dr. Bashan recommends that she fill out the column labeled Costs next. Table 19-7 shows what her complete analysis looks like.

Table 19-7	Shannon's Complete Cost-Benefit Analysis of the Anxious Attachment Schema	
Schema: Anxious Attachment — I'm absolutely convinced that anyone important to me will eventually abandon me.		
Benefits		**Costs**
This belief helps me be on the alert for any early warning sign that a new person is losing interest. I don't get caught by surprise that way.		This schema makes me jealous and clingy. People don't really like that. I'm so hypervigilant that I drive people nuts.
I won't be hurt so badly if I'm aware of what's coming.		The truth is I think that anticipating someone leaving me hurts just as bad as when I don't.
This schema makes me very good about staying in close touch with anyone who matters to me.		A lot of people have told me that I stay so close that they feel suffocated.
People think I'm great at being thoughtful.		This schema makes me feel ridiculously dependent on other people.
		I think this schema makes people more likely to leave me.

Shannon reviews the cost-benefit analysis of her anxious attachment schema and concludes, "As I really look this over, I can see where my schema has been hurting me a lot more than it has been helping. Even some of the benefits don't appear all that beneficial when I think about them. I should be able to change this schema now."

Dr. Bashan warns, "Well, I think the cost-benefit analysis is a great start. But don't underestimate the power of schemas. Changing your problematic schemas and adopting new, more positive ones is going to take a lot more work and effort."

Adopting Adaptive Schemas

The preceding "Schema Busting Strategies" section presents several techniques for reducing the frequency and impact of your problematic schemas. Now it's time to work on increasing the frequency of your *adaptive schemas,* or schemas that are less extreme and that can help you get along better with others, see the world more realistically, and see yourself more like others do. You can increase the frequency of adaptive schemas in two ways — through taking direct actions and by using schema flash cards.

Taking the direct approach

Direct actions help establish and reinforce your adaptive schemas. Direct actions are things you do to strengthen your adaptive schemas. Note that everyone, including people with BPD, sometimes act in ways that are consistent with adaptive schemas. Taking direct, supportive actions increases the percentage of time you spend with adaptive schemas and decreases the amount of time you spend with problematic ones.

If you're troubled by one of the problematic schemas in Table 19-1, look at the Adaptive Schema Action List in Table 19-8 for ideas about how to strengthen your adaptive schemas in the schema dimensions that affect you. Take note that the actions in Table 19-8 are just the start. Be creative and come up with others on your own, or work with your therapist to devise more possibilities.

Table 19-8	Adaptive Schema Action List
Self-Concept Schemas	
Adaptive Schema	*Actions for Increasing*
Balanced self-worth	* When I want something, I will assess whether asking for it will unduly annoy anyone. If not, I'll make myself start asking. * I will look toward my friend as a role model. She asks for what she wants but does so with incredible grace.
Self-acceptance	* I will intentionally make a few mistakes each week to remind myself that I'm human. * I will acquire the habit of apologizing when appropriate.
Relationship Schemas	
Adaptive Schema	*Actions for Increasing*
Secure attachment	* I will call a friend to ask her to go to lunch with me. * I will start attending that church group and make myself meet people.
Realistic view of others	* I will make a list of both the positive and negative qualities of my friends while trying to accept the fact that everyone has both. * I will ask my friend for feedback on things my boyfriend says before I demonize him. She has a realistic view of people.
World Schemas	
Adaptive Schema	*Actions for Increasing*
Reasonable safety	* I will start taking a few reasonable risks in my life, although I'll maintain some degree of caution. I can ask my therapist for feedback on what's reasonable. * I will start taking more long, interesting walks. I'll avoid obviously dangerous places, but I'll force myself to go places by myself.
Predictable	* I will try a few things that I used to think were beyond my ability to control. I'll have a Plan B and a Plan C if things don't work out. * I will start keeping track of when things work out versus when they don't. I think I usually forget about things that really do work out okay.

The Adaptive Schema Action List in Table 19-8 only scratches the surface of possibilities. Use your creativity and/or consult with friends or your therapist for more ideas. Some of the actions in our list may fit your situation, but others may not. Even if you don't see ideas that are relevant to your life in our examples, we're confident that you can come up with some of your own.

Choosing actions that you feel are doable is important. If you try out an idea that seems unmanageable, see whether you can break it down into smaller steps. You don't get extra points for making larger steps; you still get to the goal line when you go one small step at a time.

Staying on track with flash cards

Another strategy for strengthening your adaptive schemas is to use something called *schema flash cards*. These flash cards organize information from the strategies we describe throughout this chapter into convenient 4-x-6 cards. The cards also add one more element: *self-accepting statements*.

Self-accepting statements are designed for you to use when you find yourself slipping and not making the changes or taking the actions you want to take. Inevitably, you will slip and slide at times. When you do, just accept the slip and forgive yourself for being human.

See the full instructions for filling out a schema flash card in Table 19-9.

Table 19-9	Schema Flash Card Instructions
Side 1	*Side 2*
My problematic schema: Jot down the name of your problematic schema, and feel free to individualize the definition.	**My new adaptive schema goal:** Write down the name of the adaptive schema you want to strengthen, and feel free to individualize it.
Feelings: Describe the feelings you have when your schema is active.	
Childhood origins: Describe an incident or two from childhood that may have led to your schema.	**Steps toward achieving the new schema:** List one to three action steps you want to take to strengthen this adaptive schema.
Current triggers: Make note of events that frequently trigger your problematic schemas in your world today.	**Self-accepting statements:** When you slip or fail to implement your desired changes, jot down what you want to say to yourself in an accepting, forgiving manner.

Schema flash cards can help you in several ways. First, they remind you of what you want to say or do when you mess up and exhibit one of your problematic schemas. In other words, they remind you of your self-accepting statements, which is important because problematic schemas tend to erase all other realities. Think about this situation: The last time you experienced a serious setback that set off your inferiority schema, you probably couldn't recall a single positive attribute or ability about yourself. Later, after you moved past the incident, you found that some of those positive aspects were easier to recall. In addition to reminding you of your self-accepting statements, flash cards help remind you

✔ To take active actions for building your new, more adaptive schemas

✔ To look at the difference between what triggers your maladaptive schemas today versus what created them in your childhood

Fill out a schema flash card for all your problematic schemas, and read each of them often — especially when your schema triggers hit you. But remember to be patient with yourself.

Tables 19-10 and 19-11 show two sample schema flash cards that **Claire**, a 38-year-old restaurant hostess, worked out with her therapist. Use these flash card examples to guide you in developing your own.

Table 19-10	Claire's Schema Flash Card #1
Side 1	**Side 2**
My problematic schema: Anxious Attachment — I worry constantly that anyone important to me will leave me.	**My new adaptive schema goal:** Secure Attachment — I want to be comfortable with being close to people and not feel so desperate.
Feelings: I feel frightened, jealous, and clingy.	
Childhood origins: My father left my mother when I was 6 years old, and then my mother had a never-ending series of boyfriends who would try to get close to me, but later they'd leave.	**Steps toward achieving the new schema:** I will quit questioning people's motives when they change plans on me; I will work on not being so defensive with people — and I'll read Chapter 18 for help on how to deal with criticism.
Current triggers: I display this schema when anyone backs out of plans with me; when my therapist leaves town; and when anyone criticizes me in the smallest way.	
	Self-accepting statements: I'm only human. I've had this problem for many years; of course, I'll slip here and there.

Table 19-11	Claire's Schema Flash Card #2
Side 1	**Side 2**
My problematic schema: Unpredictable — I view myself as a helpless victim, unable to influence what happens to me.	**My new adaptive schema goal:** Predictable — I want to feel more in charge of my life and accept that I can't control everything.
Feelings: I feel anxious, weak, and out of control.	**Steps toward achieving the new schema:** I will take a class on personal finances at the community college; I'm going to make myself drive in heavy traffic much more often so I get used to it.
Childhood origins: My mother and her boyfriends were completely unpredictable; I never knew what would please them.	
Current triggers: Heavy traffic scares me; paying bills makes me afraid of my future; whenever someone asks me to do something, I feel obligated to do it.	**Self-accepting statements:** I want to view my mistakes as experiences to learn from.

After you fill out your own schema flash cards, discuss them with your therapist, and then work on moving toward your new, more adaptive schemas. But, be ready for a few slips and falls along the way. Read your flash cards often.

Chapter 20

Considering Medication for BPD

*P*sychotropic medications are drugs that change your mood, behavior, or perceptions. Over the last several decades, the use of these medications has skyrocketed. In fact, prescriptions for antidepressants (one type of psychotropic medication) are more common than any other category of medications.

Although most people with borderline personality disorder (BPD) take one or more psychotropic medications, surprisingly, very little research supports the use of medication for the management of BPD.

This lack of supportive research doesn't mean that medication can't be useful when you or someone you love is dealing with BPD, but it does make the decision whether to use medication more complicated. In this chapter, we lay out what science has to say about BPD and medications. We describe various classes of medication that doctors commonly use to help manage the symptoms of BPD and discuss the reasons why someone with BPD may decide to use a certain drug. We also survey the common side effects of these drugs. Finally, we offer our advice and some thoughts about saying no to medication.

Putting Medications on Trial

A scientific consensus regarding the effectiveness of medications for treating symptoms of BPD doesn't exist. At this time, no definitive studies suggest that any particular drug will cure or even eliminate symptoms of BPD. In fact, the guidelines published in 2009 by the British National Institute for Health and Clinical Excellence state that drug treatment should *not* be used specifically for BPD and that psychotherapy is the cornerstone of treatment.

The problem is that most studies of medications and BPD to date have lacked rigor and high standards of scientific excellence. The main concern is the scarcity of what scientists call *randomized clinical trials* (RCTs), which are the most accepted form of experimentation in the world of science. The problem with RCTs is that they're time consuming and costly to run. In an RCT, the study's administrators randomly assign carefully selected and diagnosed participants to a treatment. For example, if a study is looking at how Drug A improves BPD symptoms, some participants are assigned to a group that receives Drug A, while others are assigned to a group that receives a sugar pill (also known as a *placebo*). A third set of participants may be assigned to a group that doesn't receive any drug for awhile. In the best-designed studies, neither the participants nor the doctors administering the treatment know which participants are getting a real treatment and which are getting a placebo. See the "More research on medications for BPD" sidebar for more information.

More research on medications for BPD

The Cochrane Collaboration, a global nonprofit organization that searches scientific literature and evaluates the quality of research done on various disorders, offers easy-to-understand reviews of this research for free on the Internet. Go to www.cochrane.org/reviews and search for whatever disorder you're interested in. The collaboration's recent report about BPD concludes that current scientific evidence doesn't support treating BPD with medications. Renowned BPD expert, Joel Paris, MD, agrees. In his book, *Treatment of Borderline Personality Disorder* (Guilford Press), Paris argues that doctors often give people with BPD too many prescriptions. But he concludes that when doctors are considering medications for BPD, the antidepressants (specifically, the selective serotonin reuptake inhibitors or SSRIs) are a possible first choice for treating some of the symptoms. He makes this choice because of the relative safety of SSRIs and their ability to decrease the depression and anxiety that often accompany BPD.

The World Federation of Societies of Biological Psychiatry, an international group of experts, published guidelines for treating BPD in 2007. This group also found that research supporting the use of specific medications for BPD has been sparse, but, like Paris, the group suggests that certain medications may be useful for managing some BPD symptoms.

Other problems in the research of medications and BPD include vast inconsistencies among studies. These inconsistencies make comparing and contrasting the studies extremely difficult. Studies vary in lengths of treatment, in ways of measuring improvement, and in manners of recruiting participants. For example, some studies took place over a five-week period, while others occurred over a six-month period. In terms of measuring improvement, some studies used patient self-report, others used psychological test scores, and still others used ratings given by the physician who gave the medications. In terms of recruiting methods, some studies recruited people through newspaper advertisements, while others used people who were in therapy. In some studies, not enough people participated; in others too many people dropped out midstudy. Finally, studies also vary in terms of funding: In some cases, the manufacturers of the drugs being studied provided the funding for the studies, which has led many professionals to question the results because of the possibility of conflict of interest.

The bottom line is that both doctors and patients should use medication for BPD with caution. Although many people do benefit enormously from psychotropic medication, having BPD doesn't necessarily mean taking a trip to the pharmacy. Most mental health professionals agree that psychological therapy is the best form of treatment for BPD. However, the following section takes a look at the reasons why doctors may consider medications in the treatment of BPD.

Getting Help from Medications

Experts agree that psychological therapies designed for treating BPD remain the most successful approaches to helping people who have this disorder. However, at times, adding medication to the mix can make a lot of sense.

Sometimes medications can be powerful tools for people with BPD. However, most people with BPD who choose to take medications don't obtain as much relief from these medications as they hoped for. Typically, medications for BPD provide only limited relief for a limited range of symptoms. For this reason, the best form of treatment is one that includes psychotherapy.

Considerations for taking medication

Your doctor may choose to put you on medication because of other disorders or symptoms that are occurring at the same time as your BPD. Thus, if one or more of the following situations occur, your care provider may consider medication:

✔ **You have both BPD and a major depressive disorder.** Research has found psychotherapy to be an effective treatment for depression. However, for some people, medication is an appropriate adjunct to psychotherapy. For more information about depression, see our book, *Depression For Dummies* (Wiley).

✔ **You have severe, debilitating anxiety and/or panic attacks.** Psychotherapy also helps treat this problem, but some folks find that medication helps them make progress in therapy.

✔ **You have BPD and bipolar disorder.** Doctors almost always call for medication when a person has bipolar disorder, formerly known as manic depressive disorder. For more on this disorder, check out Candida Fink and Joe Kraynak's *Bipolar Disorder For Dummies* (Wiley).

✔ **You start to hear voices or see things that aren't there, or you have bizarre, paranoid thoughts.** Medications can help treat these symptoms; however, they often have significant side effects and should rarely be used for long periods of time for BPD (see the "Surveying the Medicine Cabinet" section for more info on medication options). If you have BPD (and not schizophrenia), you shouldn't need to take them for a long time because people with BPD rarely experience these symptoms for extended periods of time.

✔ **You are at risk of imminently harming yourself or someone else.** If you arrive in an emergency room for treatment because of dangerous behavior, the medical staff will probably give you medication to calm you down.

✔ **Your unique symptoms lead your medical provider to determine that a trial of medication would be beneficial.** Sometimes experienced mental health professionals have reasons to try a certain medication, especially when other treatments have failed. However, you should never feel pressured to do something against your will. To ensure that people with BPD are comfortable with their doctor's suggested treatment, we encourage them and those who care about them to become educated about the pros and cons of medication.

Precautions to consider

Prior to beginning any medication regimen, be sure to have a complete physical exam. Your doctor may want to run a blood test to look at your thyroid function, cholesterol levels, liver condition, and other health risks that can influence the medication decision. In some cases, your doctor may recommend an *electrocardiogram* (EKG), a painless test that checks how fast and regular your heart is beating.

Make sure you keep your primary care provider informed about any treatment you're receiving, including psychotherapy or medication. Before taking any medications, be sure that you talk to your doctor about the following:

✔ Any physical conditions you have, including the following:

- Diabetes
- Metabolic syndrome
- High blood pressure
- Heart disease
- Liver disease
- Thyroid malfunction
- Kidney disease
- Chronic pain
- Migraine headaches
- Allergies

- • Hormone imbalances
- • Menopause
- • Arthritis
- • Cancer

✔ Other medications (either prescribed or over the counter) that you're taking

✔ Vitamins, herbs, or dietary supplements you take regularly

✔ Heavy caffeine (and/or energy drink) consumption

✔ Your drug or alcohol use

✔ Tobacco consumption

✔ Whether you're pregnant, planning a pregnancy, or breastfeeding

✔ Your family's mental health history

✔ Previous medications you didn't tolerate well

✔ Previous medications you found useful

Surveying the Medicine Cabinet

In this section, we briefly describe the medications that doctors commonly prescribe to treat symptoms associated with BPD. At this time, however, the evidence that medications directly help people with BPD is limited at best. Nevertheless, most people with BPD take some kind of medication. So, knowing what options are available is important both for people with BPD and those who care about them. Keep in mind that researchers are constantly developing new medications and conducting new studies on side effects and general benefits. For the latest information about medications and their side effects, talk to your doctor first. You can also find information about medications on the Web at www.webmd.com.

People with BPD attempt and commit suicide at an alarmingly high rate. Therefore, doctors who treat BPD must always consider the lethality of an overdose of any drug they prescribe.

In one small study of people with BPD, researchers gave one group of patients one gram of omega-3 fatty acids (found in fish oil) and another group placebos (sugar pills). After eight weeks, researchers found a reduction of depression and aggression symptoms in the group that took omega-3 fatty acids but not in the group that took placebos. Omega-3 fatty acids may ultimately prove to be an effective and safe option to treat depression and aggression in people with BPD, but at this time considerably more research is needed.

Antidepressants

The most commonly prescribed medications for people with BPD are *antide-pressants,* which are drugs that increase the availability of certain neurotrans-mitters (or chemicals that help nerve cells communicate) in the brain. These neurotransmitters affect mood, energy, aggressiveness, impulsivity, atten-tion, motivation, arousal, and appetite.

SSRIs

Doctors frequently prescribe *selective serotonin reuptake inhibitors* (SSRIs) for people with BPD. SSRIs boost the availability of serotonin in the brain. Although most people with BPD don't have classic major depression, some research does show that SSRIs can help decrease anger and impulsivity. An important advantage to consider when using this medication is its low risk of overdose. SSRIs may take from one to four or more weeks to take effect.

Keep in mind the following concerns when you're considering SSRIs as a form of treatment:

- ✔ Side effects can include weight gain, dizziness, dry mouth, upset stom-ach, insomnia, apathy, decreased sex drive, headaches, weight loss, tremors, sweating, or anxiety. Side effects usually diminish after a month and can sometimes be managed with other medical treatments.

- ✔ Don't stop taking an SSRI abruptly. Discontinuing use too quickly can cause headaches, nausea, sweating, problems sleeping, frightening dreams, or fever and chills.

- ✔ Studies have linked SSRIs to an increased likelihood of suicidal thoughts and attempts in children, adolescents, and young adults. Doctors need to monitor moods carefully whenever someone starts a new medication, but especially younger people.

- ✔ A life threatening condition, called *serotonin syndrome,* can occur when too much serotonin is in the body. Another kind of antidepressant — monoamine oxidase inhibitors (MAOIs) — can lead to this condition when you take them at the same time as SSRIs (see the next section for more info on MAOIs). In addition, some migraine medications, pain relief medications, and dietary supplements can increase risk for serotonin syndrome.

A wide variety of SSRIs have become available in the last decade or two. People often need to try more than one to discover what works best for them. Be patient and work with your mental healthcare provider when trying SSRIs for the first time. Among the most frequently prescribed SSRIs (with their brand names in parentheses) are

✔ **Citalopram (Celexa):** This SSRI seems to have fewer side effects and is well tolerated by elderly people.

✔ **Escitalopram (Lexapro):** Prescribed for both anxiety and depression, this drug may work faster than its chemical cousin, citalopram.

✔ **Fluvoxamine (Luvox):** Also prescribed for obsessive-compulsive disorder (OCD), this drug is more sedating than other SSRIs.

✔ **Paroxetine (Paxil):** This drug is associated with weight gain, sedation, and significant withdrawal symptoms.

✔ **Fluoxetine (Prozac):** This drug tends to be more stimulating than other SSRIs and can sometimes cause insomnia. It has FDA approval for treating OCD, depression, anxiety, and premenstrual dysphoric disorder.

✔ **Sertraline (Zoloft):** This drug appears to be the safest medication for people with cardiac problems and doesn't seem to be either overly stimulating or sedating.

Other antidepressants

Because SSRIs are relatively safe and because some research supports their use with BPD, other types of antidepressants are less widely used. However, in the quest to find relief, doctors sometimes prescribe antidepressants that affect other neurotransmitters or older generations of antidepressants. These other types of antidepressants include

✔ **SNRIs:** Dual serotonin-norepinephrine reuptake inhibitors (SNRIs) work by increasing levels of the neurotransmitters, serotonin and norepinephrine. Venlafaxine (Effexor) and duloxetine (Cymbalta) are two antidepressants in this category.

✔ **NDRIs:** Norepinephrine-dopamine reuptake inhibitors (NDRIs) increase availability of the neurotransmitters, norepinephrine and dopamine. Doctors sometimes use bupropion (Wellbutrin or Zyban), one of the drugs in this category, to help people stop smoking or to treat attention deficit/hyperactivity disorder (AD/HD).For more on AD/HD, check out Jeff Strong and Michael O. Flanagan's *AD/HD For Dummies* (Wiley).

✔ **Tricyclics:** Doctors rarely prescribe tricyclics, an older variety of medications, for people with BPD because an overdose can be fatal. Side effects can also be considerably worse than those of other more refined medications and include dry mouth, dizziness, drop in blood pressure, and blurred vision.

✔ **MAOIs:** The oldest type of antidepressants, MAOIs can have serious and dangerous side effects, including dangerous spikes in blood pressure. As a result, doctors don't use them often.

Lessons from cousins

Considerable evidence links lower concentrations of the brain chemical communicator called serotonin to a variety of mental disorders, including depression and anxiety. Research also associates problems in serotonin function with impulsive aggression. Furthermore, impulsive aggression is often a symptom of BPD.

To better understand where impulsive aggression comes from, researchers have studied the connection between genes and early environment in rhesus monkeys because human beings share over 90 percent of their genetic makeup with rhesus monkeys. During their research, scientists found that some monkeys have a gene that, when activated, appears to affect concentrations of serotonin. However, when the monkeys with that gene were raised by their own mothers, the gene didn't appear to affect serotonin levels at all. By contrast, when monkeys with that gene were raised by other monkeys (not their own mothers), the gene appeared to trigger lower levels of serotonin.

Furthermore, monkeys raised by other monkeys (not their own mothers) were more likely to become impulsively aggressive than monkeys raised by their own mothers. Aggressive monkeys fought with others in their troop and acted up with their elders. As adolescents, they could've been expelled from their troops or become social outcasts. Apparently, early environmental factors interact with genetic factors and lead to later behavioral problems in monkeys. This scenario sounds a little like what happens with people who develop BPD — a less-than-ideal childhood environment increases the likelihood that a genetic risk will be activated.

Neuroleptics

Researchers originally designed *neuroleptics,* also called *antipsychotic drugs,* to help people with schizophrenia, but doctors now use them for other problems, including BPD. The following sections describe the two classes of antipsychotic drugs, which are typical and atypical.

 A rare but serious side effect of neuroleptic drugs is known as *neuroleptic malignant syndrome* (NMS). NMS causes fever, delirium, and muscle rigidity and can cause a coma. NMS can also be life threatening. Scientists once thought NMS occurred only in reaction to the older typical antipsychotic drugs. However, doctors have reported cases of NMS in people taking the newer, atypical antipsychotics. If these symptoms develop in you or someone you care about who's taking antipsychotics, seek immediate medical attention.

Typical antipsychotics

Typical antipsychotics have been around awhile, and doctors often use them in emergency rooms to calm people down. These drugs aren't usually a good choice for people with BPD because BPD tends to be a chronic disorder. Typical antipsychotics can lead to disturbing side effects with long-term use.

Tardive dyskinesia is an especially troubling side effect of typical antipsychotics that involves uncontrolled, repetitive movements. People with this side effect may make facial grimaces, smack their lips, or have rapid movements of the body, arms, or legs. Frequently, they can't control their fingers and may look like they're playing an imaginary piano. Unfortunately, treatment of this side effect can take considerable time and isn't always successful. As a result, people who already have a severe emotional distress end up with a physical condition that's extremely difficult to tolerate. Another troubling side effect that occurs mainly with typical antipsychotic drugs is called *akanthisia*. People who have this side effect describe a desperate state of inner restlessness, agitation, and anxiety. Treatment begins with discontinuing the use of the atypical antipsychotic medication and trying out other medications to reduce the symptoms.

Atypical antipsychotics

Researchers developed these newer neuroleptics with the hope of decreasing the risk of side effects such as tardive dyskinesia, but the extent to which this goal has been achieved isn't yet clear. Limited research suggests that atypical antipsychotics may have a calming effect and reduce impulsivity. Researchers have completed a few positive trials with patients who have BPD, but again, research is limited.

The following list provides the generic names followed by the brand names of some of the most common atypical antipsychotic drugs. We note in this list whether or not these drugs cause weight gain. Before beginning a prescription medication that can increase weight, your doctor should screen you for hypertension and risks of diabetes. This screening should include looking at fasting plasma glucose (blood drawn after a night-long fast), cholesterol levels, and blood pressure.

- ✔ **Aripiprazole (Abilify):** This drug is less sedating and can cause less weight gain than some of the others in this group.

- ✔ **Clozapine (Clozaril):** Side effects can be severe, including sweating, increased salivation (drooling), and weight gain. It's not usually given for BPD.

- ✔ **Ziprasidone (Geodon):** This drug is less sedating and causes less weight gain than some other atypical antipsychotics. You should take this drug with food.

- ✔ **Paliperidone (Invega):** Less sedating than other medications, this drug isn't for use with elderly patients.

- ✔ **Risperidone (Risperdal):** This drug can decrease agitation and behavioral disturbances and often causes weight gain.

✔ **Quetiapine (Seroquel):** Linked to sedation and weight gain, this drug isn't recommended for people with cardiac risks.

✔ **Olanzapine (Zyprexa):** This drug can cause weight gain. Smoking cigarettes may decrease its effectiveness. Researchers have studied this medication in randomized controlled trials, and it appears to improve symptoms in BPD.

Doctors use brand name Symbyax, a combined form of fluoxetine, an antidepressant, and olanzapine, an atypical antipsychotic, to treat bipolar disorder.

The FDA warns that atypical antipsychotics can lead to hyperglycemia or diabetes. Some of these medications appear to be worse than others. In fact, olanzapine, one of the drugs studied for treating BPD, leads to significant weight gain, which can then lead to diabetes. Furthermore, some reports suggest that these medications may increase the risk of sudden heart failure. Therefore, you or someone you love shouldn't take these drugs without considerable consideration of both the costs and benefits.

Mood Stabilizers

Mood stabilizers, also known as *anticonvulsants* or *antiseizure medications,* are drugs that prevent reoccurring seizures in people with epilepsy. In addition to preventing seizures, though, they appear to even out moodiness and, as a result, are a frequent choice for people with bipolar disorder. A few studies suggest that mood stabilizers can decrease impulsive anger in some people with BPD. Again, research is limited.

However, you can't ignore the downsides of mood stabilizers when you're considering them for yourself or someone you care about. First, while taking these medications, people need to be monitored closely for possible toxicity. And second, overdosing on mood stabilizers can be fatal.

Some of the mood stabilizers (with the brand names in parentheses) your physician may recommend include

✔ **Lithium (Lithium):** Commonly used to treat bipolar disorder, this drug is rarely used to treat BPD. Although Lithium is a naturally occurring salt, it can be deadly when levels get too high.

✔ **Valporic acid or divalproex (Depakote):** Less dangerous than lithium in terms of toxicity, this drug may help reduce aggression. Weight gain and sedation are common side effects.

✔ **Lamotrigine (Lamictal):** This drug may be useful in reducing impulsivity and anger. One side effect is a rare but possibly fatal skin reaction. It also causes less weight gain than other mood stabilizers.

- **Gabapentin (Neurontin):** Used for peripheral nerve pain, this drug may also reduce anxiety. It doesn't cause as many side effects as the other mood stabilizers.

- **Carbamazepine (Tegretol):** Fatal in overdose, this drug is used for treating resistant bipolar and psychotic disorders. It interferes with birth control pills, and people taking it need frequent blood monitoring.

- **Oxcarbazepine (Trileptal):** Chemically similar to carbamazepine, this drug is safer, but it also interferes with birth control pills.

- **Topiramate (Topamax):** Associated with weight loss, this drug can cause problems with slowed thinking. Topiramate has shown some potential to treat certain problems with addiction and impulsivity, such as alcohol addiction and pathological gambling, but, like all the other drug treatments, much more research needs to be done.

Making the Medication Decision

The quality of life for people with BPD can be quite poor. As we describe in Chapter 3, some people with BPD experience sudden shifts in mood and have severe interpersonal problems. Others hurt themselves, and some eventually kill themselves. Thus, you can understand why people search for ways to end their suffering. If taking one medication cured BPD, everyone involved would be delighted, no doubt. Unfortunately, researchers haven't yet found a drug that can take away all the pain.

Therefore, you need to keep your expectations for medications realistic. If your treatment includes taking medication, stay in close contact with your physician or psychiatrist so that he can monitor the effects of the drug as well as the effects on your mood and your general health. When you take medications, we advise you to do the following:

- Be patient. Some medications take a number of weeks to become fully effective.

- Be informed. Know what side effects to expect and discuss the benefits and risks with your physician thoroughly.

- Take your medication as prescribed. Don't discontinue medications suddenly without consulting your doctor because serious problems can result. Never take more than the prescribed amount.

- Don't drink alcohol or take illegal drugs while taking medications for BPD.

- If you experience serious side effects, consult with your doctor about possibly decreasing or eliminating some of your medication.

✔ Tell your doctor about any and all side effects you experience with a medication, including sexual side effects, even though you may feel embarrassed doing so. Sometimes side effects reduce with time; other times your doctor may prescribe a different medication to deal with side effects or add another medication to lessen the first drug's side effects.

✔ Realize that if you think a certain drug may be helpful to you, but your physician disagrees, he probably has a good reason. Many people with BPD seek medications that have addictive potential. In the end, these medications are likely to cause more harm than good.

✔ Be aware that adding additional medications won't likely result in a fully satisfactory outcome. The more medications you take, the more side effects you can expect.

✔ If you disagree with your physician, you can seek a second opinion. However, try to avoid the temptation of endless doctor shopping, because you're likely looking for a perfect doctor and that doctor doesn't exist.

Studies show that psychotherapy tends to work better than medication for BPD. Remember that psychotherapy does take awhile. Try not to expect medication miracles because you will most likely be disappointed. Hopefully, sometime in the future, researchers will find a more effective medication option for treating BPD.

Part V
Advice for People Who Care

The 5th Wave   By Rich Tennant

"I don't know, Mona — sometimes I get the feeling you're afraid to get close."

In this part . . .

At one time or another, most people have known, cared about, or loved one or more people who suffer from borderline personality disorder (BPD). If one of your friends, colleagues, or loved ones has BPD, you know the challenges that BPD causes. Well, this part is for all of you. Here we lay out strategies for handling difficult times when you're interacting with people who have BPD.

Chapter 21

What to Do When Your Partner Has BPD

In This Chapter

▶ Understanding BPD behaviors and their effects

▶ Keeping everyone safe when BPD is part of a relationship

▶ Knowing when to leave a relationship with someone who has BPD

▶ Walking away if you decide to do so

"**Y**ou have the right to remain silent. Anything you say can and will be used against you." Sound familiar? Well, you're not under arrest — you're involved with someone who has borderline personality disorder (BPD). You may even feel like you're alone in a relationship that defies logic and reason.

Living with BPD, whether you or someone you love has the disorder, feels like walking across an old board that stretches over a creek. Some steps land solid and secure, while others sway and threaten to toss you into the creek far below. You never know what the next step will feel like — a situation that leaves you confused and unbalanced. Furthermore, partners of people with BPD often feel manipulated, criticized, misunderstood, and even afraid.

This chapter is for the husband, wife, partner, or lover of someone with BPD. If you're someone who actually has BPD, you may want to read this chapter to better understand the mixed feelings your partner may be having. Therapists who work with family members of people with BPD can also benefit from reviewing this chapter's unique perspective.

To begin this chapter, we discuss common borderline behaviors. To those of you who live with and love people with BPD, we explain how to maintain emotional and physical safety in your relationship. We give you strategies for dealing with difficult communications. We also provide some hints on how to evaluate whether or not you should remain in the relationship. Finally, we tell you how to safely end a relationship with someone who has BPD if you decide to do so.

Understanding Borderline Behaviors within Relationships

If your partner has BPD, you really need to understand the nature of the disorder before you can try to improve your relationship, get professional help for understanding your own feelings, or even choose to end the relationship. We strongly recommend that you read Chapters 3 through 10 to fully appreciate what you're dealing with. Most nonprofessionals don't know a great deal about BPD. Therefore, many partners can easily begin to question their own sanities when they end up in relationships with people who have BPD.

This section discusses some of the most problematic BPD behaviors that make staying in a relationship with someone with the disorder challenging. We discuss what these behaviors feel like, and, in subsequent sections, we give you ideas for dealing with them. We hope this information helps you anchor yourself in reality again.

People with BPD don't consciously and intentionally act the way they do. Their problems have a long history and are rooted in both biology and early childhood. We present the following information to help you better understand people with BPD and deal with the challenges of their behavior more effectively.

Going to extremes

Most people, whether they have BPD or not, have a lot of good qualities mixed in with some not-so-great ones. But people with BPD can't easily see people as a mix of both good and bad. Instead, their minds focus on one or the other at any given time. Therefore, they see their partners as either angels or devils — and not much in between. One day your partner may see you as the most wonderful person who ever lived, and the next day (sometimes the next hour), your partner may view you with complete contempt.

The following story about Anthony's relationship with Beth, who has BPD, illustrates how someone with BPD can flip from adoring, seductive behavior to demonizing, hateful behavior at the drop of a hat.

> Since his divorce two years ago, Anthony hasn't gotten serious with anyone — that is, until now. He met **Beth** a couple of weeks ago, but he's already head-over-heels in love. She's cute, smart, and charming. She absolutely adores him. They become intimate quickly to Anthony's delight. And since their second date, they've pretty much been inseparable.

Beth calls or texts him throughout the day, and they get together every night that Anthony doesn't have his two young children at home. As soon as he got joint custody, he set a rule that no female would spend the night when his kids were with him. Beth doesn't like that rule, but he figures she'll just have to understand.

One Wednesday Anthony waits with the other parents in front of the elementary school. His cell buzzes — Beth texts him, "Where R U?" He enters, "P U kids." She texts, "C U L8TR." Anthony assumes that she means Thursday after work. Later that evening at home, his kids finish their homework while Anthony cleans the kitchen. Beth uses her key and walks into the house. "Daddy, who's that?" Anthony's kids say in unison.

"Uh, hi Beth, I didn't expect you," Anthony says as he reaches out a hand in front of him to keep her from giving him her regular passionate greeting.

Beth reaches into a grocery bag and pulls out an ice cream cake. "I thought the kids might enjoy a snack while we talk upstairs in your room," she suggests.

"Umm, Beth, that really isn't such a good idea. I'd love to, but I think it's too soon for my kids to deal with something like this right now," Anthony says in a soft voice.

"Oh, I get it. I'm not important to you. You really are a jerk. Why don't you just go marry your ex-wife!" Beth screams as she stomps off.

The next day Beth sends Anthony flowers at work. Anthony feels very pleased but confused at the same time.

If Anthony decides to remain in his relationship with Beth, he can expect many more seismic shifts in Beth's emotions and behaviors. Like other people with BPD, Beth flips from one extreme to the other in seconds. Often, people with BPD seem to have no memory of the previous day's hateful outbursts.

Giving you the silent treatment

Some people with BPD deal with their anger by refusing to communicate. For their partners, this silence can feel extremely abusive. The cold stares and refusals to speak frequently stand in stark contrast to the friendly façades they present to others. People with BPD may cheerfully play with children or flirt with waiters even though they make no eye contact with their partners. Partners often remain in the dark about what they did to deserve the silent treatment — perhaps they failed to fold a pair of pants correctly, put too much salad dressing on a salad, or had a bad hair day. No matter how trivial their misbehaviors are, they never know how to fix them because their partners with BPD refuse to tell them what's bothering them.

People with BPD often employ this silent strategy when their partners really want to communicate with them. Silence gives people with BPD an illusion of power, which they can use to hide the vulnerability they feel inside. Silence lets them control the amount of distance versus closeness they have in their relationships.

Bradford, recently diagnosed with BPD, has been married to Selma for about 12 years. Their story illustrates the subtle cruelty of the silent treatment.

"How did your meeting go with your boss?" Selma asks her husband, **Bradford**, as he walks through the door. "Did he apologize for being so unfair to you?"

Bradford slams the door and throws his briefcase across the floor, scattering papers. Their dog cowers and Selma says, "I guess it didn't go so great. Are you okay?"

Instead of answering, Bradford goes to the refrigerator and pulls out a container of leftover spaghetti. He begins to shovel the cold spaghetti into his mouth, dripping sauce on his chin. Selma makes another attempt to communicate, "Hey, honey, is there anything I can do? Can I get you something to drink?"

Bradford turns his back to her and finishes the leftovers. Then he gets a carton of ice cream from the freezer and finishes what's left in four huge spoonfuls. Selma, knowing what's next, sighs and says, "Okay, Bradford, I'm going to go grocery shopping. Is there anything you need?"

He doesn't reply and goes into their bathroom. She hears the shower turn on. Most likely, when she returns, he'll be asleep.

When under stress, Bradford, like many people with BPD, finds talking openly about his feelings difficult. Instead, he clams up and shows his distress to his partner. After 12 years of marriage and lots of therapy, Selma is able to take herself out of the situation by leaving the house.

Before moving on, we want to be clear about one thing: The silent treatment is abusive. It's one of the cruelest actions people with BPD can dish out to the people who love them most. Recipients — usually their partners — feel diminished, powerless, helpless, confused, and torn apart (see the "Feeling rejected and abandoned" section for more info on these feelings). Silence violates the essence of intimacy and trust.

If your partner abuses you with silence or anything else, seeking therapy can help you sort out what's going on and what you should do.

Gaslighting

Gaslighting is a term that comes from the 1940 film *Gaslight*. In the film, the main character, Gregory, manipulates a woman's home gas lights so that they dim at times that she thinks she's alone. His manipulation makes her believe that she's imagining the dimming, which leads her to question her own sanity.

Today gaslighting means providing false or distorted information with the intent of disrupting someone's ability to trust her own senses, reasoning ability, and memory of events. People with BPD may not be consciously aware of their gaslighting behaviors, but they do often distort facts, withhold information, or rewrite history so that their partners no longer trust their own reactions and memories. By making their partners feel more anxious and insecure, people with BPD often feel more confident that their partners won't leave them — this feeling becomes the motivation for their gaslighting behaviors.

John, who has BPD, uses gaslighting to confuse and unsettle his wife, Zoe. John starts by deliberately moving some garbage cans that Zoe has put out for their party. This sets the stage for his next stunt, inviting a former girlfriend to the party.

> "The food looks wonderful; the caterer did a great job," Zoe comments to her husband **John**. "People will be arriving soon."
>
> John nods, "Where are the garbage cans for people to toss plates and cups?"
>
> "I put one in the pantry, and the other one is outside on the patio," Zoe hears the first car drive up and peeks into the pantry, finding no garbage can. She also checks the patio and fails to see the other garbage can. "Did you move the garbage cans?" she asks John.
>
> "No, you probably forgot to put them out. Just go greet our guests. And try to be nice, and don't embarrass me if you can," John snaps.
>
> At the door, Zoe sees Ellen, John's former girlfriend. "Ellen," she says as she holds out her hand in greeting, "I'm glad to see you." Zoe doesn't recall John telling her that he invited Ellen, but Zoe knows not to ask.
>
> John comes out of the garage with the two garbage cans. He puts one in the pantry and one on the patio. Zoe starts to wonder if she really put them out. Zoe feels shaken by the garbage cans and the ex-girlfriend. She knows it's going to be a difficult night.

As you can see from John and Zoe's story, when people with BPD question their partners' perceptions and memories, their partners begin to question them, too. But because people with BPD only show their friends and family their good sides (while simultaneously bombarding their partners with their sinister sides), people with BPD often elicit complete support from those friends and family. As a result, their partners don't have anyone to turn to as they continue to doubt their own perceptions and memories.

Initiating isolation

Social support and connections make people feel more confident and secure. Confident, secure people trust their own judgments and know the difference between acceptable and outrageous behavior. People with BPD often attempt to isolate their partners from friends, relatives, and other sources of support — as a result, their partners feel less secure and less confident, which, in turn, means they're less likely to leave their partners with BPD. People with BPD probably aren't consciously aware of their attempts to isolate their partners, but the result is the same.

Isolation often occurs slowly and insidiously over time. It can overtake you before you even know what hit you. If you're not sure whether or not you've become isolated, consider the following questions:

- ✔ Do you find your partner's behavior so embarrassing that you avoid going out with people?

- ✔ Do you fear telling your friends and close relatives the truth about the nature of your relationship?

- ✔ Does your partner question you about where you're going, how long you'll be gone, and who you're seeing whenever you leave the house for a few hours?

- ✔ Do you feel suffocated by your partner?

- ✔ Does your partner put down your friends and family?

- ✔ Does your partner find ways to interfere with your plans to see other people socially?

If, after reviewing these questions, you're still not sure whether or not you've become too isolated, consider seeking counseling for yourself so that you can talk through your situation. Having a confidential source to help you sort out reality versus the effects of BPD can help you become more able to rationally deal with what's happening.

Shaking up the present

If your partner has BPD, you probably notice that the atmosphere surrounding your relationship is charged with electricity. Your partner flies into rages, sometimes for no obvious reason. Your partner may also respond to events with a flair for drama.

People with BPD have great difficulty regulating their emotions (see Chapter 6 for more information about explosive emotions). Some people describe people with BPD as being addicted to drama and danger. Your partner's ride on this emotional rollercoaster can send your stomach into spasms and leave you feeling frightened and helpless.

David's story depicts how some people with BPD crave excitement even though their risky behaviors may frighten the people they care about.

> The rain and wind are so fierce that cars and trucks pull off to the side of the road, waiting for the weather to let up a bit. **David's** windshield wipers are on high, but visibility is close to zero. "David, can't you pull over?" asks Ben, "I'm getting scared."
>
> "Don't interrupt me, Ben. I need to concentrate on my driving," David curtly responds.
>
> The wind picks up, and the car momentarily slides into the other lane. Ben sinks down into his seat, terrified but quiet. David increases his speed — angry at the weather but also exhilarated by the dangerous conditions. Ben feels helpless; this isn't the first time his partner has purposefully done something to frighten him.

Ben, David's partner, has learned over time that when he complains about David's risky behaviors, David explodes. Ben feels helpless to alter his partner's behavior. He also feels embarrassed to tell anyone about his concerns.

Expressing entitlement

People whose partners have BPD often feel pressured to meet unyielding, unrelenting demands. They feel they must dance to their partners' melodies because they're the only audible songs in the relationship. People with BPD typically feel entitled to have their needs met, no matter how trivial or important they are. Yet, they don't understand how their demands affect their partners.

If you do try to resist your partner's demands, your partner probably ups the ante and becomes even more demanding. Eventually, you find yourself giving in. Unfortunately, when you do give in, you reinforce the pattern of behavior, making it more likely to occur again.

The following story about Heather illustrates how someone with BPD can seem selfish because she's unable to see that she makes excessive demands of her partner.

> **Heather** is a medical technician in a busy office. She comes home tired.
>
> "Sam, what did you make for dinner? I'm beat," she asks her husband. Without waiting for an answer, she complains, "You wouldn't believe the day I had. Patients had to wait an hour for lab work, and my boss was crabby all day. Bring me a beer."

Heather lies back on the couch taking off her shoes. "Sam, did you hear me? Where is the remote? Did I tell you I hate my job? I don't know why you're not more supportive. Sam, what the hell are you doing?"

Sam mutters under his breath, "I had a bad day, too."

"What did you say? Sam, I really need a bath — can you turn on the water for me? I'll eat dinner later. Hey, where's my beer? Sam? Sam, why the attitude?

"I'll be right there, Heather, let me open you a beer and get your bath ready."

Sam feels beat up and neglected. If you asked Heather how Sam feels, she would be oblivious to his feelings. People with BPD have trouble putting themselves in other people's shoes (check out Chapter 8 for more about this particular symptom of BPD). Instead, they focus entirely on their own wants and needs.

Acting impulsively

If your partner has BPD, you probably notice that she acts without thinking. She's likely to cut herself, drink to a drunken stupor, consume risky drugs, threaten or attempt suicide, gamble, shoplift, or go on reckless shopping binges (see Chapter 5 for more information about the nature of impulsivity and BPD). After a while, you may even find that you're becoming numb to some of these outrageous episodes. On the other hand, you may never get used to these behaviors, and your heart may flip-flop repeatedly. Nothing you do seems to help slow down or stop the impulsivity cycle.

The following story about Sandra, a young woman with BPD, and her boyfriend, Aaron, shows you how a pattern of anger, drinking, and then self-mutilation can destroy a relationship.

Sandra flies into a jealous rage when she catches her boyfriend spending time on MySpace. "How dare you!" she yells. "You're disgusting."

"What are you talking about Sandra? I was just looking," Aaron replies. "What's the big deal? I wasn't doing anything."

"I'm sick of your perversions; I can't stand it around here. I'm going out so I can calm down," Sandra grabs her purse and keys.

"Please, Sandra, don't do anything stupid. You know the last time you went out you got plastered and ended up feeling pretty bad the next day," Aaron stands up and starts to go to Sandra.

"Don't even get near me," Sandra says as she throws a book aimed at Aaron's head. "I'll do what I want. You don't own me." Sandra storms out of the house and slams the front door on her way.

Aaron goes back to MySpace and imagines the day when he can finally get up the courage to leave Sandra. It won't be long.

Sandra goes to the neighborhood bar and starts drinking. After her fourth drink, the bartender, who knows her well, calls Aaron to come and get her. Aaron arrives to find Sandra leaning on an obviously uncomfortable young man at the bar. Aaron hopes to be able to lead Sandra home without another scene.

Like Aaron, partners of people with BPD sometimes rescue their loved ones from risky situations. Impulsive, risky behavior can also include sexual escapades that do little to fill the emptiness in the person with BPD but that do great harm to the relationship.

Feeling rejected and abandoned

Being romantically involved with someone who has BPD can be challenging, to say the least. People with BPD fear abandonment, but they also fear engulfment. So, at one moment, they cling to a relationship, and, at the next, they run or push angrily away.

The following story about Andrew and Anita illustrates the see-saw behaviors of a man with BPD and their effects on his new wife.

"You look beautiful tonight, Anita," **Andrew** says as he hugs his wife and plants a kiss on her lips. "I like the way you did your hair, and the dress is stunning. It's great to have a lovely young wife to show off."

"Thank you, Andrew, I know this party with your co-workers is important, and I wanted you to feel proud of me," Anita says as she pats down her hair and gathers her purse.

Andrew doesn't answer at first. He begins to wonder why Anita had to ruin a good compliment. His good mood turns sour. He turns away from her as he speaks. "Do you think I need a wife to make me look good in front of my colleagues?"

"No, Andrew, of course not. I was hoping to please you," she answers, puzzled by the tone of his question. "We don't go to many parties where we have to dress up and, um, I don't know. I'm sorry if I said something wrong."

"So, now you're telling me that I don't take you out enough. I try to please you but you're so shallow and spoiled that nothing I do is good enough," Andrew yells as he stomps down the stairs into the kitchen.

Anita follows and says, "Andrew, what are you talking about? I only want to be close to you. I want us to be able to talk and be happy."

Andrew fills the silent room with his fury. Anita shakes her head. "Am I crazy?" she thinks to herself.

Anita doesn't understand what happened. Andrew started out feeling warm and close to Anita, but then he got scared. What scared him? Maybe the idea that if he loves her too much she may leave him. Or perhaps a picture of her flirting at the party. Or the fear that she will reject him for someone better. Andrew's great fear of abandonment is based on a deep feeling of inferiority. That fear leads him to push Anita away.

Misinterpreting threats to self-esteem

People with BPD have fragile senses of who they are and what they're worth. Their delicate self-esteems shatter easily. Partners of people with BPD sometimes bruise their loved ones' senses of self, often without even knowing they're doing so. People with BPD can construe comments made with benign intent as harmful. The mind of someone with BPD spins a complex web ready to catch any fleeting remarks that it can distort.

The following story about Alyssa, a woman with BPD, and Mark, her date, is one example of how an innocent question can quickly morph into a threat to the self-esteem of someone with BPD.

"Wow, this steak is juicy and tender. Perfect. How's your pasta, **Alyssa**?" Mark asks.

"Fantastic," she replies. "Thanks for bringing me to this restaurant. I really like trying new places," Alyssa says as she smiles.

"I'm happy that we're finally going out on a date. I've noticed you at work for a long time. I thought you'd never want to go out with me. I'm glad I asked, and I'm even more glad that you accepted," Mark says as he smiles, too.

"You know, I was married until last year. I stayed away from men for awhile. My breakup was tough and I needed to work on getting myself to a better place," Alyssa confides. "But I'm ready now to get back into the dating scene, and going out with you seems to be a perfect start. Tell me about yourself, Mark."

"Well, I've worked at this company since I finished my MBA a few years back. I'm hoping to stay here for another couple of years. The company has been good to me. You know, I was made district manager last year," Mark says. "How about you, what are your hopes and dreams?"

Alyssa's face becomes serious; she's flooded by sadness. "Hopes and dreams. Those went out the window when my marriage broke up. I wanted a family. Now I have nothing."

"Oh, Alyssa, I'm sorry I brought that up. I guess I was stupid. I was talking about the future, not the past. I hope I didn't upset you," Mark says as he reaches for her hand across the table.

She pulls her hand away and says, "Don't be condescending with me, Mark. Just because you're damn perfect doesn't mean you have the right to shove it in my face."

"Alyssa, gosh, I didn't mean . . . I don't know what to say, I'm a bit confused, really. Can we start over?" Mark asks sincerely.

"No, Mark. I don't think so. As a matter of fact, I'm ready to go now. Thanks for dinner."

Mark leaves cash on the table and drives Alyssa home. He's shocked when she invites him in for a drink. He wisely declines.

Alyssa started the evening in a decent mood, and Mark's interest flattered her. Just by asking about her hopes and dreams, Mark set off a cascade of self-loathing reactions on Alyssa's part. She spiraled into an abyss and angrily shot back, "Don't be condescending with me, Mark." By the time she gets home, though, she's over her outburst and ready for a sexual encounter. This story illustrates how easily — and unknowingly — you can puncture the self-esteem of a person with BPD.

Staying Safe: Emotionally and Physically

Having a relationship with someone who has BPD becomes maximally challenging when you throw together emotional and physical safety. You probably worry about your partner's safety if she takes part in impulsive, self-destructive behaviors, such as cutting and burning or even suicidal actions (see Chapter 5 for more information about the types of self-harming acts people with BPD engage in). You may also have legitimate concerns about being abused yourself, whether that abuse is emotional or physical. The sections that follow give you some ideas for how to deal with these harmful behaviors (many of which we describe in previous sections).

We strongly recommend that you seek therapy for yourself if you're in a close relationship with someone who has BPD. This advice holds particularly true if your partner engages in either self-abuse or abuse of you or others in your family. These issues pose complex and challenging threats that can tax the coping ability of anyone.

Dealing with your partner's self-abuse

Nothing is more painful than watching your partner engage in acts of self-destruction. You probably feel guilty, responsible, frustrated, or even angry when you see these behaviors in someone you love. But realizing your own limits is important. You aren't the cause of these actions, and you certainly can't serve as your partner's therapist. Don't argue, reason, or discuss these volatile issues. Your partner will *not* be receptive to logic and reasoning during an outburst.

Now that we've told you what not to do, here are a few ideas about what you can do:

✔ Remind your partner about any alternative strategies for coping that she may have written down (see Chapters 15 and 16 for examples of emergency preparedness plans and flash cards). However, don't suggest alternative strategies for the first time during an outburst.

✔ Remember that your partner's actions aren't about you. In other words, don't take them personally.

✔ Remain calm.

✔ Call your partner's therapist if she has one.

✔ Calmly tell your partner that you're going to leave for awhile — if the behaviors don't appear to be life threatening. This action works best when you've already told your partner that you plan to leave for awhile the next time she engages in serious self-abuse.

✔ Call an ambulance or the police if the behavior looks like it may escalate to violence.

✔ Remind your partner of previous coping strategies that seemed to work.

✔ Call your own therapist and make an appointment to discuss your options for the future.

What you can't do is assume responsibility for your partner's actions. Obviously, you want to avoid keeping guns hanging around the house, but you can't get rid of every sharp object or potential weapon.

Knowing what to do when you're the recipient of abuse

Only rarely do people with BPD consciously and intentionally set out to cause harm to their partners. Rather, they respond to fears with amazing emotional intensity and strike out as a form of self-defense. But, at some level, what their intentions are doesn't matter because the results are the same for their partners whether or not they intended to hurt them in the first place.

If you're in real fear for your physical safety, the only good plan is to pick up any kids who are involved, take a few crucial documents (if you have them), and get out of the household. Don't threaten that you'll leave; just do so and call the police — preferably after you're out of the house.

Whether your partner intends to be malicious or not, being abused is never okay. If you aren't sure whether your partner's behavior is over the line, seek therapy to help you figure out the situation. Abuse comes in a wide variety of forms, including inducing guilt, gaslighting, isolating, being overly demanding, and giving the silent treatment (see the "Understanding Borderline Behaviors within Relationships" section for more examples). To make situations more difficult, abuse isn't always easy to recognize. Furthermore, abuse has a nasty habit of escalating slowly over time.

Whether you've sought therapy for yourself or not, you can get a better handle on what's going on by keeping a secret log of the interactions between you and your partner. People with BPD can make you feel crazy and an objective account of your interactions can help you find clarity. The key is to write out exactly what each of you said and what happened, almost like you're writing a police report. Over time when you review your compilations, you may be able to more fully appreciate how much abuse you've been allowing yourself to receive.

If you do have a therapist and the two of you conclude that remaining in your relationship seems like the best course for now, here are a few strategies for minimizing the number of verbally abusive assaults:

✔ Inhibit your own anger; expressing it will simply escalate the conflict.

✔ Don't argue or try to reason.

✔ Don't fight back, but don't agree that you warrant the abuse.

✔ If you do talk, keep the conversation simple. Stay focused on the present.

✔ Try to express empathy for the likely underlying emotion, which is probably fear, anxiety, or vulnerability. For example, you can say, "I know you're probably feeling very frightened. I'm open to talking about your fear."

✔ Tell your partner, "I can't really deal with this issue right now. I need to take a walk for awhile."

✔ Don't accept the blame for the outburst. Abusive behavior isn't acceptable even when something you said triggered it.

✔ Don't threaten to leave permanently. You can always decide to do so later.

✔ Agree to talk later when everyone feels calmer.

✔ Agree to disagree.

✔ Don't reinforce the attack by capitulating or begging.

In addition, after the verbal abuse abates, don't accept apologies. Rather, point out to your partner that the episode hurt you and that you want her to work hard to minimize such incidents.

Walking Away from BPD

Partners of people with BPD think about ending their relationships over and over and over again. Most partners admit to vacillating between love and hate in parallel with the vacillating feelings of their borderline partners. At times, many partners wish the whole problem would just disappear, and some even fantasize that their BPD partners simply die. As the song goes, "breaking up is hard to do," but breaking ties with someone with BPD is not only hard, but frightening and painful, as well.

Debating the decision

Deciding whether to remain in a relationship with a partner who has BPD is often surprisingly difficult. Even though you may have suffered abuse and unimaginable conflicts, your partner may have been charming, intelligent, loving, caring, and generous at many other times. Many people with BPD can sense when you're contemplating a split, and, in response, they often turn up the affection at that point. Furthermore, you may feel horrendous guilt and/ or worry for your kids, for your partner, or for yourself. So, how do you dig yourself out of this dilemma?

An excellent way to find clarity on difficult decisions like this one is known as the *split chair technique*. You can use this technique to help you figure out what to do when you just can't seem to sort things out in your head. The procedure is fairly simple and goes as follows:

1. **Place two similarly styled chairs facing each other.**

2. **Call one of the chairs your *stay in the relationship* chair.**

3. **Call the other chair your *get out of the relationship* chair.**

4. **Sit in the *stay* chair first.**

   Talk out loud to the imagined other side of you sitting in the other chair. Explain to that part of you why remaining in the relationship is the best course right now. Point out every argument you've ever used, and notice how you feel during this segment.

5. **Now switch and sit in the *get out* chair.**

   Argue against what you just said, and toss in any additional reasons you can think of for why you need to get out of the relationship. Notice how you feel during this part.

6. **Rinse and repeat. In other words, keep switching chairs until you feel you've drained the argument dry.**

7. **Consider redoing this exercise a number of times until you feel ready to stick with your decision, no matter what it is.**

Mental health professionals have used this technique to help people get out of their most difficult predicaments for many decades. You can use it for a variety of life's dilemmas. The following story about Julia clarifies how this strategy works in practice.

> Julia has been married to **Thomas,** who has BPD, for the past seven years. Thomas has verbally abused Julia more times than she can count. He's never actually hit her, but she's been terribly frightened by the intensity of his anger. He's been violent with their dog and has put his hand through walls. Thomas can exude sweetness, charm, and affection, but his emotional abuse has drained Julia of self-esteem, energy, and happiness. Thomas and Julia have seen four therapists for couple's counseling; things get better for a few months and then deteriorate again. The last therapist diagnoses Thomas with BPD and predicts that if Thomas doesn't get help for himself, the marriage won't last.
>
> So Julia sees a therapist herself to help her sort out what to do. Her therapist suggests the split chair technique. Here's what Julia comes up with the first time she tries the technique:
>
> **Stay chair:** Thomas can be very loving. He gives me whatever I want and is generous with money. He can be kind to others — especially strangers.

He can talk to anyone when he feels like it. He seems to stay friendly with many of his previous girlfriends. We travel all the time and get to see many exotic parts of the world. I also care about him. He needs me.

Get out chair: You never know when Thomas will lose his temper. Sometimes it's over trivial things. I've hosted parties or gatherings when he's so mad that he leaves. He doesn't treat my friends or family with respect (he puts on a show only when he feels like he needs to — like when we're in public). He has no friends of his own — only people he's known in the past. I think he still sees some of his girlfriends for support, but he'll never admit it. He flirts with strangers in front of me and denies what he's doing. On some of our trips, he becomes angry and withdrawn. Yes, I care about him, but, at some level, I don't trust him or know him. I believe he's wounded, but I can't reach him. Yes, he needs me, but he's afraid to get close — it's like we're in two separate worlds.

Stay chair: When I look back at what I said, it sounds so superficial. Like I'm staying with him because he can sometimes be nice. But, the truth is, I don't trust him. I never know when I might displease him. Okay. This is supposed to be the chair that I keep focused on staying, but I'm drifting. What does that mean?

Get out chair: It means that I'm struggling to hold onto the idea of staying — that staying is feeling less and less like what I want to do. Do I really think his generosity with money is that important? Why am I still waiting?

Stay chair: I stay because I'm scared.

Get out chair: At least I'm on the right issue. So, what am I so scared about? Don't I have friends? I have a good job, too. And I know my family will help.

Stay chair: I've seen how he treats his former wife; I don't want to be treated that way.

Get out chair: Yes, that won't be fun. But what about that can't I deal with?

Stay chair: I'm running out of things to say.

Julia repeats this exercise five more times in the next two weeks. Each time, her *stay chair* arguments grow weaker. She consults an attorney, who advises her on ways to leave the relationship safely.

Like Julia, many people stay in relationships because their partners with BPD can be passionate, exciting, affectionate, and generous. But, when the tide turns, they struggle to reconcile the contrast. Friends and family sometimes only receive access to the outward, good side of the person who has BPD. The fact that friends and family think the partner with BPD is wonderful leaves the partner who doesn't have BPD feeling more than a little crazy as she hears people who matter to her heap praise on the partner, whom she thinks may be abusing her, either verbally, emotionally, or physically.

Leaving abusive relationships if you decide to do so

We're not trying to tell you to leave your partner who has BPD. Sometimes staying in the relationship makes sense; especially when kids are involved, when no serious abuse is happening to anyone in the family, when the person with BPD is seeking therapy, and when at least a few signs of improvement show up over time. However, if your rendition of the split chair technique that we discuss in the preceding section tells you that you need to leave, you need to consider one more issue — your personal safety. We recommend that you follow the following guidelines if significant abuse has been a part of your relationship:

- Don't tell your partner that you plan to leave.

- Talk to your therapist or your attorney about local resources (including domestic violence shelters).

- Put together a bag with copies of important papers, such as account numbers, birth certificates, health records, school records, insurance policies, and your marriage license, as well as a set of car and house keys.

- Pack a suitcase with a couple sets of clothes for you and your children.

- Store these bags somewhere that your partner can't find them or at a friend or neighbor's house.

- Withdraw some cash and keep it somewhere safe.

- If your abusive partner finds out that you're planning a getaway, you're at higher risk of abuse, so be careful.

- If you're using the Internet to plan your escape, be sure to exit the browser completely, delete your browser history, and turn off the computer when you're done.

- Even better; use the computer at a public library.

- Consider using a code word with children and friends so they know when they need to call for help.

- Don't turn to drugs or alcohol for courage.

- Leave a note that explains how to contact you through your attorney.

- Don't have one last confrontation. Leave when your partner is out of the house and very unlikely to return during your exit.

We realize that many of these recommendations may sound harsh or even Draconian to you. However, if you're truly at risk for abuse based on past history, not taking these steps can put your safety in serious jeopardy.

Keeping your children from being exposed to violent conflict is extremely important. Witnessing violence inevitably harms kids.

Leaving nonabusive relationships if you decide to do so

On the other hand, not every relationship with someone who has BPD is seriously abusive. Sometimes people decide to leave a relationship simply because it's extremely unsatisfying. If you're in a similar situation, you may wish to consider the following guidelines:

- ✔ Plan ahead. Discuss legal issues with an attorney before you talk with your partner.

- ✔ If you're certain of your decision, don't make further attempts at reconciliation.

- ✔ Remain calm. Deliver your message clearly, but don't say it over and over again. Your partner doesn't need an elaborate explanation. Keep the message simple, short, and focused.

- ✔ Unless your partner's issues have softened and become milder over time, we generally recommend that you avoid further contact after you leave. Obviously, in the case of children and shared custody, you don't have a choice in the matter.

- ✔ When you tell your partner about your decision, don't allow his or her negotiations or promises to change deter you.

- ✔ Follow through by leaving soon after you have your discussion with your partner. Remaining in the household can be risky even when abuse hasn't occurred before. Consider having a few friends or relatives available as an emergency backup if things go worse than you anticipated.

- ✔ Expect that your partner with BPD will likely be extremely upset and distraught because of her fears of abandonment. *This reaction isn't your fault, and you can't prevent it.* You may receive a bombardment of e-mails, text messages, begging, calls, threats of suicide, or even stalking. Consult with a therapist for help with these issues. You may even need to inform police about especially threatening behaviors on the part of your ex-partner.

Once you have left, realize that you'll likely go through some degree of mourning the loss of what could've or should've been. People with BPD can be loving, exciting, and interesting, so the loss may be great even though you know you really needed to leave. Again, we suggest seeing a therapist if you find the emotions from ending the relationship difficult to deal with.

Chapter 22

Befriending People with BPD

In This Chapter

▶ Looking for early warning signs of BPD

▶ Seeing the more serious symptoms

▶ Tossing out a lifeline and saving yourself

▶ Handling serious threats

▶ Dealing with guilt when ending a BPD relationship

We've never seen a person with borderline personality disorder (BPD) wear a T-shirt that announces to the world, "I have BPD!" Okay, one or two of those shirts are probably around somewhere, but they're definitely not a common sight. Come to think of it, maybe we could design one and make millions — or maybe not.

Thousands, if not millions, of people function in this world without divulging their diagnoses to co-workers and even friends. People with BPD don't necessarily stand out in a crowd. They look the same as everyone else. After all, they don't have any outward physical signs of the disorder, and many days in many situations, they don't act differently than other people, either.

At first, people with BPD generally don't have major social problems. As a matter of fact, sometimes they're especially charming and interesting. Often, a person befriends someone with BPD without having an inkling that he or she has a personality disorder. Later, events and emotions often turn in totally unexpected directions.

In this chapter, we take a look at the first signs of BPD within a friendship. We explore some of the issues that can become more serious and problematic. Then we supply some pointers on how to help your friend without falling into the dangerous rapids yourself. Finally, we look at how to handle serious threats to the safety of you or someone you care about and how to end a relationship with someone with BPD if you decide to do so.

Recognizing Warning Signs of BPD

The sooner you detect signs of BPD in a new friend, the better off you are. Recognizing that a friend has BPD early in your relationship may help you avoid making excessive commitments and/or becoming enmeshed in a friendship that can engulf your entire life.

In case you're wondering, we aren't suggesting that you avoid any relationship with someone who has BPD. But, we do suggest that you learn as much as you can about the disorder and its effects on the people who have it. If you know what you're getting into before you get heavily involved in a relationship with someone with BPD, you can set limits, learn not to take everything personally, and decide how involved you want to be.

So what signs should you look for in a new friendship? The following warning signs can help you determine whether or not you want to take your new relationship a little more slowly than you have taken other relationships:

- **Too close:** Your new friend self-discloses unusually intimate details early in the relationship.

- **Too much flattery:** You know you're a good person and everything, but when a new friend starts slinging out flattery like slop to a pig, you may have a problem. Don't be beguiled by praise.

- **Too much time:** You like spending a lot of time with a new friend, but you, like most folks, have a pretty busy life. Be wary about requests for more contact with you than your previous friends have wanted.

- **Too much texting/phoning:** Yeah, our kids text a lot, and sometimes we do it, too. But a new friend with BPD may be inclined to text you 40 times a day. Be careful with this excessive contact.

- **Too probing:** You want to share your life with friends — but not all your friends — and trust should evolve slowly over time. If your new friend asks you too many personal questions early on, heed the warning sign.

- **Unreliable:** Someone with BPD often cancels or arrives late for events, dates, get-togethers, and so on. This issue isn't a big deal unless it occurs chronically. If a new friend frequently cancels dates, understand that this behavior signals a lack of respect for your time. Always canceling or arriving late can also be a sign of narcissistic personality disorder (see Chapter 3 for more information about this and other personality disorders).

- **Too critical:** Most people with BPD don't criticize a friend excessively in the beginning of a new relationship. However, if your newfound friend indulges in a lot of harsh criticism of other friends or past relationships, ask yourself whether you may be next.

✔ **Long history of broken friendships:** If you seem to be the only friend this person has at the moment, and if your friend recounts numerous past friends, you have to wonder, right?

The preceding list of warning signs is by no means a method for diagnosing your friends! These signs are solely characteristics that can lead to trouble in your new relationship at some point. A true diagnosis of BPD requires a mental health professional. If you've gotten into a friendship that exhibits several of the preceding warning signs, we recommend that you consult with such a professional.

Becca's story shows how easily someone can slip into a destructive relationship with someone who has BPD. Becca has never known someone with this disorder before and finds herself ensnared by something she doesn't understand.

> Becca notices **Amber** standing by herself at the trail head. Becca has been a member of the outdoor singles' group for awhile. Recalling how hard getting involved is at first, she walks over to Amber and introduces herself. Amber smiles broadly and tells her how nervous she feels about joining a singles' group. "My divorce was finalized last week, so here I am," Amber says, "I'm hoping to meet a whole new group of friends. My ex-husband has convinced everyone we know that I'm crazy and that I drink too much. So, not only did I lose my marriage, but I also lost every single one of my friends."
>
> Becca replies, "I'm sorry to hear that. You can be sure that you'll meet lots of people here. We try to mix up our activities. Sometimes we hike locally, and we do a lot of volunteer work fixing up trails. Some of us ski in the winter, too."
>
> "Becca," Amber gives her a hug, "I'm so glad I met you. I know we're going to be best friends. Would you walk with me a ways so we can talk? I really need to tell you something."
>
> "Sure, Amber," Becca says, a little caught off guard, "I'll make sure that I introduce you to some of the others. What do you need to tell me?"
>
> "Well," Amber begins, "I thought you should know who my ex-husband is in case there's any trouble."
>
> "Oh my God, Amber, did he abuse you?"
>
> "No, but he got pretty mad. He's an attorney, a very prominent attorney, and he was really mad at me. You see, when we were together, well, the sex was pretty good. But, he worked crazy hours and you know what happens. I got bored and lonely, too. So, I was out one night and met a guy. Then, you know, we started seeing each other. Buddies, you know. Nothing serious. Then my ex found out. I told him it was meaningless sex. That I still loved him. But then he got so mad that I couldn't help it. I ended up telling him about the other affairs I had while he was working. He had no right to divorce me. I was a good wife, don't you agree, Becca?"

Becca isn't sure she really agrees with Amber, but she says, "Well, I guess we all have problems."

Amber grabs her hand, "I knew you'd understand. How about we go out after the hike and get a few drinks? Look at that guy over there; he's cute. How many of these guys have you had sex with?"

Becca feels a tad uneasy but likes going out for drinks with new friends, so she says, "Sure, that sounds like fun. I'm not sure how many guys I've had sex with, but not all that many."

Over the next few weeks, Becca starts spending more and more time with Amber, and her disquieting feelings grow. She's not sure what to do.

Becca didn't know where to take this relationship. Amber got too close too fast. And she spilled unusually intimate details about her life to a stranger. Finally, she flattered Amber by saying, "I know we're going to be best friends." If Becca had known what to look for and recognized the warning signs in Amber's behaviors, she might have had a better idea of what to do in this situation. For instance, she might not have gone out for drinks with her after the hike, or she might have trusted her uneasy feelings and ended the relationship before it started.

If a new acquaintance comes on strong like Amber, you may decide to start a new friendship anyway. However, we recommend that you proceed slowly and cautiously. If you agree to a friendship, you'll probably want to set some limits early on. For example, don't set up frequent get-togethers, and be cautious about what you share with your new friend about your personal life.

Detecting Serious Symptoms

You may have found a new, seemingly best friend and not seen any signs of a personality disorder. Or perhaps you ignored the signs. Or maybe your friend was better than most at keeping her issues out of view at first. Some people with BPD become quite adept at hiding their issues, although, in time, their attempts inevitably fail. Someone or something will eventually trigger your new friend's BPD symptoms. The trigger can be something as simple as you don't have enough time to spend with your friend one day, which leads your friend to fear abandonment. Or it may be a mix-up in communication that cascades into rage and anger. The one exception is the person with BPD who has emerged from highly successful treatment — in which case, he doesn't have anything to hide anymore. Check out Chapter 3 for more detailed information about the array of serious symptoms that folks with BPD exhibit.

At some point in your relationship, your friend starts down a path strewn with reprehensible behavior. You feel yourself swirling downward, sucked in by an enormous whirlpool fueled by inexplicable behaviors, guilt, worry, and confusion. Never fear, we're about to toss you a lifeline. The following list covers many of the serious signs of BPD (see the next section for ideas about how to deal with these nefarious symptoms):

- **Excessive demands:** Now, we're talking *serious* demands here. For example, your friend may start out by merely asking for a few more favors than most of your other friends do. But, then the requests escalate into more intense demands, such as calls in the middle of the night to deal with serious emotional distress. Or a demand that you take your friend to the emergency room to avert a suicide attempt.

- **Expectations that you choose a side:** People with BPD have many conflicts in their intimate relationships, so watch out if your friend bombards you with details about these conflicts and asks you to take his side.

People with BPD often misreport what's going on in their relationships because of their tendency to see people as all good or all bad. Don't get sucked into taking their side in conflicts with their intimate partners. You weren't there, so you can't know what happened.

- **Unexpected anger or rage:** Many people with BPD have trouble regulating their emotions. Small issues quickly escalate into outbursts.

- **Substance abuse:** A lot of people like to drink socially. Moderation is often difficult for people with BPD. Be wary of friends who get drunk frequently or who use dangerous drugs. Medication abuse is also common in people with BPD.

- **Unnecessary risks:** If your friend is a reckless driver, engages in highly risky sports, or does anything that frightens you, these behaviors may be results of their BPD disorder. Don't be seduced into joining them.

- **Self-harm:** If your friend engages in self-destructive behaviors, such as cutting, burning, or purposely self-inflicting any other kind of pain, your friend has a serious problem. Threats of suicide fall into this self-harm category, and you shouldn't trivialize them.

If your friend threatens suicide, make sure that he sees a professional right away. If he refuses to get help, deciding how serious his threat is isn't up to you — call 911 for help.

Handling Friends with BPD

So, what should you do if your friend has been diagnosed with BPD or if he or she shows serious signs like the ones in the preceding section? Basically, dealing with a friend with BPD falls into two categories — what you *can* do and what you *can't* do.

What you can do

A friend with BPD can be funny, kind, enthusiastic, bright, and interesting. You may want to maintain a relationship with a friend with BPD because he exhibits those qualities. But, that same friend may also seem to take advantage of you and involve you in situations that seem unhealthy. To stay friendly but to stop feeling stepped on, consider the following points:

✔ **Be calm.** A friend with BPD is likely to provoke you from time to time with obnoxious behavior (see Chapter 3 for a full list of potential symptoms and problematic behaviors associated with BPD). If you get irritable or angry, you only make things worse. Being calm, on the other hand, can communicate a good message to your friend. Remaining calm, however, doesn't mean you can't set reasonable limits or boundaries with your friend.

✔ **Set reasonable boundaries.** Know what your personal limits are. Sometimes people with BPD can make you think your limits are excessive, if not a little crazy. If you find yourself confused about your own rights and limits as a friend, ask someone who doesn't have BPD for feedback. Another good way to evaluate your boundary decisions is to ask yourself what you'd tell someone else in your situation. After you know what's reasonable, say it and stick with it. Waffling only invites abuse.

✔ **Remind yourself that your friend isn't intentionally malicious.** People with BPD don't consciously and methodically set out to anger or hurt you. BPD has deep roots in childhood, culture, and biology. People don't choose to develop BPD. Thus, you want to depersonalize your friend's obnoxious behavior — remember that it's not about you.

✔ **Keep your expectations reasonable.** Of course you want to appreciate your friend's positive qualities, but you also have to expect a certain degree of criticism, disapproval, rejection, and unpredictability. As we describe in a preceding bullet, you need to know what's acceptable to you, and when you see something that isn't, know how you want to respond. You can't expect people with BPD to demonstrate only their positive qualities all the time.

✔ **Think about what information to share.** You may have a few trusted friends with whom you feel comfortable sharing your most deeply held secrets. In general, we don't recommend that degree of openness and trust with someone who has BPD. Unfortunately, the impulsivity associated with BPD (see Chapters 3 and 5 for more information on this particular symptom) is likely to lead to breaches of trust. People with BPD may sincerely agree to keep something confidential, but they often find themselves talking without thinking later on.

The following story about Haley and Michelle demonstrates the kind of limit setting you may need to do with a friend who has BPD.

Haley has been good friends with **Michelle** for many years. They work downtown and often meet for lunch. Although Michelle has BPD, she's constantly striving to work on her issues and has been in therapy for the past four years.

Haley works out three times a week at a local gym. One day at lunch, Michelle asks Haley if she can start working out with her. Haley agrees. Over the course of the next few months, Michelle frequently cancels at the last minute, and when she does show up, she's chronically late. At other times, Michelle asks Haley to change her gym schedule to accommodate her, and Haley usually tries to do so. But Haley feels annoyed and starts to avoid Michelle.

Then Haley reevaluates her commitment and friendship with Michelle. She thinks about some of Michelle's positive qualities, such as her great sense of humor, her willingness to help when needed, and her political knowledge. However, she realizes that she needs to set limits with her friend about the gym so that she doesn't reject her.

Haley decides that she'll stick to her gym schedule and not count on Michelle to show up. She tells Michelle that to keep herself healthy she needs to go to the gym three times a week at certain times. If Michelle is late, Haley will go on without her. If Michelle wants to change the day and time, Haley probably won't go along unless it's really convenient for her. Michelle feels angry about Haley's limit setting, but she agrees, not having any other real choice. Haley later sets limits with Michelle about several other issues in their relationship.

If you have a friend with BPD, carefully consider the issues that you could improve by setting limits like Haley did. You can't expect the moon from your friend, but you certainly have the right to stand up for yourself, to not accept abuse, and to not allow someone else to consistently trample your time and schedule.

 Friendships are two-way streets. You may not receive as much from a friend who has BPD as you do from your other friends, but you have to get something positive from the relationship for it to be healthy. Friendships are choices — if you feel *trapped* by a friendship, talk with a friend, a spiritual advisor, or even seek therapy for yourself to figure out what's going on.

What you can't do

People with BPD often seek support from others whenever they can. They have chronic, deep emotional distress and desperately look for relief. In many cases, asking friends for special favors and advice isn't unusual. Sometimes they even plead with their friends to intervene on their behalf in conflicts. As the friend of someone with BPD, you can easily find yourself feeling engulfed by the friendship and feeling intense guilt about not always being there for your friend.

We cover what you can do to help maintain a relationship with someone with BPD in the previous section, and now we offer some advice about what to avoid in that same friendship.

- **Don't be your friend's therapist.** In general, you want to help your friends. You probably even give advice to your friends on occasion. But we're going to give you some advice — don't let yourself take on the role of your friend's therapist! Even when you think you know what your friend should do, don't offer that advice because people with BPD need much more than suggestions for what to do. When you start acting like a therapist, you soon find yourself overwhelmed and drained.

- **Don't mediate between someone with BPD and others.** People with BPD get in numerous conflicts with other people — co-workers, spouses, partners, and friends. And when they do, they try to gather support for their cause. They may ask you to intervene on their behalf or serve as a mediator. Don't agree to such requests. You're probably not a trained mediator, anyway, and, as a friend, you can't bring objectivity and neutrality to the table.

The following story about Brandon and Peter illustrates how people with BPD can convince their friends to intervene in their personal problems. Brandon jumps into trying to help his friend Peter and later regrets it. Remember that the situation is rarely as black and white as someone with BPD describes it to be.

Brandon and **Peter** sit next to each other at the new-employee orientation for physician assistants. Peter is changing jobs to be closer to home, and Brandon is a new graduate. By the end of the day, they discover that they're both avid golfers. They exchange phone numbers and set up a golf date for the following week.

Brandon and Peter's friendship grows quickly despite family obligations and busy schedules. One day after golf, Peter shares with Brandon that he's having trouble with his wife. Surprised, Brandon asks him what's going on. Peter tells Brandon, "I give my wife everything, but it isn't enough; she wants me to agree to a big house. We can't afford it, but she won't listen to me."

Brandon is pretty sure he knows how much money Peter makes because they're both in the same position at the same hospital. He asks Peter, "What does she want? A mansion?"

"No, she wants a four-bedroom house with a family room for the kids," Peter replies.

"Well, you should be able to afford that with your salary and bonuses, Peter," Brandon says.

"I could, but she has a spending problem. As a matter of fact, she's out of control. Brandon, would you consider talking to her? I just can't get through to her at all, and she respects you," Peter pleads.

"Gosh, Peter, I'd feel pretty funny talking to your wife about her spending. And I'm not sure what I would say," Brandon answers.

Peter responds, "You'd just have to tell her that she shouldn't be looking at new houses in this economy. You might tell her a bit about budgeting. Nothing deep, that's all."

Brandon reluctantly agrees. Peter's wife is angry that her husband discussed their problems outside the marriage. First, she tells Brandon that it's none of his business. Then, she tells him that this isn't the first time that Peter has used his friends to address their marriage problems.

During the conversation with Peter's wife, Brandon learns that Peter has a serious gambling problem and that he has been diagnosed with BPD. Brandon doesn't know who to believe. He regrets ever getting involved.

Peter, like many people with BPD, sometimes manipulates people to solve his personal problems. He doesn't tell the entire truth, and Brandon finds himself in over his head. Thus, you should avoid getting in the middle of your friends' conflicts even when they make you feel guilty or responsible.

Dealing with Dangerous Situations

When you're friends with someone with BPD, you may rarely see the darker times. People with BPD sometimes keep their symptoms hidden from certain people for long periods of time. However, the closer your friendship becomes, the more likely your friend with BPD is to let his true feelings show.

The most difficult and frightening times are those in which your friend with BPD threatens to hurt or kill himself. How do you manage to help your friend without getting hurt yourself? The following points can help:

- Know that self-mutilation and suicide threats are common symptoms of BPD. You're not responsible for your friend's pain.

- Tell your friend that you understand that he's hurting and that the threat of hurting himself is part of his disorder.

- Attempt to distract your friend, and encourage him to do something that has helped him in the past.

- Stay disconnected. Don't get emotional or try to use logic to figure out the situation.

- Refuse to witness the self-abuse or mutilation.

- Get help. If you feel that your friend may act dangerously, call for help. If your friend has a therapist, start there. Don't wait this out. Your friend has made a threat, and you have to take him seriously. Don't hesitate to call the police if you're fearful for your friend's life.

✔ Get information and education about BPD (start by reading the rest of this book). If you decide to stay in the friendship, consider joining a support group for families and friends of people with mental disorders, such as National Alliance for the Mentally Ill (NAMI). (For more information on this group, check out www.nami.org.)

Ending a BPD Relationship

If you're in a relationship with someone who has BPD, you may decide to pull the plug on the relationship at some point. Your friend may have worn you out with demands and requests for advice and help, or he may have drained you dry with drama day in and day out. If you do decide to end the relationship, you may wonder how to do so, and you may wrestle with guilt over abandoning someone who has so many needs. We cover these issues in the next two sections.

Making your exit

You can probably think of countless ways to leave a friendship — after all, Paul Simon came up with a whopping fifty ways to leave a lover. His point was that any method works, and that's true when you're leaving someone with BPD, too. But we offer a few specific words of advice to keep in mind when you decide to end a relationship with a friend who has BPD.

✔ **Make the message short and clear.** Don't recite a laundry list of reasons; someone with BPD isn't likely to hear or process it anyway.

✔ **Don't reason with your friend.** The moment you say you're ending the friendship, your friend won't be able to listen to logic or reasoning.

✔ **Tell your friend in a public place.** This piece of advice may seem a little unfair. After all, your friend may feel emotional and be embarrassed to express himself in front of others. However, you're safer when people are around. If you're absolutely certain that your friend has no history of rage or violence, you can consider a private conversation.

✔ **Writing a letter is okay.** Especially if your friend has ever shown rage or other signs of potential for violence, you can communicate in writing.

✔ **Don't waffle.** After you've made the decision to the end the relationship, don't let your friend talk you out of it. People with BPD hate feeling abandoned, so your friend may try out all sorts of ways to convince you to remain friends. Remind yourself beforehand that you've made your decision and that you will stick to it — no matter what your friend says or does. Waffling will only prolong the pain for both of you.

- ✔ **Remain calm.** Your friend may become very emotional whether it be tears, fears, or anger. You may want to practice what you'll say and how you'll say it by yourself or with another friend before your confrontation.

- ✔ **Don't go back later.** Your friend may surprise you and remain calm, accepting what you have to say. In this kind of situation, the temptation to reconsider may increase. Perhaps your friend will attempt to reconnect in a few weeks or months. Again, if your reasons for ending the relationship were sound, don't be swayed to reenter the relationship.

Ending friendships is never a fun thing to do, but you have a right to expect a friendship to make you feel good. Don't let a friendship make you feel miserable. After all, life's too short for that.

Wrangling with guilt

Most people who decide to end any friendship feel a certain amount of guilt in doing so, but those who end relationships with people with BPD feel especially guilty because they recognize that their friends need a lot of help. They may think that they were just as responsible for encouraging and fostering the relationship as their friend with BPD was, and that may be true. But even when you played an important role in bringing this person into your life, you aren't forever beholden to your friend. Consider the following points:

- ✔ You probably didn't realize your friend had BPD when the relationship began. Even if you did, you likely didn't foresee the destructive impact the friendship had on your life.

- ✔ You have a right to friendships that don't leave you in a constant state of worry.

- ✔ Even if your friend with BPD has done many wonderful things for you, you can't conclude that you owe that person a lifelong friendship in return. Many people with BPD are skilled at extending themselves in extraordinary ways to their friends, especially at the beginnings of relationships. But they all too often inflict an inordinately large emotional toll in other ways at the same time.

- ✔ Your guilt may boil over if your friend threatens self-harm or suicide when you try to end the relationship. Please realize that such threats amount to emotional blackmail. You can't hold yourself responsible for someone else's self-destructive behavior. Consult with a therapist if you feel overwhelmed in your relationship or in ending it. Also, read the "Dealing with Dangerous Situations" section earlier in this chapter.

We're not recommending that you end a relationship with someone who has BPD in all cases. Some of these friendships provide a reasonable balance of good and bad qualities but truly feel worth it overall. If you're struggling with making the decision whether or not to end a relationship, consider filling out a Cost-Benefit Analysis Form, which you can find in Appendix B.

Chapter 23

Parenting Children at Risk for BPD

In This Chapter

▶ Recognizing early warning signs of BPD

▶ Taking a look at the causes

▶ Getting the help you need

▶ Loving and setting limits at the same time

▶ Looking after yourself and everybody else

People in the mental health field debate at what age you can first diagnose someone with borderline personality disorder (BPD) and other
personality disorders. BPD consists of a pattern of unstable relationships,
impulsivity, and moodiness (as discussed in Chapter 3), all three of which are
common behaviors in teenagers. The two sides to this debate are

> ✔ The argument for *not* making a diagnosis until age 18 is based on the fact
> that children and adolescents change so much over the course of their
> development.

> ✔ The argument *for* making a diagnosis, when the symptoms are present,
> is that you can start appropriate treatment early.

In our opinion, whether or not the diagnosis is *official,* treatment for the
symptoms of BPD can start in adolescence. Furthermore, the presence of risk
factors and early signs of BPD warrant some family interventions.

In this chapter, we examine the early warning signs of BPD. We discuss some
risk factors that parents should be aware of and give advice on how to get
help. Finally, we provide some tips to the parents of children and adolescents
who may be developing BPD.

Heeding Early Warning Signs

The differences between a 2-year-old, a 12-year-old, and an 18-year-old are huge. Children grow, mature, and change quickly. At the same time, some consistencies occur across ages. For example, a mother may describe her 2-year-old boy as fearless because he runs instead of walks, climbs onto things, and gets into a lot of mischief. That same boy at age 12 may show the same trait of fearlessness, but his actions may have changed to rock climbing, water skiing, and taking off alone on long walks. At age 18, he may be interested in extreme sports, show no fear of talking in public, and demonstrate unusual independence. The trait of fearlessness, like many traits, carries on throughout the boy's life, but it shows up in different ways at various ages.

Much like the fearlessness in the preceding example, overly reactive emotions, a major symptom of BPD, can show up early on in a child's life. Toddlers with this trait may have a hard time going to bed without having a tantrum, they may have trouble sharing with other kids, and they may get extremely emotional when they're separated from their caregivers. At school age, children with emotional instability may get overly upset when they receive negative feedback, engage in frequent squabbling with classmates when they disagree with them, and have meltdowns when they're frustrated. Teens with such emotional instability may have frequent bouts of anger, anxiety, or rage. From these examples, you can see that certain traits can persist over the course of childhood, adolescence, and adulthood.

Identifying problem behaviors

The following list represents worrisome behaviors and reactions that your kids may exhibit from time to time. Even if your child hasn't been diagnosed with BPD, these symptoms are worth checking out and addressing.

- **Intense emotional overreactions:** The slightest frustration can set off these reactions. For example, your kid may overreact when she misses the bus, gets a B on a test instead of an A, forgets her homework, or isn't allowed to stay out late one night. The emotional reaction to events like these may include crying, screaming, rocking, throwing a fit, or swearing.

- **Defensiveness in response to perceived slights:** Your child or adolescent may respond with severe rage, outbursts, or despondency when she isn't picked for a team or a school play, when a friend doesn't invite her to a party, when a teacher criticizes her, or when she experiences a similar rejection.

- **Paranoid thinking:** When your teen walks into the school cafeteria and sees that the kid she wanted to sit next to has no seat saved for her, she may respond with jealous outrage that her friend would deliberately reject her in that way. Behaviors like this one may point to a paranoid style of thinking. Other examples of responding to situations in a para-noid manner include believing that others are plotting against her, thinking that the teachers have it in for her, or worrying that people are always watching her.

✔ **Cutting:** If you ever see scars, open wounds, or other signs of cutting along your teen's arms, legs, or torso, seek a mental health consultation as soon as possible. The only exception is if you hear a logical, plausible, coherent story that explains why the marks are on your teen's body — and you don't see a reappearance of them.

✔ **Other self-mutilation:** Other signs of self-mutilation behavior include burns, pin marks, and repeated "accidental" actions that result in bodily harm. You need to realize that your teen probably won't be able to disclose these behaviors easily and may very well lie to keep you from knowing what's going on. More often than not, teens cover up self-harming behaviors to avoid feeling intense shame from letting their parents know about their troubles.

✔ **Intense, unstable relationships:** Okay, teens often have fairly unstable relationships. But most kids have a few friendships that last for years. If your child or adolescent has a pattern of acquiring friends, feeling unusually intense about those friends, and then dumping them for inex-plicable reasons, you may want to encourage your teen to seek out help.

✔ **Threats of violence:** Kids sometimes say they "hate" their parents. Occasionally, they may even scream that they want to kill them. However, if your child starts to destroy property, take swings at you, or threaten violence to friends or teachers, you need to take these threats seriously. We strongly recommend that you and your child consult with a mental health professional.

✔ **Eating disorders:** Eating disorders vary from being excessively con-cerned about gaining weight to drastically limiting food intake to binging (eating unusually large quantities of food at a single sitting) to purging (self-induced vomiting or excessive laxative usage) to exercising exces-sively to control weight. If you notice these or other signs of eating dis-orders in your child, seek out a professional evaluation because these disorders can be deadly.

✔ **Impulsivity/sensation seeking:** Teens and impulsivity go together like French fries and ketchup. However, the kind of impulsivity we're talking about here is more extreme than what most teens do. Many teens exper-iment with a shoplifting incident or two, but getting caught once usually ends their experiments for good. Problematic impulsivity in teens refers to behaviors like repeated, serious shoplifting, promiscuous sexual behaviors, unusually reckless driving, uncontrolled spending, heavy substance abuse (as opposed to experimentation), and frequent damag-ing of property. Again, many teens bang up a fender now and then, but you should be concerned if car accidents occur as a result of wild, reck-less driving. If you're not sure whether your teen's behavior falls into this category, check with a professional.

Pursuing a diagnosis

Many children show these sorts of emotional responses or behaviors at times. Kids go through stages or have reactions to stress that seem pretty extreme. Furthermore, teenagers show many of the symptoms of BPD at some point. What teenager isn't at least occasionally impulsive, dramatic, emotionally reactive, and irritable? For a mental health professional to diagnose teens with BPD, the symptoms must be over the top and out of the ordinary, and they must persist across multiple situations. In other words, just because your teen is rebellious and grouchy doesn't mean he or she has BPD.

Parents want to understand and help their children. However, parents love their children so much that they can't be totally objective in their visions of them.

If your child or teen shows some of the warning signs we describe in the preceding section, you may want to consult with a mental health professional who has experience with diagnosing children and adolescents. Although an experienced professional may avoid giving a diagnosis of BPD to a child or adolescent, you need to understand that some type of treatment may still be useful. Talk to the therapist about what types of treatment are available.

Looking at Risk Factors

We suggest that you read Chapter 4 for detailed information about the various risk factors for BPD, especially if your child exhibits a few of the warning signs we describe in the "Identifying problem behaviors" section of this chapter. If your child not only shows troubling behaviors similar to those of BPD, but also has several risk factors for developing BPD, your concerns should increase. In that case, you need to seek a professional consultation sooner rather than later. Risk factors of particularly acute concern include the following:

- ✔ **Family turmoil:** Divorces, serious marital conflict, financial struggles, and frequent moves are examples of stressors that can afflict families — especially children.

- ✔ **Genetics:** If one of your child's close relatives has BPD or some other serious mental disorder, your child's risks increase.

- ✔ **Abuse or trauma:** If your child has been abused by one or more parents, relatives, peers, or teachers, the risk of BPD occurring in your child increases.

✔ **Early separation or loss:** Children who experience the loss of a parent, sibling, or close relative, especially multiple times, have a higher risk of developing a serious emotional problem such as BPD.

✔ **Inadequate parenting:** Sometimes when parents are very young or when their own parents served as challenging, difficult role models, they simply don't know how to parent effectively. Ineffective parenting also increases the risks of BPD occurring in your child.

Note that some of these risk factors directly relate to parents, whether as a result of parental conflict, poor parenting, or abuse. Does this mean we're blaming parents for their kids' BPD? In a word, no. The causes of BPD are many, and figuring out the specific cause for any given person is impossible to do.

However, we aren't completely letting parents off the hook, either. If you feel like you've blown up at your kids more often than you would've liked, not known how to handle your kids' challenging emotions, and/or been in a high-conflict marriage, you can probably profit from consulting a mental health professional for assistance. Raising kids is a daunting job, and most parents feel inadequate at times. When your child shows signs of an emotional disturbance, the task grows exponentially in difficulty — whether you contributed to the cause or not.

Even if you haven't been a perfect parent (whatever that is), and even if you contributed to your child's problem, now is the time to step up to the plate. Be part of the solution, not just the problem.

Finding the Right Help

Researchers haven't completed many studies on what works for children and teens with BPD symptoms. Part of the reason for this lack of scientific study is the reluctance most professionals have in diagnosing kids under the age of 18 with BPD — instead, they often diagnose kids who exhibit BPD symptoms with other more "kid-appropriate" disorders. So your child may present with BPD symptoms but receive a diagnosis of one of the following disorders rather than BPD:

✔ **Conduct disorder:** This diagnosis involves a pattern of behavior that includes destruction of property, aggression, rule breaking, and deceitfulness.

✔ **Oppositional defiant disorder:** Kids with this disorder exhibit a pattern of hostile behaviors, including arguing with adults, becoming easily angered, blaming others, and being touchy or easily annoyed.

Special ed for kids with BPD

Children and adolescents with symptoms of BPD often have trouble in school. If your child's emotional problems impair her learning, your child may qualify for help or accommodations at school under the special education umbrella. The category of *emotionally impaired* may allow your child to be part of an individualized program in school to better meet her unique needs. To qualify, your child has to undergo a complete educational and psychological evaluation. A teacher, a school psychologist, and other school professionals generally complete these evaluations.

Various parent organizations can help you better understand the special education programs that many public schools offer. Go to one of the following Web sites for more information:

✔ www.ed.gov/parents/needs/speced/resources.html

✔ www.ed.gov/parents/needs/speced/edpicks

✔ www.wrightslaw.com

✔ www.parentpals.com

✔ www.cec.sped.org

✔ **Bipolar disorder:** Bipolar disorder is a complicated diagnosis that generally includes alterations of mania (for example, feeling grandiose, sleeping poorly, or talking too fast) and depression. See Chapter 3 for more information, or read *Bipolar Disorder For Dummies* by Candida Fink and Joe Kraynak (Wiley).

✔ **Attention deficit/hyperactivity disorder:** AD/HD includes problems with controlling impulses, interrupting others, waiting, fidgeting, focusing, and making careless mistakes.

More than one-third of adolescents hospitalized for psychiatric reasons have at least some features of BPD. A minority of these kids will receive the BPD diagnosis in later years, but most of them won't. Nevertheless, you can use the same strategies professionals use for treating BPD to address many of the symptoms of other problems.

Getting the correct diagnosis is less important than getting a good picture of the symptoms your child or adolescent suffers from. If your child or teen has symptoms of BPD, you should look for a mental health professional who can address the presenting problems. For example, if your teen has trouble with substance abuse, you may need to seek a program or therapist who specializes in teenage substance abuse. If your teen acts impulsively, you may need someone who can help your teen develop a behavioral plan or possibly a prescribing professional who can determine whether your child has AD/HD or some other kind of impulsivity problem. Furthermore, if your child has symptoms of depression, you need to address that symptom by seeking a professional who has experience in dealing with youth depression.

Loving Tough

If one of your kids has serious symptoms of BPD, you may discover that this child easily becomes the center of the family's universe. You may find yourself considering how each activity, decision, or plan will impact your emotionally challenged child. Will she approve, or will your decision set off a firestorm of rebellious rage? If you go out for the evening, will your kid be safe? Will she harm the baby like she has threatened to do a few times? You want to do the right thing for everyone involved — which includes you, your emotionally challenged child, and the rest of your family. You want to show love and support for your child, but you also have to set limits. Doing both isn't easy.

Supporting without fostering

Some parents feel that with enough love, they can solve the emotional problems in their children. They worry that they may hurt their children's self-esteem if they don't give them unconditional positive feelings. They hesitate to show disapproval, fearing that doing so may trigger rage, self-harm, or suicide. So they praise whenever they can and make excuses for their kids' obnoxiousness. They tiptoe around their children's misbehavior. Such parents defend their kids from the criticism that teachers, coaches, and other kids' parents give them.

Unfortunately, these efforts are misguided. Kids don't benefit from never having to deal with the reality of their behavior. Parents who make excuses and overly protect their kids only delay the inevitable consequences — broken relationships, self harm, substance abuse, or even jail. Thus, kids whose parents protect them from accepting responsibility for their actions are much more likely to end up having to be accountable in the court of life one day — from bosses, friends, or judges.

One reason parents wrestle with reprimanding their kids with BPD symptoms is that, frankly, their kids make doing so very difficult. When kids rage, they often shift to a warm and loving mode (for a little while, at least) when you give them what they want. Psychologists call this phenomenon *negative reinforcement*. Negative reinforcement occurs when you take something unpleasant away after a behavior occurs. Kids with BPD symptoms often take away their negative rage when you give them what they want, and, as a result, you feel very reinforced for caving in.

Solid self-esteem is based on reality, not false praise and flattery. Confidence comes from hard work and follow-through. Kids don't learn either of these important concepts when you constantly cater to their demands.

Telling your kids — even those with serious BPD symptoms — that you love them is important. However, you also need to tell them when their behaviors are unacceptable. This strategy is called *setting limits*.

Setting limits

Kids with symptoms of BPD often throw tantrums, disobey rules, and stop listening to their parents. In turn, parents become angry and frustrated when their children refuse to do what they ask them to do. Obviously, this kind of situation isn't good for parents or children. But how do you set limits when you haven't been consistently doing so up to this point?

We have some suggestions for dealing with typical BPD behaviors in your children:

- ✔ **Enlist help.** If setting limits hasn't come naturally to you in the past, a therapist can help a lot. Therapists can guide you through the process of setting limits for your emotionally challenged child and provide a reality check when you're uncertain about how to set limits. We especially recommend a therapist who has been trained in *cognitive behavioral therapy,* which involves teaching specific new ways of thinking and behaving as well as setting limits and consequences on behavior. For more information, consider reading *Cognitive Behavioural Therapy For Dummies* by Rob Willson and Rhena Branch (Wiley). (In case you were wondering, *behavioural* with a *u* is the British spelling.)

- ✔ **Be specific.** Tell your child exactly what you want her to do or not to do. For example, don't tell your kid to stop being a brat, but rather, tell her that you want her to speak to you without sarcasm.

- ✔ **Be clear.** State explicit consequences for inappropriate behavior. For example, tell your kid that you will hold back a specific amount of her weekly allowance for every infraction of your new rule.

- ✔ **Hold firm.** After you've made a rule, follow through with it. Don't waffle — waffling only makes things worse. Don't bother setting a rule or a consequence that you can't follow through on. So, for example, don't prohibit TV time completely if you don't have a way to disable the television when you're out at night.

- ✔ **Be calm.** If you feel angry, walk away and deal with the situation when you calm down. People with BPD symptoms need to see a model of calm and the ability to deal with difficult emotions. After all, you don't want to model a BPD behavior.

- ✔ **Don't use reasoning.** By all means, give your reason for a rule when you set it. Give it once, and don't get hooked into an emotional dialogue about your reasons every time an inappropriate behavior occurs. Don't lecture — your kid knows the reasons.

✔ **Don't listen to arguments.** This point elaborates on the previous one. Kids love to use arguments, such as "all the other kids do it," or "you're not fair," or "my brother doesn't have to do this," and so on, to induce guilt and convince you that you're being unreasonable. Getting sucked into these arguments makes things worse because your child feels she can influence or control you when you stay engaged in the argument.

In addition to following the preceding suggestions, we recommend that you read *The Kazdin Method for Parenting the Defiant Child: With No Pills, No Therapy, No Contest of Wills,* by Alan Kazdin (Houghton Mifflin) and *Your Defiant Teen: 10 Steps to Resolve Conflict and Rebuild Your Relationship* by Russell Barkley and Arthur Robin (Guilford). These books give you loads of information about how to deal with the difficulties that kids and adolescents with BPD-like behaviors present.

You may be wondering how to hold firm when your kid escalates to incredible levels, such as threatening bodily harm to siblings — or perhaps making suicidal threats.

We'd really like to give you some quick and easy solutions to these dilemmas, but the truth is you won't find any. Kids and adolescents who have BPD often learn to put their parents in maddening, unsolvable binds and, thus, end up wielding shocking power over everyone in the family. Is there anything you can do to cut this Gordian knot? Read the next section to see what we suggest.

Dealing with a dangerous or out-of-control child

Don't even think about trying to deal with problems and threats involving potential bodily harm without seeking the help of a skilled therapist. Your therapist can help you develop a game plan for even the worst of threats.

If your child makes one of these high-level threats for the first time — and you haven't yet involved a therapist — consider taking a trip to the hospital emergency room for an evaluation. Yes, you're likely to have a long, tedious wait. However, that wait alone is a useful consequence that your child has to face for having made the threat. If your child made the threat to manipulate you, you lessen the probability that your child will try something similar again by implementing this consequence. If your child was serious in her threat, you're in the right place to get immediate treatment. In either case, the ER can give you a referral for a competent therapist.

In addition, consider some of the following options for dealing with out-of-control, dangerous threats and behaviors:

- ✔ **911:** If you're afraid of imminent danger, call 911.

- ✔ **Inpatient treatment:** Your therapist or the ER usually arranges such treatment to stabilize an out-of-control child and arrange for the next stage of treatment. Mental health professionals don't usually encourage inpatient treatment on a repeated basis.

- ✔ **Residential treatment:** In this approach, kids are sent to a controlled, residential setting, usually for an extended period of time (generally at least a month). At these settings, kids receive individual therapy, group therapy, social skills training, miscellaneous therapies, education, and structured consequences for their behavior. Mental health professionals don't recommend this approach as often as some others largely because of its high expense and uncertain outcomes.

- ✔ **Treatment foster care:** With this approach, parents temporarily give up physical custody of their kids so that foster parents trained in dealing with serious emotional issues can attempt to improve behaviors. Although somewhat radical, this strategy can be a lifesaver sometimes. Also, your state may pay for the costs. Go to the relevant department in your state (sometimes called the Department of Children Youth and Families, Department of Human Services, or Department of Social and Health Services) to find out whether your state offers this treatment free of cost, or at least at a discounted price.

- ✔ **Therapeutic boarding schools:** Again, this strategy is quite expensive. However, these schools are equipped to deal with complicated behavioral and emotional problems, so the benefits of this form of treatment may outweigh the costs.

- ✔ **Wilderness therapy programs:** These programs usually last from one to two months and involve teaching kids how to get along with others in challenging conditions. Kids are also taught confidence building skills through physical activities such as rope skills courses, rock climbing, and living outdoors. They can provide a much-needed respite for parents, and they sometimes teach adolescents cooperative survival skills.

- ✔ **Other out-of-home placements:** Sometimes a caring uncle, grandparent, or close family friend may be willing to take on the care of your emotionally challenged child for awhile. If your child has a good, solid relationship with that person and both parties are willing, this option may prove useful.

Whatever option you choose, the point is to find the care and assistance that will allow all your family members to feel safe. You can't let a child with serious BPD symptoms put you or your other kids in danger.

Taking Care of Everyone Else — Including Yourself

We assume that you have ensured the safety of your family, as well as that of your child with emotional problems. Physical safety comes first. But, after you've established basic safety, you must attend to the needs of everyone in the family, not just your kid with BPD symptoms. Many times, a marriage or partnership can come unglued by the stress of having a child with serious BPD symptoms.

You can't let your emotionally challenged child act like a black hole that sucks all the attention, focus, and satisfaction out of your family. Parenting a difficult child takes energy. A strong partnership and family connection help you recharge. In this vein, making sure the family engages in a reasonable number of pleasurable pursuits is important — whether the child with BPD symptoms tags along or not.

Parenting Adult Kids with BPD

Most people with adult children can look back on their parenting years and think of many things they would change if they could. Regret is especially poignant when your adult child has BPD. No doubt you can compile a long list of mistakes you made.

But one thing you can't do is make up for where you may have gone wrong by trying to fix your adult child's life. If you try to do so, you may just make things worse. Your child is now an adult and has to be responsible for his or her own life and recovery.

Yet, your BPD adult child is likely to try and enlist your help, whether in the form of finances, advice, or solutions. Here's our advice to you:

✔ Make sure your child is in treatment before considering giving help.

✔ If you do decide to provide help, that help should be *limited* and it should be help that you've discussed with the professional who's involved in your child's treatment.

Remember that limiting your help is actually in your adult child's best interest because people with BPD need to figure out how to live their own lives. Continued dependency merely reinforces their old patterns.

✔ Never try to be your child's therapist or counselor.

Yes, dealing with an adult child with BPD — or any child with BPD, for that matter — can be extremely difficult and energy draining. However, by following our suggestions, you can improve your child's ability to cope. And you can pave the way for getting your child appropriate treatment. Finally, you can improve the atmosphere for the entire family by not allowing your child's issues to dominate.

Chapter 24

Advice for Adult Children of BPD Parents

In This Chapter

▶ Grieving for your lost childhood

▶ Setting boundaries for a parent with BPD

▶ Getting support from others

*R*aising healthy children takes sacrifice, energy, and commitment. Parents with BPD typically lack the resources they need to provide a healthy environment for their kids. This lack of resources doesn't mean they can't be wonderful parents — sometimes. But all too often they become overwhelmed by their own emotional issues and either neglect, or in the worst cases, abuse their kids.

If your parent has BPD, you probably have more than your share of difficult memories. You may recall times when you felt abandoned or when you had to take on excessive responsibilities. You may also remember exciting adventures or periods of time when your parents placed you on a pedestal. A parent with BPD can alternate from being better than the best of parents to the worst of the worst — having a parent with BPD can be quite a ride.

We don't recommend attempting to diagnose any family member with BPD or any other emotional disorder. Although we give you information about BPD symptoms (see Chapter 3 for details), matching your parent's behaviors to these symptoms doesn't qualify as a diagnosis. Even describing your parent to a professional can't result in a formal diagnosis because professionals can't diagnose someone without seeing him. Nevertheless, this chapter can be useful for adult children who are aware that their parents demonstrate BPD-like features or for those who know their parents have been diagnosed by a professional.

After you grow up, you must deal with your childhood memories as well as any ongoing issues with your parents. In this chapter, we show you how to accept what happened and how to move forward from the past when one of your parents has BPD. We describe how to understand a parent who has BPD and how to set realistic expectations for your relationship with that parent. We also give you ideas on how to set boundaries so that you can live a life without chaos. Finally, we offer some advice on obtaining support that may help you get to a better place.

In this chapter, we use *parent* rather than *parents* because being raised by one parent with BPD is far more common than being raised by two. Obviously, exceptions to this rule do show up from time to time.

Mourning the Childhood You Didn't Have

Perhaps you watch television or movies and see stories of wonderful, nearly idyllic families — families made up of children and parents who play together, talk to one another, solve problems together, and show warmth and love toward one another. Maybe you feel cheated because, unlike these TV families, your family was unstable and full of conflict. Well, the families on television and in the movies aren't real. Most families have their ups and downs, their strengths and their weaknesses.

But, if you grew up in a family with a BPD parent, your ups may have been higher, and your downs were surely lower than most. Chaos and stress probably permeated the atmosphere. You have good reason to feel like you missed out on something. The following sections can help you understand the effects your parent with BPD may have had on you. Not everyone will have had the same experience because BPD symptoms vary from person to person. By exploring the impact BPD had on your childhood, you can move past your past and start living a better life for yourself in the present.

Understanding the impact of BPD on children

Children raised by a parent with BPD are at greater risk for depression, substance abuse, behavior problems, and other emotional disorders than children raised by parents without a personality disorder. This high risk makes sense when you consider that their parents' BPD symptoms likely expose them to chronic conflicts, threats of violence, substance abuse, and unpredictable emotions throughout their childhoods. The interactions between mothers or fathers with BPD and their children negatively impact normal development. Table 24-1 lists some common ways that parents with BPD relate to their children and some of the impacts that these patterns can have on those children.

Parents have BPD for a variety of reasons, including biological, social, and psychological factors (see Chapter 4 for more info on the reasons for BPD). Most parents want to raise healthy children, but a personality disorder like BPD often gets in the way. We present this table so you can better understand how you may have been affected by your troubled parent, not as ammunition for blaming your parent.

Table 24-1	The Possible Impact of BPD Parents on Kids
BPD Parent Behaviors	*Possible Effects on Kids*
Up and down relationships: A BPD parent may change partners multiple times.	The unpredictability may lead to feelings of intense insecurity, anxiety, and worry, as well as fears of abandonment.
Explosiveness: BPD parents often have fiery arguments, temper outbursts, and even violence or abuse.	This parental model may prevent kids from learning how to regulate their own emotions. Kids become extremely aggressive or depressed.
Splitting: Parents with BPD may lavish their kids with praise and love one day and bombard them with blame, criticism, and scorn the next day.	Splitting may lead children to have unstable self-esteems — feeling better than others at times and much worse on other occasions.
Problems understanding others: BPD parents may not have the ability to read and understand their children, and, thus, they may lack empathy.	Children have trouble understanding their own emotions and those of others.
Dissociation: Parents may be in another world and unable to respond to their children's needs.	Children feel neglected and may ultimately develop a sense of emotional deprivation, or sometimes they may overcompensate by feeling excessively entitled.
Impulsivity: Parents with BPD may give in to substance abuse, gambling, promiscuity, or other impulsive behaviors.	Children may experience overwhelming worry or exhibit similar behaviors themselves.
Self harm: Some parents with BPD exhibit self-harm through suicide attempts, actual suicide, or self-mutilation.	Children may become depressed or develop similar behaviors of their own.
Neediness: Parents with BPD may be unable to meet their own daily obligations and thus turn to their kids and burden them with excessive responsibilities.	Such kids may develop anxiety or even obsessive-compulsive disorder. They may also become quite resentful and angry.
Boundary violations: Parents with BPD violate parent/child boundaries by demanding that their children become their best friends or even provide for the parents' emotional needs more than for their own.	Such children may overly focus on the needs of other people or become so confused about their roles that they struggle to interact well with peers.

You may notice that many of the effects on kids shown in Table 24-1 are consistent with emerging BPD symptoms. This trend makes sense because having a BPD parent increases the likelihood that children will develop BPD. Their risk also increases for most other emotional disorders, such as anxiety and depression.

At the same time, you need to realize that you could have a parent with BPD and end up with no major emotional problems at all. BPD has many causes; thus, predicting who will get it based only on one's parents is impossible. You may not have inherited the relevant genes, or you may have had other positive influences that mitigated against your chances of ending up with the disorder.

Reviewing your relationship with your parent

The preceding section illustrates how BPD in a parent can affect kids in various ways. However, even more valuable to understand is exactly how *your* parent with BPD (or BPD-like traits) affected you and *your* childhood. In all likelihood, you've either experienced grief over these effects or you will at some point in the future. After all, having a parent with BPD means you lost something very significant — specifically, the childhood that all kids want to have.

And, unless you've had professional help with this issue, that grieving process may have yet to surface.

Coming to terms with your grief through Grief Exploration Questions

You can begin to resolve grief by reviewing all facets of the relationship you had or still have with your BPD parent. Consider answering the following Grief Exploration Questions about this relationship:

- ✔ What was your childhood like with this parent?

- ✔ What did you value about your parent, and what was problematic for you?

- ✔ What did you learn from your parent (including good and bad)?

- ✔ What resentments do you carry today from your relationship with this parent?

- ✔ What about that parent do you feel grateful for?

- ✔ How would your life be different today (in both good and bad ways) if your parent hadn't had BPD?

✔ What things could your parent not provide for you that you found through someone else (such as your other parent, a friend, a relative, or a teacher)?

Taking a close look at remembrances from the past, such as old photo albums, school report cards, letters, or long-forgotten diaries can facilitate your review.

Take time to mull over your answers to these questions. Notice your feelings as you do. You may experience some angst or pain as you ponder these issues. Discussing your answers and feelings with a highly trusted friend or perhaps your siblings (if you feel close to them) may be useful to you. If your feelings are especially painful or difficult, consider seeking professional help to resolve them.

The point of grieving is to fully appreciate the meaning of your relationship with a problematic parent. As you understand this relationship — the good, the bad, and the ugly — you may find yourself more able to let go and move on. Carrying resentment and anger only causes you harm — holding on to these emotions doesn't change your past or your future.

Expressing your feelings

After you've thoroughly processed your childhood relationship, consider writing a letter to your parent with BPD. We generally don't recommend actually sending the letter to your parent because the point isn't to change your parent or extract an apology. Rather, the intent is to give you an outlet through which you can express your feelings. On the other hand, if you're working with a therapist who recommends sending such a letter, you may find value in doing so.

The following story about Ella, who is now 32 years old, illustrates what can happen when an adult child actively reflects on her childhood with a mother who has BPD.

> **Ella** remembers celebrating her 12th birthday in a hospital's emergency room. Her mother had taken another overdose of medications, and the wait on a Saturday night was long. As her mother faded in and out of awareness on a gurney, some of the nurses learned of her birthday and bought her a pastry from the vending machine. They found a couple of used birthday candles at the nurses' station and sang happy birthday to her at around 2 a.m. Ella's mother had been diagnosed with BPD, and this was her fourth hospitalization after attempting suicide.
>
> Years and many sessions of therapy later, Ella still worries about her mother. But now she feels ready to say goodbye to the resentment and anger that have poisoned her life. After reviewing her answers to the Grief Exploration Questions, she writes this letter to her mom:

Dear Mom,

Hope you're doing okay. I know I don't call you very much, and when I see your name on my caller ID, I don't answer. You probably feel pretty hurt by that and I'm sorry.

I remember all the family therapy we had when I was a teenager. We never seemed to be able to spend any time talking without one of us getting mad. I lost a lot of years not being able to get over my anger and resentment of you.

But lately I'm doing better, and I wanted to get a couple of things off my chest. First, there's nothing scarier to a child than having a mother try to kill herself. I can't tell you how frightened I was. At the same time, I was furious with you, with the doctors who didn't seem to help, and with everyone else in the world. I was just so angry and scared. That's pretty much how I felt — all the time.

I never once thought about how much you must have suffered, too. And I blamed myself for not being able to help you. Now I understand that I couldn't help or understand; I was too young. I've learned a lot about borderline personality disorder, and now I see that you probably did the best you could and that I couldn't do anything to make you better. I do recall how much fun you could be when you felt well. I know you tried. And a few times you were there for me. Maybe at some point I'll try calling you again from time to time. But for now, I need to maintain some space.

Love, Ella

Although Ella felt ready to write this letter to her mother, she didn't send it because her mother remained unstable. Ella felt better after writing the letter to her mom, even though it didn't change anything, because doing so allowed her to let go of some of her bitterness and resentment. Her grief over her lost childhood slowly began to lessen.

Moving on with Your Life

You can't redo your past, but you could remain stuck in it forever if you don't figure out how to forgive and let go. Forgiving doesn't mean forgetting or saying that what happened was okay. Instead, forgiving means allowing yourself to move forward.

So, now what? You're an adult with your own life to lead. If your parent with BPD still causes you strife and turmoil, you have some work ahead of you. You need to set better boundaries with your parent to protect yourself and the life you're living now whether it involves friends, work, a partner, a spouse, and/or kids of your own.

Setting boundaries

Boundaries are the limits that people draw around themselves and their lives to keep others from constantly interfering. When you're clear about your boundaries, others usually respect them. For example, we have boundaries about phone calls — we generally don't answer the phone after 10:00 p.m. unless the caller ID indicates a close friend or family member. We answer then because those friends and family members know that we don't like answering the phone late unless it's something very important or urgent. Our friends and family respect this boundary that we set.

People set boundaries around a variety of issues, including needs for space, time alone, privacy, and intimacy. People with BPD don't always understand interpersonal boundaries or the need to respect them. Thus, you may have to be unusually clear in communicating your expectations to parents who have BPD.

To set boundaries with a BPD parent, consider the following issues:

- ✔ **Decide what's important.** Ask yourself what you want to set boundaries around. Some people consider their personal time paramount. Others feel that privacy is critical. Some may decide that any contact with their parent would be overly toxic. Remember, deciding what's important to you is *your* decision.

- ✔ **Realize your rights.** This issue is often difficult for adult kids to grasp. As an adult, you have a perfect right to lead your own life. You and only you can be the ultimate judge of what you need and want. Your friends, your other parent, your siblings, or others may pressure you to rescue your parent with BPD. You've probably been down that road many times before and found only dead end after dead end. So, you need to make the decision as to what works for you. Make *your* life your priority.

- ✔ **Deliver the message.** Vagueness, ambiguity, and lack of clarity don't help you set good boundaries. You must give your message as clearly as possible, and don't pull any punches. You also don't need to be mean or rancorous. For example, you may tell a parent, "I won't take your phone calls at work anymore — if need be, I will hang up. My work simply can't be interrupted." Or, perhaps you tell your parent, "You can't drink at my children's birthday parties. If you arrive with alcohol on your breath, I will insist that you leave. I mean it." You may also want to tell your parent, "I'm not going to discuss my marriage with you any longer."

    And you don't need to explain why you're setting these or any other boundaries. We aren't telling you what boundaries to set, but we want you to make them clear and explicit like the preceding examples.

✔ **Deal with the emotional fallout.** You can't expect your parent to celebrate your new boundaries. Your parent with BPD is likely to feel insulted or rejected by you. Your parent may try to blackmail you with guilt. Don't let your parent persuade you to change your mind. Opening the door a crack encourages your parent to barge through, leaving you feeling flattened and violated.

✔ **Adjust your boundaries as needed.** Setting boundaries with a problematic parent isn't a one-time deal. You may feel a need to put up more barriers when your parent is behaving especially badly. In some cases, your parent may improve over time, which allows you to loosen the limits a little. At other times, your needs may change, which leads you to put up either higher or lower barriers.

Setting clear boundaries for the first time can be challenging. Read the next section for ideas on obtaining support for your efforts.

Soliciting support

Living with someone who has BPD is very difficult. Being the child of someone with BPD can be exquisitely painful. Think of a small child bringing a band-aid to a parent who has purposefully cut himself. The feelings of helplessness and terror must be overwhelming. You don't have to wonder why adult children of parents with BPD are at greater risk for having emotional problems themselves.

So, if you suffer, know that you're not alone. Others have walked the same path and gotten through it. Get help. Here are a few options:

✔ Seek therapy from a professional who has experience dealing with BPD.

✔ Join support groups and learn about the disorder that disrupted your life.

See Appendix B for additional Web sites and resources.

Chapter 25

Advice for Therapists of People with BPD

• •

In This Chapter

▶ Recognizing early signs of BPD

▶ Letting go of your ego and focusing on your client

▶ Setting serious limits — and sticking to them

▶ Taking care of yourself

• •

*T*he complexity of borderline personality disorder (BPD) can send shivers down the spines of mental health therapists. Clients with BPD present with multiple issues, including impulsive behaviors, relationship problems, substance abuse, emotional dysregulation, and a high risk of suicide. In fact, 10 percent of people with BPD eventually do commit suicide. The treating mental health professional feels a great deal of anguish and pain when a client's life ends through suicide.

No wonder many therapists feel unprepared to meet the challenges of a person with BPD. Other therapists unknowingly accept people with BPD into their practices and become enmeshed in an entangled complex relationship that eventually spins out of control. Thus, they may find themselves providing unusual amounts of help, giving special considerations, or feeling angry and annoyed with their BPD patients without even knowing why.

At the same time, treating people with BPD can be uniquely rewarding. Changes may come more slowly than they do in other cases, and obstacles may seem more daunting. But, hanging in there and giving someone with BPD the tools and skills she needs for a better life gives you, the therapist, an opportunity to use all your talents and training. And nothing is more satisfying than seeing someone's life turn around with your help.

In this chapter, we give you some guidelines for recognizing BPD in your patients early. We discuss how to be in touch with your own thoughts and feelings, as well as how to keep them from interfering with the therapy you're doing. We also make note of the importance of setting reasonable limits with all your patients, including those with BPD. Finally, we recommend various ways of taking care of yourself. Therapists need to make sure they meet their own needs in various ways if they hope to have the energy and reserves they need to take care of challenging patients.

Detecting BPD in the Early Stages of Therapy

The sooner you know that a new patient has BPD, the more likely you are to be able to manage the therapeutic complexities involved. However, many patients with BPD work hard to keep their therapists in the dark about their condition. Reasons for this behavior vary from person to person, but in part, BPD patients may fear rejection from you, their new therapist. This fear isn't entirely groundless because some therapists prefer not to work with patients with BPD. Thus, some BPD patients report having been rejected by several therapists in the past.

If you don't feel comfortable treating BPD, try to avoid starting a therapeutic process before making a referral. Doing so can cause unnecessary harm to your client by exacerbating abandonment concerns. Usually a phone interview or an agreement to one to three evaluation sessions prior to starting therapy can keep you from taking on someone you shouldn't.

Our reason for recommending that you detect BPD early in therapy has less to do with needing (or wanting) to avoid working with BPD patients and more to do with maximizing your awareness of what may be tricky *hot buttons* for your patient. By hot buttons, we mean core issues, such as the following:

- ✓ Fears of abandonment
- ✓ Self-esteem problems
- ✓ Problems with identity
- ✓ Feelings of emptiness
- ✓ Need for constant stimulation
- ✓ Substance abuse issues
- ✓ Problems with boundaries
- ✓ Rage
- ✓ Feelings of entitlement
- ✓ Dysregulated emotions
- ✓ Tendencies to engage in self-harm
- ✓ Relationship struggles
- ✓ Dissociation

See Chapter 3 for more details about BPD symptoms. When you're aware that your BPD patients may have exquisite sensitivity to any of these issues, you can follow a more careful course in your therapeutic dialogues with them. Knowing what to avoid and what to address in your dialogues with BPD patients helps prevent ruptures in the therapeutic process.

We suggest that you consider the possibility that clients *may* have BPD when they display the following behaviors, especially in the first few sessions:

- ✔ Report that their past therapists didn't understand them
- ✔ Give you a long list of previous, inadequate therapists
- ✔ Say their problems are too great to be solvable
- ✔ Miss, cancel, or change appointments, especially at the last minute
- ✔ Desire special considerations, such as after-hours appointments or forgiveness on bills
- ✔ Try to make sessions run over the time allocation
- ✔ Idealize you — the new therapist — or a previous therapist (including subtle or blatant seductive behaviors)
- ✔ Treat you, the new therapist, as a special friend or discuss a previous therapist in those terms
- ✔ Appear overly sensitive to your moods or state of health
- ✔ Ask seemingly innocent questions about your family
- ✔ Try to make connections outside of therapy, such as bumping into you at stores or local events
- ✔ Reveal knowledge about you that isn't widely known
- ✔ Report past suicidal behaviors and threats
- ✔ Report past self-harming behaviors, such as cutting

Obviously, the preceding bullets don't represent a diagnostic checklist for BPD — we assume you already know the basics of BPD diagnoses. But, if you're unsure about the diagnosis of an especially complex case, seek professional supervision and consultation. You may even want to refer the client to a psychologist with expertise in assessment for a complete psychological evaluation before proceeding with treatment.

In addition to looking for these signs in your patients, you need to tune into your own feelings. You may find yourself starting to reveal personal information without even knowing why. Or, you may feel attracted to or simply quite warm toward some clients with BPD symptoms. You may find yourself forgiving last-second cancellations and special requests. You need to be aware of your thoughts and feelings, especially those that are similar to the ones we mention here. Of course you care about your clients, but you have to be careful when you feel something out of the ordinary.

If you don't keep a check on your feelings, you could easily become ensnared in an inappropriate relationship.

Working as a mental health therapist can be a lonely job, especially when you have a private practice. Because of legal and ethical reasons, you can't go home and tell your family about your day. You have to keep your daily experiences to yourself, which can be a difficult task at times. We recommend that all mental health practitioners have either peer supervision groups (with colleagues) or regular consultations with other professionals. Doing so is a major part of maintaining good practice, but it's especially crucial when you're working with clients with BPD.

Maintaining Objectivity

We, like most mental health therapists, have come across clients who ask for help and then, in the same breath, say that they're helpless. People with BPD often present contradictions like this one. The first few sessions may sound something like the following:

- Save me; you can't.
- Help me; I'm helpless.
- I can trust you more than anyone in the world; I won't tell you how I feel.
- Give me tools, and I'll break them.
- Give me support, and I'll find ways to test you.
- Don't ever leave me; I hate you.
- Be nice to me; I'll destroy you.
- You can't help me; you're my only chance.
- I'll do anything for you; I'm going to kill myself.

Do any of these scenarios feel familiar? Do you have a sick feeling in the pit of your stomach? We understand. Being a therapist for someone with BPD is a very difficult task.

However, if you fear dealing with BPD issues like these, you need to get therapy and/or supervision, because avoiding having any BPD patients in your practice is pretty tough. After all, a variety of studies have estimated that around 10 percent of all outpatients have BPD. And, the reality is that 25 percent or so of therapists eventually lose one or more patients to suicide. That percentage is a little higher for psychologists and even higher for psychiatrists, who usually see many more patients.

If these statistics create overwhelming fear, you may want to consider another occupation. However, assuming that you're interested in treating even the difficult patients with BPD (after all, you're reading this book), you need to consider a few issues. First of all, 90 percent of all people with BPD don't commit suicide. Second, therapy does help people with BPD, and so does the passage of time. Third, the outcome of any client, with or without a diagnosis of BPD, ultimately has as much to do with the client's efforts as those of the therapist. The next two sections may help you hold onto the objectivity that is so critical when you're dealing with challenging clients.

Keeping your therapist ego on the shelf

Therapists by and large love to help people, which is a major reason why they're therapists! Providing people with the care, support, and therapeutic guidance they need to reduce their distress and helping to make their lives fuller and more meaningful are very rewarding parts of the job.

However, providing psychotherapy to people can't be about enhancing your own ego. Yes, you want to feel good about what you do, and yes, you probably feel better about yourself when your hard work pays off with a client. But you can't measure your own worthiness by how each individual client does in therapy.

Psychotherapy is a two-way street. As a therapist, you can only set the optimal conditions for enhancing the likelihood of clients making useful changes in their lives. When someone doesn't go along with your plan, you need to know that you're not a bad therapist or an unworthy human being.

In other words, if you allow your own ego to become intertwined in the relationships you have with your clients who have BPD, you'll likely lose the objectivity you need to be an effective therapist. By letting your personal feelings take over, you may find yourself allowing boundaries to blur as you feel increasingly frustrated, annoyed, and upset with your challenging client.

If you let your feelings override your objective thoughts, you may end up doing the very thing your BPD clients fear the most (but expect at the same time) — abruptly abandoning them because of your own emotional struggle. Alternatively, you may allow yourself to become enmeshed in an inappropriate, unethical relationship that can range from becoming close friends to building a sexual liaison. Either relationship ultimately proves harmful to any client — especially clients with BPD. If you doubt the truth of this statement, ask a few of your colleagues who have experience treating serious personality disorders about their thoughts on the issue.

In addition to keeping your ego and feelings in check, you also need to fully understand what's reasonable to expect from a therapeutic relationship if you want to be an effective therapist. We discuss this topic in the next section.

Keeping therapist expectations within bounds

Every therapist needs to understand what to expect from a career as a mental health professional. Some of the advantages you can expect from such a career include reasonably good pay, some degree of autonomy over your work schedule, respect in the community, intellectual stimulation, and a variety of interesting colleagues to work with. More important than these, however, is the great satisfaction that therapists usually report feeling after having played a role in improving their clients' lives.

On the other hand, what you can't expect from this career is nurturance, support, friendship, or great gratitude from your clients. Many clients may feel appreciative, yet they often don't express that emotion fully. Some clients may leave after a couple of sessions and give you no feedback at all. For other clients, you may plant seeds that won't germinate until years after your work is over. In fact, many clients may repeat your ideas back to you some weeks or months after you first offer them, attributing the notions to their own insights — a situation like this is wonderful because it means they're making progress!

Understanding Boundaries

Psychotherapists need boundaries, or they may lose control over some of the relationships they have with clients. Generally speaking, you want to discuss a number of issues and boundaries with new clients, as well as provide a form for them to sign that states they understand and agree to these limits. The details of these limits vary from therapist to therapist, but your list should generally include a review of the following items:

- ✓ **Timeliness:** You should set out some expectations regarding showing up on time with every new client. Of course, traffic or other unexpected delays occasionally arise, but you can deal with those issues on a case-by-case basis.

- ✓ **Financial arrangements:** You should either collect the co-payments or insurance deductibles the patient owes at the time of service or bill the patient regularly. Whichever method you choose, make sure you go over it with your new patient. Allowing bills to accumulate significantly is typically a big mistake.

- ✓ **Cancellation/no show policies:** Therapists vary on how they decide to deal with this issue, but you need to lay out the details of your own policy at the beginning of therapy and explain that you expect your new patient to adhere to this policy.

✔ **After-hours availability:** This issue is especially controversial in the mental health field, and practitioners debate on how to deal with it. We have no simple answer for you, but whatever your policy is, you need to make it clear to every new client. All clients need to know what to do in the event of an emergency, so make sure your policy includes such cases.

✔ **Dual relationships:** Mental health professionals strongly discourage dual relationships and rarely consider them ethical. However, the issue can get quite subtle and perplexing. As a rule of thumb, you don't want to have any relationships with your clients outside therapy that include financial transactions, friendships, sexual liaisons, exchanges of other services, or favors.

✔ **Self-disclosure:** What therapists decide to disclose about themselves to clients — and whether they decide to disclose anything at all — is another controversial area. We encourage therapists to seek supervision and consultation with colleagues on this issue. If you do decide to judiciously disclose a few personal stories or anecdotes, make sure they're limited. Also, make sure you only tell personal stories for sound therapeutic rationales — never do so for your own needs.

✔ **Bartering:** Although some professional groups consider this practice acceptable under a few circumstances, we discourage bartering (accepting items or services in return for therapy) in general. The process can quickly turn sour.

✔ **Gifts:** Clients often feel quite grateful to their therapists. Sometimes they want to express their gratitude with small gifts. Often, homemade goodies (cookies and such), a small box of chocolates, an inexpensive coffee cup, or a card are acceptable. However, you should be clear that you can't accept expensive gifts, no matter how well intended they may be.

In addition, therapists or the agencies they work for should provide each new client with a consent form that discusses reasonable expectations of therapy, appropriate therapeutic goals, confidentiality issues, client rights, and professionals' obligations to their clients.

Limits, rules, and boundaries may sound rather straightforward and simple on paper. However, these issues can quickly become very complex and confusing in practice. Some of your clients are bound to complicate matters at some point. People with BPD, for example, sometimes have an exquisite sense of how to thread the needle, leaving you bewildered. See the story of Linda and her therapist Jim in the section "Dealing with Boundaries" for an example of a subtle attempt to cross boundaries. The best advice we can give you is to make sure you document all issues related to boundaries, seek continuing education and consultation, and be careful. In addition, we strongly recommend that you go to www.kspope.com where you can find an extensive collection of resources about therapeutic boundaries.

Dealing with Boundaries

Therapists sometimes get caught in nets of negativity, or alternatively, tugs for crossing boundaries with patients. When either of these situations happens, treatment can turn into a battle of wills instead of a helping relationship. These traps ensnare all therapists from time to time, but you can do your best to minimize them in several ways.

A few guidelines for avoiding these pitfalls include the following:

✔ **Don't become defensive.** You may become the symbol of everything that's wrong in mental health care in your client's mind. Or, you may become the equivalent to the client's mother, father, ex-partner, teacher, or some other person who caused substantial angst or disappointment. In any event, clients will criticize you, sometimes very aggressively, from time to time. You must realize that the criticism isn't about you in most cases, and when it is, you need to be open to hearing it. You may be able to learn something from your client's rampage. Defensive counterattacking on your part quickly leads to a therapeutic rupture that you may not be able to repair.

✔ **Look for something to validate.** Almost any criticism has a sliver of truth in it. Focus on finding the part of the criticism you can agree with. Look for reasons why your client is behaving in self-defeating ways, whether with you or with others. Usually a reason does exist, and that reason isn't entirely unreasonable!

✔ **Reflect empathy.** Even when you feel annoyed or aggravated, you can probably find something about your client or her words that you can feel empathy for. Express that empathy and understanding to your client.

✔ **Ask your client for more information.** Even when you feel attacked, ask for clarification. Most people calm down when you seem genuinely interested in fully understanding their concerns.

✔ **Listen to your gut.** If you feel uncomfortable, squeamish, pulled, or bullied, you need to slow down, back off a little, and reflect. Your feelings are trying to tell you something — try to figure out what that something is. Don't get caught up in a rapid fire exchange that feels out of control.

✔ **Put an issue on the shelf for awhile.** Sometimes an issue may be so hot that your client isn't ready to hear anything you have to say. In those cases, saying something like the following is perfectly acceptable: "I understand the way you're feeling right now; would you be willing to take another look at this issue in a future session? I have a feeling we're a little stuck at the moment."

Therapists are human beings, and as such, they're imperfect. If you feel confused or upset, step back and ask the client for more clarification. Your guidance and responses don't have to be instantaneous.

The following story about Jim, an experienced social worker, illustrates some of the boundary struggles a therapist can face with his client. Jim finds himself getting into battles with his patient, Linda. He also finds himself expressing feelings of friendship without even understanding why. He seeks help from his clinical director, who asks for an audio tape of the therapy session.

Sometimes, as a therapist, you may want to bring in a supervisor to help you better understand a particular client and what you can do to help that client. You can enhance this supervision by using video- or audio-taped sessions. Most patients or clients agree to the taping if the only use is for clinical supervision. As the session progresses, the client soon forgets that the camera or tape recorder is even there.

Here's the dialogue from Jim's recent session with Linda.

> **Jim (the therapist):** Hello, Linda, I'm glad to see you today. I heard that you were in the ER this weekend after cutting yourself. I'm glad you weren't admitted.
>
> **Linda (the client):** You're lucky I'm alive. No thanks to you or your stupid hospital. They made me wait four hours before anyone would see me. By the time I got to talk to the doc, I was so tired that I just wanted to go home and go to bed.
>
> **Jim:** Well, we've talked about this before, Linda. Sometimes just waiting awhile until the overwhelming feelings go down can keep you safe. You don't always need to be admitted.
>
> **Linda:** You know what, Jim? You're just a whore for the insurance company — trying to keep costs down by turning away psych patients.
>
> **Jim:** That's not true, Linda. We do what's right for our patients. My obligation is to keep you safe. Not to save money.
>
> **Linda:** Don't be condescending to me. I've been around a long time. I used to be able to get a bed and a few days rest in your hospital. Now, it's full of homeless criminals. The people who really need help are sent home.
>
> **Jim:** Now Linda, that's not fair to me. You know I'm trying to help you.
>
> **Linda:** Not fair. Look, I've been coming here for years, and that's the treatment I get from you?
>
> **Jim:** Okay, Linda, can we stop here? I think we both need to step back and figure out what's going on.

Linda: Oh, I see, you've finally had enough of me and want to get rid of me as a client. Right?

Jim: No, no, not at all. I really like you. Really. But you're not hearing me or realizing that I'm trying really hard to help you.

Linda: You really like me? I'll bet you wouldn't even have a cup of coffee with me if you ran into me on the sidewalk, would you?

Jim: That's not true. Of course, I would. I really care about you.

Linda: Well, that's reassuring.

Jim's supervisor listens to this segment of the tape. He asks Jim where he thinks things first got off track. In retrospect, Jim realizes that his first mistake occurred when Linda told him that she had to wait for four hours and was exhausted from the ordeal. Because Jim was feeling defensive, he failed to express empathy for her plight. Then, when she called him a "whore from the insurance company," he argued with her. Instead, he may have found a way to agree that insurance can be frustrating.

Jim further derailed when he directly argued with his client by telling her that what she said was untrue and unfair to him. His mistake gave Linda an opening to ask whether he cared enough about her to have coffee sometime. Jim was totally flustered, and not wanting to make things worse, agreed to her vague request to consider violating boundaries.

Jim and his supervisor discuss some alternative approaches (which we note at the beginning of this section) he can take to work with Linda in future sessions. The supervisor points out that these ideas may not always work but that they will help Jim maintain appropriate boundaries. Even if Jim and Linda can't repair their therapeutic relationship, the alternative approaches Jim wants to use will send Linda a more appropriate message, which can help her in future therapy if she chooses to seek it. If they can repair their therapy relationship, all the better. Here's a partial transcript of the next session.

Jim: Hello, Linda, how are you doing this week?

Linda: Much better Jim, how are you?

Jim: Good. If there's nothing pressing going on in your life that we need to deal with immediately, I'd like to propose that we talk a little about our session last week. Would that be okay with you?

Linda: I'm sorry I got on your case about the ER and called you a whore; I know you care about me.

Jim: Well, Linda, I want to say that I got a little defensive and shouldn't have. You have every right to express your opinions, whether they're negative or positive.

Linda: I like it when a man can admit mistakes, Jim.

Jim: Let me explain. I took a wrong turn that may have hurt our therapeutic relationship. I was feeling uncomfortable about arguing with you, so I went a bit the other way.

Linda: Oh, no, Jim. I can really trust you now. I know that you care about me in a special way. I'm more than just an ordinary client to you.

Jim: Linda, I care about you in the same way I care about all my clients. I want to be able to help you help yourself. I'm sorry I misspoke.

Linda: What do you mean, misspoke?

Jim: Well, when I agreed with you that I could consider having coffee if I ran into you somewhere, I wasn't thinking. In fact, doing something like that would cross a barrier that I just don't think is a good idea.

Linda: What? I wasn't asking you to have an affair with me; it's just coffee, for gosh sakes!

Jim: I understand that coffee sounds very innocent and trivial. I just make it a rule not to socialize in any way outside of therapy with any of my clients. I care about them, but therapy takes place in the office.

Linda: Gosh, you're incredibly uptight.

Jim: I know it sounds a little rigid. Maybe it is, but I've found it works better for me that way.

Linda: So you don't really think I'm special, is that it?

Jim: Everyone's special, Linda. And so are you.

Linda: That sounds like a lot of BS to me, Jim.

Jim: I understand that. But do you feel you can accept what I'm saying and continue working with me?

Linda: I think so. But I'll think about it and let you know.

At Jim's next supervision session, his supervisor compliments him on his work. He relates that Jim kept his cool, looked for ways to agree with what Linda said without endorsing everything, and held his boundaries firmly. He tells Jim that he thinks the relationship may be close to back on track, but only time will tell.

When you communicate your boundaries clearly and honestly, most clients can hear the message. If clients can't accept what you're telling them, letting go of your boundaries will only make things worse.

Taking Care of Yourself

An important component of taking care of other people involves taking care of yourself. Too many therapists let their lives get out of balance. They worry excessively about their clients, work reprehensible hours, and disparage themselves when their clients don't improve like they think they should.

For people who spend much of their lives focused on meeting the needs of other people (in other words, you!), looking after themselves and meeting their own needs aren't always as easy as they may think. Here are a few suggestions we offer you, a therapist, for taking care of yourself:

- ✔ **Seek social support.** Spend time with friends and family.

- ✔ **Take part in hobbies and outside activities.** Try out some new activities, such as hiking, travel, or crafts.

- ✔ **Exercise.** You tell your clients to exercise, don't you? Well, what about you? Try a range of ideas until you find a few activities you enjoy enough to stick with them. Don't restrict yourself to a single form of exercise, such as jogging. Your body does better when you cross train.

- ✔ **Learn new things.** Take adult education classes at a local college or university.

- ✔ **Read new books.** Of course you read professional books and articles. But consider reading outside of your field. In addition, read for entertainment.

- ✔ **Prioritize your health.** Staying healthy takes some energy, time, and commitment. Practice self-control.

Part VI
The Part of Tens

The 5th Wave   By Rich Tennant

"The kids love it when Chuck meditates."

In this part . . .

The Part of Tens chapters appear in all *For Dummies* books. They provide helpful tips on dealing with some of the difficult issues we discuss throughout this book. We wrote these chapters specifically for the sufferers of borderline personality disorder (BPD). We show you ten quick ways to calm down when your emotions start running high. We give you some hints on how to say you're sorry. And, finally, we review ten techniques that either don't work at all or are insufficient for addressing BPD issues.

Chapter 26

Ten Quick Ways to Settle Down

In This Chapter

▶ Using your senses to calm yourself down

▶ Interrupting your emotions with a variety of activities

▶ Changing scenes to improve your mood

People with borderline personality disorder (BPD) frequently become intensely emotional. They may react to small stressors, such as waiting in line at a grocery store, getting stuck in a traffic jam, or hearing negative feedback, with great big emotions. Psychotherapies for BPD help patients by teaching them skills for regulating negative emotions. Here are some quick tips for bringing intense emotional highs back down to earth. Pick a couple and try them out.

Most people need a lot of practice before some of these strategies become effective. Practice them when you're *not* upset.

Breathing Away Distress

Deep breathing helps calm people down. When in distress, people breathe rapidly but shallowly. In Chapter 16, we discuss breathing meditation, one good method you can use to calm down. However, getting results from meditation usually takes considerable practice over time.

Here's an easier, faster breathing method that can help you dissipate distress. You can practice this method anywhere, anytime.

1. **Empty your lungs by breathing out.**
2. **Take a deep breath; feel the air flowing in through your nose, then moving into your chest, and finally expanding your abdomen.**
3. **Hold your breath for a couple of seconds.**
4. **Breathe out very slowly through your mouth — try to push all the air out.**
5. **Repeat Steps 1 through 4 ten times.**

Chilling Your Hot Emotions

Do you sometimes feel like you need to "chill out," as younger folks say? Cooling down the body can douse your fiery hot feelings, too. Here's a strategy you can try:

1. **Get a piece of ice from your freezer.**

2. **Hold it with one hand, and press it against your wrist.**

3. **When your hand or wrist starts to hurt, change hands, and hold it against your other wrist.**

4. **Repeat Steps 1 through 3 until the ice cube is melted.**

5. **If you are still upset, you can repeat the process with another cube, but usually one will work.**

Picking Up Your Pace

This method of settling down involves a little exercise. If you have health concerns or haven't exercised for awhile, check with your doctor to make sure this strategy is okay to try.

1. **Buy a jump rope, or make your own.**

2. **Get a kitchen timer, and set the time for 45 seconds.**

3. **Now jump rope for 45 seconds.**

   If you're in really good shape, jump for 2 minutes.

4. **Count your jumps to keep your mind off other things.**

After you finish, you won't be thinking about whatever is (or should we say, "was"?) bothering you. You'll be catching your breath!

Massaging Away the Blues

Massage therapy has been a recognized medical treatment for many centuries. It has grown in popularity over the past few decades as a way to relax. Once a pleasure for the rich, massage therapy offers physical and mental benefits to many different people today.

Usually a professional therapist performs massages. However, if you don't have the time or money to pay a professional, you can give yourself a mini-massage instead. Take some lotion or oil and rub it into your feet and ankles. Be sure to knead each toe and each heel. Do the same on your shoulders, elbows, and hands. Ahhhh, feel the relaxation.

Surfing for Distraction

If your job primarily consists of sitting in front of a computer all day, this strategy may not be a great idea. But for many people, 30 minutes of surfing the Web can be very entertaining. Look up a topic you're interested in, such as vacation destinations, financial planning, homes for sale in your neighbor-hood, or exotic pets, and find the fascinating array of information right at your fingertips. Focusing your mind on something carefree or interesting can help you calm down.

Reading a Great Book

Reading can take your mind away from your troubles and put you into another world. If you enjoy reading, always have a few books available. For most people, reading takes more concentration than watching television, which, in general, makes books more effective than TV shows at distracting your mind. Furthermore, you won't find any commercials in books. Our personal preference is to have a nonfiction book for the early evening and then a good mystery for the late hours.

Mellowing Out in a Movie

Movies can also sweep you away to another place. You can buy a movie, rent a movie, watch one on a cable channel, or even download one straight from the Internet. Whichever method you choose for getting your movie, be sure to make some popcorn to go along with it — low fat, skip the butter. Mmm, crunch, crunch, crunch.

Playing to Improve Your Mood

If you have kids or grandkids, take some time to play. Go to a park, or play a board game. Your kids will love spending time with you, and your mood can benefit from playing, too. After all, being in a bad mood while playing hopscotch or capture the flag is pretty hard to do! Call your young nieces, nephews, or cousins, and offer to watch them for a couple of hours so that their parents can have a break. If you don't have kids around, play with a dog or other animal. Dogs love to play. If you don't have a dog or other pet, you can volunteer to be a dog walker at the local animal shelter. Or, consider being a temporary foster parent for a dog that's waiting placement. Dogs can bark you down from a bad mood anytime.

Phoning a Friend

If you've ever seen *Who Wants to Be a Millionaire?*, you know all about the lifeline that allows participants to call a friend when they need help. When you're upset, friends can be a real lifeline for you, too. However, be careful that you don't let your bad mood cause you to attack your friend for not listening well enough or for not agreeing with you 100 percent. Tell your friend that you just want to vent a little. If you do start feeling angry with your friend, cut the conversation short — you certainly don't want to add to your woes.

Be careful not to overdo this strategy because you don't want to burn your friends out. Friendships sustain themselves only when they're two-way streets.

Getting Outside

A couple of years ago, we wrote a book called *Seasonal Affective Disorder For Dummies* (Wiley). Seasonal Affective Disorder (SAD) is a type of depression associated with the short days of winter. One of the best ways to decrease the low moods of SAD is to go outside.

Even if you don't have SAD, going outside can help improve your mood. Take a walk in a nice park or on a street that has interesting houses. Go to a dog park and watch the dogs run around. Attend an outdoor sporting event. Whatever you do, just get outside.

Chapter 27

Ten Ways to Say You're Sorry

*W*e have great compassion for people with borderline personality disorder (BPD). We know painful emotions permeate their lives. Guilt and regret are two especially powerful emotions that often plague people with BPD.

We also know that folks who love people with BPD often feel terribly hurt and confused. Some have endless optimism that their loved ones with BPD will improve. Others give up and move on. Either way, people with BPD feel better when they take personal responsibility for the role they've played in hurting the people who care about them. Part of getting better involves being able to tell the people you have hurt, "I'm sorry." This chapter offers ten ways to tell your loved ones that you're sorry.

Saying the Words Out Loud

A simple but, at times, excruciatingly difficult way to communicate remorse is by speaking the words out loud. For some people, apologizing seems almost impossible. If you feel overwhelmed by this challenge, talk to your therapist about it. Try role-playing in one of your sessions. Then ask yourself the following questions:

✔ What does saying I'm sorry mean about me as a person?

✔ How can saying I'm sorry help me and the other person?

Saying you're sorry actually suggests that you're a brave person — someone who can own up to mistakes. Saying you're sorry can help the one you hurt as well as yourself. Although apologizing won't negate past wrongs, it's a move in the right direction — especially if you commit yourself to continuous growth.

Asking for Forgiveness

Saying you're sorry is only half of the picture. The other part is asking for forgiveness. Sounds pretty easy, right? "Please forgive me."

People who've been hurt by people with BPD have likely been told, "I'm sorry," or "Please forgive me," more than once. Asking for forgiveness must come with a spoken or unspoken pledge to work at making life better for both you and the person you hurt. In other words, when people with BPD ask for someone's forgiveness, they must be starting or getting treatment and learning the skills that will improve their relationships. After all, asking forgiveness is a promise to work on reducing the hurt.

Running an Errand

You've heard the expression, "Actions speak louder than words." Well, being professional writers, we're not sure that we agree 100 percent, but, in the quest for making amends, you need to think hard about this concept.

For example, consider running an errand for someone you care about and think you may have hurt with your BPD. This errand can involve picking up the groceries, filling up the gas tank, going to the post office, picking up the kids from school, or taking the tax forms to the accountant. The task doesn't have to be difficult, but it should be something that your partner, family member, or friend usually does for herself.

Sending Flowers

Almost everyone likes flowers. And getting flowers from someone you care about feels good. You don't have to spend a fortune. A small bunch from the grocery store can brighten up moods and get your point across. If you can't afford the cost of a bouquet, buy a single flower.

Sending a Card

A card can also be a thoughtful way to express your feelings, whether you want to ask for forgiveness, say you're sorry, or tell someone how special he or she is. Make sure you spend some time looking at and reading the card before you buy it. You probably don't want to send your partner a card designed for someone's third birthday, even if it does look pretty cute.

Doing a Chore

Again, the chore doesn't have to be a big deal. Just make sure that it involves something that your friend, partner, or family member usually has to do. For example, you can clean the garage, make a special dinner, pay the bills, wash the car, pick up around the house, or file financial papers. Whatever you choose to do for someone you care about, do it without complaining or bragging about what you did.

Writing Your Thoughts

Writing out your thoughts can be one of the most meaningful ways to show and explain your feelings. Your loved one will appreciate the time you spent thinking about him or her. Here are a few pointers:

- ✔ Never send anything that you wrote in the middle of the night without proofing it in the morning.
- ✔ Don't send a letter that's basically self-defense and justification.
- ✔ Don't write your letter after you've been drinking.
- ✔ Remember that when you write something, whomever you give it to can save it forever.

Finding a Poem

Sometimes you can't express yourself in a way that fully describes your feelings or passions. Poetry sings a message. If you haven't read poetry since high school (okay, that goes for about 90 percent of the population), go to your local library or bookstore and browse for a couple of hours with a cup of coffee. Whether or not you understand everything you read, a few of the poems will surely inspire you.

Borrow the book from the library or buy it from the store. Copy the poem in your best handwriting or type it on the computer. Add a few comments about what meaning the poem holds for you and what you think about the person you're giving it to. Send the poem and your comments to the person you may have hurt.

Sending a Small Gift

Small gifts are another way to express your feelings. In many ways, small is truly better than large. Large gifts generally come with implicit strings attached, whether you intend them or not. Small gifts, especially gifts that may have special meaning to the person you wronged, have much more power and, yet, no strings.

If you want to express your regret or sorrow with your therapist, we generally recommend avoiding gifts whether small or large. Many therapists work under ethical codes that discourage accepting gifts, and they aren't necessary anyway. Simply express your feelings verbally or in writing.

Making Amends: Giving or Volunteering

Sometimes your past actions from long ago continue to plague your mind with guilt and regret. Often, the person you hurt has moved on, died, or simply isn't available for you to make amends directly. In these cases, consider designing a plan for making amends.

Such plans can entail making a contribution to others. The contribution may be giving money, spending time, or providing a skilled service to someone or a group of people who need help. A few of our favorite charitable activities include becoming a dog walker at the Humane Society, working at a local food bank, tutoring people who want to learn English, and participating in a community trash pickup. You can also donate money to a group that's important to either you or the person you're making amends with. Call your local Red Cross or United Way office for more possibilities. You can't undo the past, but you can feel better about who you are becoming today by contributing to others.

Saying you're sorry, asking forgiveness, and making amends are only useful when you accompany them with a commitment to make things better — not a promise of perfection, but a sincere effort.

Chapter 28

Ten Things You Shouldn't Do

The first 300 pages or so of this book tell you what to do when you or someone you know has borderline personality disorder (BPD). Now that we've almost reached the end of the book, we've saved a little space for some tips on what *not* to do for your BPD. Some of these items are quite harmless and may provide a little relief from pain, depression, or discomfort. However, you won't find any research that proves that any of the following techniques are comprehensive enough to tackle BPD.

BPD is a serious emotional disorder. It's important to get appropriate help. See Chapter 11 for the types of treatments and professionals for dealing with BPD and Part IV for an exploration of treatment ideas.

Expect Quick Fixes

We're sorry if you expected to read this book and be cured of your BPD. Effective treatment of BPD takes time. In most cases, treatment takes at least a year and often even longer. BPD is a complex disorder that requires consistent hard work. Don't be fooled by someone who promises a quick fix. You won't find any ten-day miracle cures for BPD — at least none that actually work.

On the other hand, people with BPD who are ready to look at all their symptoms in an honest way and work hard to get better can enjoy significant improvements fairly rapidly. Not surprisingly, however, breaking old habits and permanently learning new, better ways of living usually takes considerable time.

Stay Stuck

When people with BPD tell us that they've tried everything to get better and nothing has worked, we know they're stuck. Because so many treatment options have emerged over the years, few, if any, people have really tried them all. Thus, we tell our clients that doing nothing is, in fact, making the decision to stay the same.

We've never met anyone with BPD who loves having the disorder. If you have BPD, you can find programs that can help you. If you live in a location where no therapists are trained in treating BPD, consider asking a local therapist to request supervision from someone who has knowledge and experience with the disorder so that you can get the help you need. The bottom line: You can find treatment for your BPD, and you can feel better.

Choose Chiropractic Medicine

Most chiropractic doctors believe that the spine and overall health are related. People who go to chiropractors report relief from headaches, back pain, neck pain, and other muscular or skeletal pains. Often covered by insurance, this type of healthcare has gained popularity over time. However, some chiropractic practitioners promise much more than relief from physical pains — some of them promise improvements in mental health. Chiropractic medicine has its place in the care of many health issues; however, no research justifies it as a treatment for BPD. So feel free to seek this kind of treatment for your body's physical aches and pains, but don't expect it to cure your BPD.

Stick Pins and Needles

Imbalanced internal energy is the premise behind *acupuncture,* an ancient Chinese medicine that many trained acupuncturists still practice today. Acupuncture treatment consists of inserting very fine needles into different places in the body to rebalance energy flow. Many people claim that acupuncture helps decrease chronic mental and physical pain. Some research supports the use of acupuncture for substance abuse, as well.

We advise you not to make acupuncture a primary treatment for BPD because evidence to support acupuncture's effectiveness in treating BPD just doesn't exist. However, if you find that it helps reduce pain or stress, or improves your mood, by all means, consider it *in addition* to your other treatments.

Find a Life Coach

We like coaches. Coaches can help you stay focused on your goals and cheerlead your efforts. However, BPD is a serious mental disorder. Treatment requires highly skilled professionals trained in specific therapies for treating BPD.

We encourage you to postpone hiring a life coach until you've benefited from professional mental health treatment. If you decide you want to have a coach at that time, be sure to talk with your therapist first.

Fill Up Emptiness with Food or Drink

One of the symptoms of BPD is a strong feeling of inner emptiness. If you suffer from this symptom, you feel like something important is missing. (See Chapter 7 for more information on this particular symptom of BPD, and look to Chapter 17 for ways you can treat it.) Often, people experiencing this emptiness hope that food or drink will fill the void. Unfortunately, that approach doesn't work. Furthermore, after eating or drinking too much, people with BPD add guilt and remorse to their plate of negative feelings.

This common feeling of emptiness isn't a hunger of the body; it's a hunger of the mind. Working on getting better, improving relationships, and leading a meaningful life will satisfy the hunger — not food or drink.

Try Too Hard

Most people come to therapy with great anticipations and expectations. Just walking through the door for the first time to get help can set off feelings of optimism and hope. Those positive feelings can be quite strong. We wish we had a magic wand that could instantly fix the people who walk into our office, but breaking old habits and learning new ones takes time — not magic.

To get the most out of your therapy, you need to find the balance of learning to accept where you are in the present and where you want to be as you move forward. Trying to go too fast, too hard only bogs down your progression.

Pace yourself. Give yourself the space to work through your issues. Remember that the turtle wins the race through persistence and hard work — be the turtle.

Gaze at Crystals

Some people believe they can tell the future, solve crimes, and heal people by staring at a crystal ball. Some crystal gazers advertise that they can defeat depression and relieve daily stress. After surfing the Web for about an hour, we found out much more than we ever wanted to know about the powers of crystal balls. Apparently, different crystals have different powers. One Web site suggested putting a particular crystal in a glass of water overnight and then drinking the water the next day as a tonic.

Well, if you want to look at shiny rocks, go ahead. But please don't hope to cure BPD with crystals. You just won't find any evidence that proves crystal gazing can cure the disorder.

Get the Wrong Therapy

Throughout this book, we promote getting psychotherapy for BPD. By far, the treatments we review are your best bets for getting better. However, some psychotherapy approaches don't appear to be effective or haven't yet been well researched for treating BPD. We recommend that you choose a therapist who conducts evidence-based treatments specifically targeting BPD.

Now, we're not saying that some of these other treatments don't have benefits, but we are saying that we don't have enough information to say that they do. Would you buy a new type of furnace to heat your home if it has never been tested in the lab? Or a car that has never been tested on the road? The same idea holds true for therapy.

Ask potential therapists how they treat BPD and what therapy they use. If they can't answer these questions, find someone else. They should at least mention one or more of the approaches to treatment that we discuss in Chapter 11.

Hope That Medications Will Cure BPD

Researchers are constantly developing new medications. In the future, scientists may find a medication that helps or possibly even cures BPD. But at this time, no such medication exists. People with BPD sometimes benefit from medication for specific symptoms, but you should use medication only in conjunction with psychotherapy.

Part VII
Appendixes

The 5th Wave By Rich Tennant

"I'm looking for someone who will love me for who I think I am."

In this part . . .

Here we offer numerous resources for more information and help. We also provide several blank forms and exercises that we reference in other parts of the book.

Appendix A

Resources for You

• •

In this appendix, we list a variety of books, Web sites, and organizations that provide useful information about borderline personality disorder (BPD). We also include resources for other disorders, such as anxiety, obsessive-compulsive disorder, and depression, that frequently occur along with BPD. We don't intend this list to be comprehensive, but we think you'll find its content useful.

Books about BPD for the Public

✔ *Borderline Personality Disorder: A Patient's Guide to Taking Control* by Gina Fusco and Arthur Freeman (W.W. Norton)

✔ *Borderline Personality Disorder Demystified: An Essential Guide for Understanding and Living with BPD* by Robert O. Friedel (Da Capo Press)

✔ *The Borderline Personality Disorder Survival Guide* by Alex Chapman and Kim Gratz (New Harbinger Publications)

✔ *The Dialectical Behavior Therapy Skills Workbook: Practical DBT Exercises for Learning Mindfulness, Interpersonal Effectiveness, Emotion Regulation & Distress Tolerance* by Matthew McKay, Jeffrey Wood, and Jeffrey Brantley (New Harbinger Publications)

✔ *The Essential Family Guide to Borderline Personality Disorder: New Tools and Techniques to Stop Walking on Eggshells* by Randi Kreger (Hazelden)

✔ *I Hate You — Don't Leave Me: Understanding the Borderline Personality* by Jerold Kreisman and Hal Straus (HarperCollins)

✔ *Lost in the Mirror: An Inside Look at Borderline Personality Disorder,* 2nd Edition, by Richard Moskovitz (Taylor Publishing Company)

✔ *Reinventing Your Life: The Breakthrough Program to End Negative Behavior . . . and Feel Great Again* by Jeffrey Young and Janet Klosko (Plume)

✔ *Sometimes I Act Crazy: Living with Borderline Personality Disorder* by Jerold Kreisman and Hal Straus (Wiley)

✔ *Stop Walking on Eggshells: Taking Your Life Back When Someone You Care About Has Borderline Personality Disorder* by Paul Mason and Randi Kreger (New Harbinger Publications)

✔ *Understanding and Treating Borderline Personality Disorder: A Guide for Professionals and Families* by John Gunderson and Perry Hoffman (American Psychiatric Publishing)

✔ *Why Can't I Get What I Want?: How to Stop Making the Same Old Mistakes and Start Living a Life You Can Love* by Charles Elliott and Maureen Lassen (Davies-Black)

Books about BPD for Professionals

✔ *Affect Regulation, Mentalization, and the Development of the Self* by Peter Fonagy, Gyorgy Gergely, Elliot Jurist, and Mary Target (Other Press)

✔ *Borderline Personality Disorder: A Clinical Guide,* 2nd Edition, by John Gunderson and Paul Links (American Psychiatric Publishing)

✔ *Cognitive Therapy for Personality Disorders: A Schema-Focused Approach,* 3rd Edition, by Jeffrey Young (Professional Resource Press)

✔ *Cognitive Therapy of Personality Disorders,* 2nd Edition, by Aaron Beck, Arthur Freeman, Denise Davis, and Associates (The Guilford Press)

✔ *Cognitive-Behavioral Treatment of Borderline Personality Disorder* by Marsha Linehan (The Guilford Press)

✔ *Escaping the Self: Alcoholism, Spirituality, Masochism, and Other Flights from the Burden of Selfhood* by Roy F. Baumeister (Basic Books)

✔ *Psychotherapy for Borderline Personality: Focusing on Object Relations* by John Clarkin, Frank Yeomans, and Otto Kernberg (American Psychiatric Publishing)

✔ *Psychotherapy for Borderline Personality Disorder: Mentalization-Based Treatment* by Anthony Bateman and Peter Fonagy (Oxford University Press)

✔ *Schema Therapy: A Practitioner's Guide* by Jeffrey Young, Janet Klosko, and Marjorie Weishaar (The Guilford Press)

✔ *Skills Training for Treating Borderline Personality Disorder* by Marsha Linehan (The Guilford Press)

✔ *Treatment of Borderline Personality Disorder: A Guide to Evidence-Based Practice* by Joel Paris (The Guilford Press)

Books about Anxiety and Depression

- *Anxiety & Depression Workbook For Dummies* by Charles Elliott and Laura Smith (Wiley)

- *The Anxiety & Phobia Workbook* by Edmund Bourne (New Harbinger Publications)

- *Depression For Dummies* by Laura Smith and Charles Elliott (Wiley)

- *Feeling Good: The New Mood Therapy Revised and Updated* by David Burns (HarperCollins)

- *The Feeling Good Handbook: Using the New Mood Therapy in Everyday Life* by David Burns (Plume)

- *Mind Over Mood: Change How You Feel by Changing How You Think* by Dennis Greenberger and Christine Padesky (The Guilford Press)

- *Obsessive-Compulsive Disorder For Dummies* by Charles Elliott and Laura Smith (Wiley)

- *Overcoming Anxiety For Dummies* by Charles Elliott and Laura Smith (Wiley)

- *The Worry Cure: Seven Steps to Stop Worry From Stopping You* by Robert Leahy (Three Rivers Press)

Web Sites with More Information

As you know, the Internet changes constantly. However, the following sites have been around awhile and provide some quality information about BPD and other emotional and personality disorders:

- **About.com: Borderline Personality** (http://bpd.about.com): This site is loaded with articles, blogs, and news about BPD.

- **Academy of Cognitive Therapy** (www.academyofct.org): This organization promotes the research and practice of cognitive therapy for the treatment of all types of personality disorders. The organization certifies therapists with skills in this approach and lists practitioners around the world.

- **The American Psychiatric Association** (www.psych.org/): This organization is made up of medical specialists and offers information about BPD and other mental disorders.

- **The American Psychological Association** (www.apa.org/pubinfo): This professional and scientific organization offers an array of fact sheets and information about BPD and other emotional disorders.

✔ **Association for Behavioral and Cognitive Therapies** (www.abct.org): This professional organization promotes training, research, and development of scientifically validated treatments for emotional disorders, including BPD. The Web site provides referrals to qualified therapists across the globe.

✔ **Borderline Personality Disorder Resource Center** (http://bpdresourcecenter.org): This site, sponsored by New York-Presbyterian Hospital and The University Hospital of Columbia and Cornell, contains statistics, research, and resources for families and professionals of people with BPD.

✔ **BPD Central** (www.bpdcentral.com): This site focuses on BPD and provides support groups, links to other resources, and information for choosing BPD therapists in the United States and some other areas of the world.

✔ **National Alliance for the Mentally Ill** (www.nami.org): This alliance is the largest organization of family members, friends, professionals, and people with mental disorders in the United States. The organization provides support and education to families and advocates.

✔ **National Education Alliance for Borderline Personality Disorder** (www.borderlinepersonalitydisorder.com): This comprehensive site contains information about BPD for families and professionals; it also provides an up-to-date BPD conference schedule and a list of recommended books.

✔ **National Institute of Mental Health** (www.nimh.nih.gov): This site offers educational materials, research summaries, and a vast array of statistics on various mental health issues, including BPD. It also posts announcements on clinical trials for various mental health problems.

✔ **Psychcentral** (www.psychcentral.com): This site provides a wide range of information about psychological issues, including BPD. It also houses a large number of interesting psychology-related blogs and is one of the most-visited psychology-related Web sites. Currently, we run a blog called "Anxiety & OCD Exposed" on this site.

✔ **WebMD** (www.webmd.com): This site is basically an online medical encyclopedia. It covers both physical and mental health issues. It's a great resource for finding out about symptoms and treatments for almost anything you can think of, including BPD.

Appendix B
Forms to Help You Battle BPD

• •

*T*his appendix contains a few forms that you can use in conjunction with some of the exercises that appear throughout this book. We give you instructions for using each form and tell you which chapter each form relates to. Feel free to make copies of the forms for your own use.

Cost-Benefit Analysis

You can do a *cost-benefit analysis* to help you make all sorts of decisions in life. In fact, we've often used this strategy in our clinical practices as well as for tricky decisions in our own lives. You can see the cost-benefit analysis in action in several chapters throughout this book. In Chapter 12, we use the cost-benefit analysis to help a client decide whether to seek treatment for BPD. In Chapter 19, we apply the same strategy to help a woman who suffers from BPD challenge her problematic schemas. And, in Chapter 22, we suggest that you use this approach to help you decide whether to end a relationship with someone who has BPD. Follow these steps to complete a Cost-Benefit Analysis Form:

1. **On a page in your notebook or computer document, or on the Cost-Benefit Analysis Form that appears in this appendix, write down the decision you want to make, the problematic schema you may want to change, or any other dilemma you're facing.**

2. **Underneath the dilemma you wrote down in Step 1, make two columns. Label the first one "Benefits" and the second one "Costs."**

3. **In the Benefits column, write down all the conceivable benefits that taking one side of the issue can possibly bring you.**

   Be creative and think of any possible way that taking this side of the issue can or even may help you. Benefits can come in various forms, including emotional, interpersonal, financial, and physical.

4. **In the Costs column, write down all the ways that taking this same side of the decision can, will, or may cost you. Costs can include emotional, financial, physical, and interpersonal stressors or damages.**

5. **Write down a few thoughts or reflections about the costs and benefits you've come up with — if you want to. If you're already working with a therapist, discuss your results with him or her.**

Cost-Benefit Analysis Form

Decision, Problematic Schema, or Dilemma

Benefits	Costs

My Reflections:

_____

_____

Impulsive Awareness

Chapter 15 describes the benefits of monitoring your impulsive actions. Use the Impulsive Awareness Form to increase your awareness of your impulsive tendencies. Follow these steps to monitor your impulsive actions (see Chapter 15 for more complete instructions). Use a separate form for each of your impulsive tendencies, and record the tendency you're studying at the top of the form on the line next to "Impulsive Awareness Form."

1. **Describe each time you act impulsively, without thinking.**

2. **Recount where you were and what you were doing before you acted impulsively.**

3. Explain how you felt — before you acted impulsively.

4. Write down what you thought or hoped would happen as a result of your impulsive behavior.

5. Express how you felt after the impulsive behavior. Did you achieve your goals?

6. Jot down your conclusions from this exercise underneath My Reflections.

Impulsive Awareness Form: *Record Impulsive Issue Here*

1. Describe each time you act impulsively, without thinking.

---

2. Recount where you were and what you were doing before you acted impulsively.

---

3. Explain how you felt — before you acted impulsively.

---

4. Write down what you thought or hoped would happen as a result of your impulsive behavior.

---

5. Express how you felt after the impulsive behavior? Did you achieve your goals?

My Reflections:

Schema Monitoring

In Chapter 19, we discuss the concept of schemas and the problems that schemas can cause for you and the people around you. You can use the Schema Monitoring Form to start changing your problematic schemas. Follow these steps to start monitoring your schemas (see Chapter 19 for more complete instructions on using this form):

1. **When you feel distressed, try to figure out what event seemed to trigger your feeling.**

   Jot down at the top of the form what that event was. The event can be something that actually happened to you or an image that came into your mind.

2. **Jot down in the middle column what thoughts, perceptions, interpretations, or meanings the event had for you.**

   In other words, make note of what thoughts were going through your head when the event actually occurred.

3. **In the right-hand column, make note of how you feel about the event.**

   If you have trouble labeling your feelings, consider reading Chapter 6, which explains bodily sensations and words that describe feelings.

4. **Refer to Chapter 19 for a list of problematic schemas and their definitions to discover whether one of your own problematic schemas is related to your thoughts and feelings about this event.**

   If a problematic schema is related to your feelings, make note of that schema and the related feelings in the first column of the Schema Monitoring Form. You may conclude that more than one schema seems to apply, which is okay. Jot down however many schemas seem to be involved. Briefly describe your schema based on the definition in Chapter 19, or individualize how that schema seems to apply to you.

Schema Monitoring Form

Event: _____

Schema and Definition	Thoughts	Feelings

Event: _____

Schema and Definition	Thoughts	Feelings

Event: _____

Schema and Definition	Thoughts	Feelings

Then and Now

In addition to the schema monitoring exercise, you can find another important method for challenging your problematic schemas in Chapter 19 — this one deals with identifying the difference between the past and the present. People generally develop their problematic schemas in childhood. Later in their lives, events that are only tangentially similar to the events of their childhoods continue to set these schemas off. The Then and Now Form helps you see the difference between the past and the present so that you can address the problematic schemas that you developed in childhood. Follow these steps to complete this form (see Chapter 19 for more complete directions):

1. **Write down your problematic schema in the left-hand column. (See Chapter 19 for a list of problematic schemas.) Describe how this particular schema plays out in your life.**

2. **Jot down one or more recollections from your childhood that may have helped create this schema in the second column.**

3. **Write down the events or happenings that tend to trigger this schema for you in your current life in the third column.**

4. **Remind yourself that you're older today, that the current triggering events aren't usually as significant as the events that created your schemas, and that, with time, your mind will see the difference between the events of your childhood and those of the present. Write down your thoughts and reflections underneath My Reflections.**

Then and Now Form

Problematic Schema	Image(s) of Childhood Origins	Current Triggers

My Reflections:

Index